CONVERSATIONS
WITH
CARTER

CONVERSATIONS
WITH
CARTER

edited by

Don Richardson

LYNNE
RIENNER
PUBLISHERS

BOULDER
LONDON

Published in the United States of America in 1998 by
Lynne Rienner Publishers, Inc.
1800 30th Street, Boulder, Colorado 80301

and in the United Kingdom by
Lynne Rienner Publishers, Inc.
3 Henrietta Street, Covent Garden, London WC2E 8LU

Library of Congress Cataloging-in-Publication Data
Carter, Jimmy, 1924–
  Conversations with Carter / edited by Don Richardson.
  Includes index.
    ISBN 1-55587-801-6 (hc)
    1. Carter, Jimmy, 1924– —Interviews. 2. Presidents—United
States—Interviews. 3. United States—Politics and
government—1977–1981. I. Richardson, Don, 1938– . II. Title.
E873.A3 1998
973.926'092—dc21   97-50176
                                                                   CIP

British Cataloguing in Publication Data
A Cataloguing in Publication record for this book
is available from the British Library.

Printed and bound in the United States of America

∞   The paper used in this publication meets the requirements
    of the American National Standard for Permanence of
    Paper for Printed Library Materials Z39.48-1984.

5 4 3 2 1

CONTENTS

Part 3   Post-Presidential Conversations

PHOTOGRAPHS

INTRODUCTION

This is not so much a book about Jimmy Carter as it is a book by Jimmy Carter. It is a book of conversations in which Carter, under the prompting and probing of journalists and others, reveals his inner self. It's a book in which Carter tells us who he is and what he stands for. It's a book from which we can learn about Carter from Carter himself.

Jimmy Carter emerged from nowhere to become the thirty-ninth president of the United States. At least, that was the view of many in the national news media. Although he had been governor of the largest Southern state east of the Mississippi River, he was not nearly so well known as George C. Wallace. In early 1976, few took Carter's candidacy seriously. It was not until after his strong showing in the Iowa caucuses that the media began to notice him. Even then, few people gave his run for the Democratic nomination, let alone the presidency, much chance of success.

There were many hurdles to be overcome in pursuit of his goal of being president. He was from the South. Many Americans assumed that the South was accurately represented by George Wallace. The country had seen Wallace standing in the schoolhouse door at the University of Alabama and had heard him declare that we would have "segregation now, segregation tomorrow and segregation forever." Americans remembered the efforts of Arkansas governor Orval Faubus to keep the public schools of Little Rock segregated. It was Mississippi governor Ross Barnett who made white supremacy his principal campaign issue and who was widely quoted as saying, "The Negro is different because God made him different to punish him." Was it not safe to assume that all Southern governors were cut from the same cloth?

In addition to the Southern stigma, Carter was a farmer. The political cartoonists made great sport of Carter's agrarian background,

1

depicting him in a variety of comic-rural situations. Few people could conceive of a south Georgia peanut farmer ascending to the highest office in the land.

Finally, Carter had no legal training and relatively little political experience. By the time he began his run for the presidency, he had served two terms in Georgia's legislature and one term as governor. His knowledge of national politics came from reading rather than first-hand experience.

The media were not alone in discounting Carter's chances for success. So did mainstream Democrats. At first, most Democratic leaders did not take him seriously. Then, as more delegates lined up in the Carter column, apprehension arose for the party leadership, who either publicly or privately supported Henry "Scoop" Jackson, Morris Udall, and Hubert Humphrey. Some even supported enigmatic California governor Edmund G. "Jerry" Brown. Carter got little help from the Democratic National Committee. Various groups arose to stop Carter, including the ABC Movement—"Anybody But Carter." None of these efforts were successful, however, and Carter continued his determined run for the Democratic nomination. He ran in all 29 primaries and won 19 of them. It was perhaps only when Carter began his address to the Democratic Convention—"My name is Jimmy Carter and I'm running for president"—that the realization set in that Jimmy Carter could, in fact, be our next president.

For the most part, the campaign against Republican nominee Gerald Ford was a nonevent. Polls gave Carter a comfortable double-digit lead for most of the race. It was not until Carter told *Playboy* magazine, "I've looked on a lot of women with lust. I've committed adultery in my heart many times"—that the race became close. In the *Playboy* interview, Carter spoke of someone who "shacks up with somebody out of wedlock" and refers to a "guy who screws a whole bunch of women." The conservative Christians felt that this was not language a born-again Southern Baptist should be using. In fact, good Southern Baptists shouldn't even be thinking these thoughts, let alone talking to *Playboy* about them. Although the interview is extensive and informative, the world only remembers that Carter lusted in his heart. Shortly after the *Playboy* interview was published, Carter lost 15 points in the polls. When the votes were counted, however, Carter had been elected president of the United States by a margin of only slightly more than 2 percent of the popular and 10.5 percent of the electoral vote.

Carter's next order of business was to set up a transition team to make specific preparations to administer the executive branch of the U.S. government. One of the very earliest tasks was to compile a list of campaign promises. On November 30, 1976, Stuart Eizenstat and

David Rubenstein sent a memorandum to President-elect Carter that began: "Attached is the compilation of campaign promises that you requested. The compilation should prove helpful in reviewing the nature and extent of your public commitments."

These promises were collected and published in a work commonly called the "Promises Book," and they became the agenda for the Carter administration. The broad, major areas in which promises were made include economy, natural resources, human and urban needs, justice, general government, special groups (including elderly, handicapped, labor, small business, veterans, American Indians, and arts), foreign policy, and defense policy. Subsumed under these major headings in the "Promises Book" were 52 subheadings. There were a total of 111 pages of promises to be kept.

This laudable effort showed Carter to be an honest man who wanted to deliver on his promises. His list of promises was also restrictive because it committed his administration to an extensive, diverse, and, in fact, impossible set of goals. Carter, by going public with his promises, in effect, knitted his own noose. The national news media, which had never warmed to Carter, delighted in pointing out what he failed to achieve and gave little play to what he did achieve. This was the story of his presidency. Accomplishments were little noted and failures were given broad coverage. A major research project by John Orman published in the *Presidential Studies Quarterly* in 1984 revealed that Carter received more negative periodical press coverage than any other president this century. Orman noted that Carter "scored 46 months in a row of negative reporting."

As president, Carter was judged by a standard of morality and perhaps achievement that had never before been applied to a president. He, in part, brought this on himself. He campaigned on a platform of doing things differently, of not lying to the American people, of bringing a new standard of morality to the executive branch. He succeeded in doing that. In fact, his administration might be considered an oasis of morality in a desert of improbity. The press, reluctant to believe anyone could be "that good," spent much time and effort looking for flaws. Consequently, Carter and his staff received uncommon scrutiny from the media. The most insignificant misstep was treated as a national crisis. For instance, when Bert Lance was accused of illegal banking practices, the media had a field day. There was almost daily coverage on network news; Lance's picture was on the cover of *Time* and *Newsweek;* and newspapers devoted front page stories to the "Lance Affair." All this in spite of the fact that a 394-page report released on August 18 by the comptroller of currency cleared Lance of having done anything illegal. He was later acquitted of all charges. Lance was hounded out of Washington by the media.

Carter's most devastating setback was his failure to be elected for a second term. The Iranian hostage crisis and the ill-fated effort to rescue the hostages figured heavily in his defeat. So did runaway inflation. Republican nominee Ronald Reagan, although probably not as smart as Carter and certainly not as politically experienced as Carter, had one great advantage: he was, according to the press, "the great communicator." Reagan made people feel safe and comfortable. With his benign grandfatherly appearance and his well-modulated voice, he talked about simple themes and told the American people that there were better times ahead.

Carter, on the other hand, consumed, processed, and stored information as perhaps no other president ever has. He had the ability to deal with multiple complex issues. But he still had difficulty communicating his thoughts to the people. He was not a gifted public speaker. He didn't make people feel particularly comfortable and, in fact, in one of his most famous speeches—which was dubbed by the media "The National Malaise" speech—told the American people on July 15, 1979, "This is not a message of happiness or reassurance." It is likely that Reagan simply out-communicated him for the presidency.

Carter was bitterly disappointed by the loss, but he did not let that disappointment hamper his post-presidential career for very long. That career consists of teaching classes at Emory University, serving as diplomat-without-portfolio to many nations of the world, authoring 12 books, responding to calls from troubled nations to assist in peace negotiations, and administering the Carter Center in Atlanta.

During the 21-year span covered by this book, Carter participated in more than two hundred interviews. He was probably more accessible to the media than any president in history. During his four years in office he conducted 59 press conferences and met with scores of domestic and international journalists. Interviewers included well-known media personalities, lesser-known reporters, and some just "plain folks"—mainstream Americans. In almost all of the interviews, Carter's answers were open, forthright, and honest. In some he seemed deliberate and circumspect, as one would expect when issues of national security were involved.

Almost without exception the pre-presidential conversations involve an effort to find out who Jimmy Carter really is. Since he was virtually unknown, people had no idea where he stood on most issues. In fact, his political rivals for the nomination accused him of deliberately obscuring his stand on major issues. It is more likely, I think, that so early in the campaign Carter simply had not solidified his position on many issues. All that notwithstanding, the U.S. public had an increasingly voracious appetite for information about Jimmy Carter, and the conversations multiplied.

The tone of the interviews necessarily changed during the presidential years. Carter entertained a variety of interviewers in the White House and, in an effort to be responsive to the U.S. citizenry, he even conducted a two-hour telephone call-in program on CBS Radio called, "Ask President Carter." The program was moderated by Walter Cronkite, who introduced the program by saying, "This is a unique occasion, in the sense that it marks a new approach to communication between the president and the people of the United States. It is indeed historic—unique, historic—and we must also say an experiment since the president has never taken part in this sort of broadcast." Carter responded to questions from 42 people from 26 states. It was reported that more than nine million people tried to get through to the president. This conversation with the people of the United States took place on March 5, 1977, fairly early in the Carter administration. Although no judgment is made regarding the success or failure of the experiment, it should be noted that it was never repeated.

As president, Carter conversed with many journalists, some of whom had highly specialized and very restrictive agendas. He met with European newspaper journalists, Israeli journalists, Egyptian journalists, representatives of the U.S. Jewish Press, black media representatives, and Hispanic journalists, among others. Toward the end of his administration, his availability to the press was dramatically reduced. For instance, in the last nine months of his administration, he conducted only two of his 59 press conferences, and in the last four months, none.

The post-presidential interviews have appeared in a variety of sources and touch on diverse topics. Most deal with the "good works" in which Carter has engaged in his life after the presidency. He is arguably the most active ex-president of this century.

Some of the post-presidential interviews deal with Carter the man. The best example of this kind of interview was Carter's conversation with Robert Fulghum conducted on December 19, 1996, and broadcast on C-SPAN. That interview, perhaps more than any other, reveals Carter the man. Fulghum's questions are insightful and interesting, Carter's answers candid and forthcoming.

Only a small percentage of the total number of Carter conversations could be included in the context of this book. The major criteria for selection were whether the interviews were interesting and representative. A secondary criterion was the name recognition of the publication source and/or the interviewer. In almost all cases, the conversations appear as originally published. In two cases exceptionally long interviews have been edited. Those are noted in the text of the book.

Perhaps these conversations will prompt journalists, historians, and others to take a fresh look at Carter. Through these conversations we see a very decent human being with a stronger commitment to a religious faith than most of us can hope to achieve, who at age 73 continues to expend enormous amounts of energy promoting peace, resolving conflicts, helping the less fortunate, and generally doing more than could be reasonably expected of any one person to improve the lot of the people of this planet.

He is resolute, decisive, and effective. Why has he changed from the days of his presidency? The answer is he probably has not. Only the tone of what is reported by the media has changed, and since we rely on the media to tell us how things are, we assume Carter has changed. Maybe it is time to not only reassess Carter himself, but also the Carter presidency in light of current insights into "the man."

—Editor

PART 1

PRE-PRESIDENTIAL
CONVERSATIONS

1

A TALK WITH CARTER, MAY 16, 1976

Los Angeles Times, Bill Moyers

Despite his narrow loss in Nebraska last week to Sen. Frank Church, the former Georgia governor remains the clear Democratic front-runner. Yet to many voters of both parties, Jimmy Carter is something of an enigma. One of his most revealing interviews was held recently with President Johnson's former press secretary, Bill Moyers, who, like Carter, was raised a Southern Baptist and who once studied for the ministry. The following dialogue is drawn from their broadcast discussion, which was produced for public television by WETA in Washington and WNET in New York.

BILL MOYERS: What drives you?

JIMMY CARTER: (Long silence) I don't know. I—exactly how to express it. As I said, it's not an unpleasant sense of being driven. I feel like I have one life to live. I feel that God wants me to do the best I can with it. And that's quite often my major prayer. Let me live my life so that it will be meaningful. And I enjoy attacking difficult problems and solving of solutions and answering the difficult questions and the meticulous organization of a complicated effort.

MOYERS: How do you know—this is a question I hear a lot of young people—how do you know God's will?

CARTER: Well, I pray frequently. And not continually, but many times a day. When I have a sense of peace and just self-assurance—I don't know where it comes from—that what I'm doing is the right thing, I assume, maybe in an unwarranted way, that that's doing God's will.

MOYERS: I've been intrigued as to why you almost suddenly gave up a military career (in 1953) and went back home to Plains, Georgia.

CARTER: Well, up until that time, I guess I was a naval officer who enjoyed my work. I had the best jobs in the Navy. And then my father had terminal cancer, and I had to go home to be with him about the last month of his life. I hadn't seen him since I was about 17 years old. This was 10, 12 years later.

MOYERS: Did you regret that, those last 11 years of your father's life? You had really not been in close touch with him.

CARTER: Well, I would like, obviously, in retrospect, to have been more with my father. I never thought he would die so young. But I've never regretted a day that I served in the Navy. That was an opportunity for me that paid off.

MOYERS: What do you think it did for you or to you? Did it stamp this discipline that everyone tells me about? This respect for authority.

CARTER: Yes, I think so. Obviously, the Naval Academy is quite heavily disciplined. And a life on a ship—particularly as a junior officer—is a heavy discipline; to move in the submarines is a heavier discipline. And then I met (Hyman G.) Rickover, who knew me as one of his maybe four young naval officers who had come in on the Seawolf and the Nautilus, which were the two submarines that were built with atomic power. And he demanded from me a standard of performance and a depth of commitment that I had never realized before that I could achieve. And I think second to my own father, Admiral Rickover had more effect on my life than any other man.

MOYERS: Can you step back as the civilian Commander-in-Chief from this heavy influence of the military and of an admiral in your life?

CARTER: I can.

MOYERS: Can you?

CARTER: Yes, yes. There's no aspect of a militaristic inclination now on my part. I feel free of that completely. But the self-discipline has stuck with me. I have a constant drive just to do the best I can, and sometimes it's disconcerting to other people, but it's not an unpleasant thing for me. I don't feel that I've got to win, or that I, you know, that I'll be terribly disappointed if I don't win. I feel a sense of equanimity about it. If I—if I do my best and lose, I don't have any regrets.

MOYERS: People say to me, "Jimmy Carter appears to be so full of certainty and conviction." Do you ever have any doubts? About yourself, about God, about life?

CARTER: I can't think of any, you know. Obviously I don't know all of the answers to the philosophical questions and theological questions that—you know, the questions that are contrived. But the things that I haven't been able to answer in a theory of supposition, I just accept them and go on. The things that I can't influence or change.

I do have, obviously, many doubts about the best way to answer a question or how to alleviate a concern or how to meet a need. Or to how—how to create in my own life a more meaningful purpose and to let my life be expanded in my heart and mind. So doubts about the best avenue to take among many options is a kind of doubt. That is a constant presence with me. But doubt about my faith? No. Doubt about my purpose in life? I don't have any doubts about that.

MOYERS: I ran into a friend who's a lawyer in a large firm in New York, and he said, "Could I ask you to ask Jimmy Carter something?" And I wrote it down. He said, "What bothers me about Jimmy Carter, the human being, is that he strikes me as a decent but provincial and narrowminded man from the South who's lived most of his life in that environment. And I'd like to know how a man like that expects to lead a pluralistic society, not to mention the Western world."

CARTER: I'm not sure that you have to have lived in many different places to understand a pluralistic society. I've had a changing career myself. I started out as an isolated farm boy living in—as a minority member—in a predominantly black neighborhood. I moved from that to a smaller town and then from there to a junior college, from there to Georgia Tech and then to the Naval Academy.

I've traveled extensively in foreign countries all my adult life.

I've read extensively in history of our country, the purpose of the President, the interrelationship between the President and the Congress. And I've had a chance, as governor, to deal with a multiplicity of problems from different kinds of people.

MOYERS: What do you think of the three or four lessons that we have to take away from this last decade, if we don't get into trouble again?

CARTER: One is to strip away secrecy of government in every possible way we can, to open up the deliberations of the executive and legislative branches of government.

MOYERS: Would you let the minutes of the Cabinet meetings be made public?

CARTER: There would have to be some exclusions. States have done this. When you have staff members advising a superior, that ought to be an area that would be kept private, because you've got to have the freedom of debate.

The second thing is to make sure that we have in our government an access of the people in other ways. I would like to see, for instance, Cabinet members go before joint sessions of Congress to be examined and questioned about foreign affairs, defense, agriculture and so forth.

MOYERS: You would send your secretary of state up to a joint session of Congress to actually answer questions from the floor?

CARTER: Yes, I would. If the Congress would accept this, I will be glad to have it done.

The President ought to tell the truth always. I see no reason for the President to lie, and if any of my Cabinet members ever lie, they'll be gone the next day.

MOYERS: If anybody came forward with the evidence in this campaign that you had lied, would you quit?

CARTER: I think I would, because I haven't told a lie.

MOYERS: If anybody came forward with evidence that while you were in the White House that you had lied, would you resign?

CARTER: Well, I can't say that. But there will be times when I'm asked a question that I might refuse to answer. But if I give an answer, it will be the truth. I think we ought to also have—I've forgotten the original question . . .

MOYERS: The question was, what are the three or four lessons we mustn't forget from the last 10 years if we don't make the same mistakes. You said strip away secrecy.

CARTER: I would never again get militarily involved in the internal affairs of another country. Unless our own security is directly threatened.

MOYERS: If North Korea invaded South Korea, would you get involved?

CARTER: Well, we're already involved there. And we have a commitment made by the Congress, the President, the people and the United Nations in South Korea. I would prefer to withdraw all of our troops and land forces from South Korea over a period of years— three, four years, whatever. But, obviously, we're already committed in Japan. We're committed in Germany.

MOYERS: Well, where then does the Carter Doctrine apply?

CARTER: Well, it would apply in retrospect to South Vietnam. It would apply in recent months to the attempt in Angola. It would apply possibly in the future in a place like Rhodesia. I just wouldn't do it. I don't think the American people need it. We don't have to show that we're strong. We are strong. And I wouldn't get involved militarily.

Another thing we must do in this country is to make the government mechanism work. It's an ineffective, bloated, confused, unmanageable bureaucracy there. It hurts our people worse than anything I can think of almost—even compared to integrity in government, the competence of government is missing.

MOYERS: I read your proposals and the record of your administration in Georgia on that—and I've read a lot of your speeches and analyses—the effect of which, it seems to me, is to centralize the executive branch of the government. Don't you find people wary of centralized authority after the Lyndon Johnson administration and the war in Vietnam and Richard Nixon and Watergate?

CARTER: When you throw Johnson, Watergate, Vietnam in the question, obviously, people are very wary about that. They're all wary about what occurred with Watergate, with Vietnam, with the CIA, with Johnson, with Nixon—of course they are. But it's not the fact that the government is well organized, managed, a clear delineation of authorities and responsibilities. I did it in Georgia, and not only did we save a lot of money and make it more economical and efficient—that was to some degree important—but the main thing is we opened up government so the people could understand it and control it.

MOYERS: That brings up the quote that you use in the beginning of your autobiography from someone we both admire—Reinhold Niebuhr—"The sad duty of politics is to establish justice in a sinful world." Do you think this is a just society?

CARTER: No, no, I don't. I think one of the major responsibilities I have as a leader and as a potential leader is to try to establish justice. And that applies to a broad gamut of things—international affairs, peace, equality, elimination of injustice in racial discrimination, elimination of injustice in tax programs, elimination of injustice in our criminal justice system and so forth. And it's not a crusade. It's just common sense.

MOYERS: The profile that emerges is of a man who's into everything and pushing and pressing. How does that square with the reports we're getting of an anti-government, anti-Washington mood in the country which you seem to represent?

CARTER: I've never expressed deliberately any anti-Washington feeling or any anti-government feeling. I'm not going to disrupt anything when I get here to Washington, if I'm elected. I'm not anti-Washington at all. And when I come here, I think I'll get along fine. But I would be a very activist President. I never have said I wanted a small government. I want one that, when it performs a function, does it well and performs a function in the ways that alleviate the problems of those who have not had an adequate voice in the past.

MOYERS: How do you see the Presidency? What's the purpose of the President?

CARTER: I think the nation's best served by a President who is strong and aggressive and innovative and sensitive. Working with the Congress. Is strong, independent, in harmony for a change, with mutual respect for a change. I don't think the Congress is capable of leadership. That's no reflection on the Congress, but you can't have 535 people leading the nation. I don't think the Founding Fathers ever thought that Congress would lead this country.

There's only one person in this nation that can speak with a clear voice to the American people. There's only one person that can set a standard of ethics and morality and excellence and greatness or call on the American people to make a sacrifice and explain the purpose of the sacrifice, or answer difficult questions or propose and carry out bold programs, or to provide for defense posture that would make us feel secure, a foreign policy that would make us proud once again, and that's the President. In the absence of that leadership, there is no leadership, and the country drifts.

So strong President, yes. But an autocratic President, an imperial Presidency, no.

MOYERS: Let me go back to some personal questions. You said once that you were strongly influenced by a sermon whose title was: "If you were arrested for being a Christian, would there be enough evidence to convict you?" What is the evidence that the rest of us can see of a Christian?

CARTER: (Sigh) I don't know. That's a hard question to answer, because I don't think I'm better than anyone else. I reckon there's my own shortcomings and sinfulness and need to improve, and need for forgiveness among the people around me, and God.

I was going through a state in my life that was a very difficult one. I had run for governor and lost (in 1966). Everything I did was not gratifying. When I succeeded in something, it was a horrible experience for me. And I thought I was a good Christian.

And one day the preacher gave this sermon—I don't remember a thing he said—I just remember the title which you described—"If you were arrested for being a Christian, would there be any evidence to convict you?"

And my answer by the time that sermon was over was "No." I never had really committed myself totally to God—my Christian beliefs were superficial. Based primarily on pride, and—I'd never done much for other people. I was always thinking about myself, and I changed somewhat for the better. I formed a much more intimate relationship with Christ. And since then, I've had just about like a new life. As far as hatreds, frustrations, I feel at ease with myself. And it doesn't mean that I'm better, but I'm better off myself.

MOYERS: Tom Ottenad, who's a very well-known writer for the St. Louis Post Dispatch, said recently, "In a ruthless business, Jimmy Carter is a ruthless operator. Even as he wears his broad smile and displays his Southern charm." And the question that arises, and I've been inside the White House—I know some of the influences that work on a man trying to do the right thing—can you be ruthless in the way I think he means it here? And a Christian?

CARTER: I presume—well, I'm a Christian, no matter what.

He was talking about the campaign. And I don't know what he meant by ruthless. I don't think I've ever deliberately hurt one of my opponents to gain an advantage.

I think I can be tough in making decisions that were difficult. And I can be tenacious under difficult circumstances. One of the major criticisms of me by my opponents in the (Georgia) Legislature, who've never yet been assuaged, is that I can't compromise. And that's a common criticism. I often had to compromise, but I didn't compromise in a back room. My preference was to spell out my position openly—"This is what I propose; this is the reason for it; this is the mess we have now; this is what we can accomplish"—try to work harmoniously with the legislature; try to give them all the credit they could, and then fight to the last vote. And I never was much able to get in a back room and compromise away the things I believed in.

And that's a very legitimate source of criticism for me. I'm not a good compromiser.

MOYERS: I think what some people in this town are talking about is the unwillingness of Woodrow Wilson to compromise on the League of Nations. The unwillingness of Lyndon Johnson to compromise on the war, or Richard Nixon on the opposition of the war, and a feeling that a disciplined, principled man, convinced of his own rightness, or having a private pipeline to God, in a sense, is going to say, "I'm right." And the town won't function because of his inability to compromise. Is that a legitimate danger?

CARTER: I don't believe so. I can see that would be a legitimate concern, but I think the concern will be proven unjustified. They have a right to be concerned, but I don't think they need to be.

I'd like to quote one other thing—you've gotten into theology—Paul Tillich said, that "religion is a search for the relationship between us and God, and us and our fellow human beings." And he went on to say that, "when we quit searching, in effect, we've lost our religion." When we become self-satisfied, proud, sure, at that point we lose the self-searching, the humility, the subservience to God's will, the more intimate understanding of other people's needs, the more inclination to be accommodating, and, in that instant, we lose our religion.

So, the fact that a person has deep religious convictions doesn't necessarily mean that that person always thinks that he's right, that God's ordained him to take a dominant position. Although I have prayed a good bit, and do, I've never asked God to let me be President.

MOYERS: If we learned anything the last few years, it has been that good intentions in the use of great power are no guarantee that that power will be used wisely. That the character of the man is less important to the safeguards against the abuse of power than the checks and balances on the office and on the power. And here Jimmy Carter is coming along saying, "I want to do all these things because I believe they're right. I want more power because I want to do good things. And trust me, I won't abuse the power."

Now, after the last 10 years, why should someone believe you? They may trust you. They may know that you are sincere and well intentioned, and yet they know it is power that often changes the man, and not the man who changes power.

CARTER: I know. I can see that. That's why I go back to what I said originally. You need to have an open government. You need to tell the truth. A minimum of secrecy. Let the people have a maximum part in the evolution and consummation of our domestic and foreign policies. That gives you a safety net under an incompetent or distorted President—the people themselves. And I think had we told the people the truth about Vietnam, we would have been out very early. Had the people had the truth about Watergate, it would never have happened.

MOYERS: You want checks. You want balances. You want safeguards.

CARTER: I don't object to those. I don't object to a strong, aggressive Congress. A strong, aggressive Supreme Court. And a strong, aggressive President—if what goes on in our government is known by, debated by, questioned by, controlled by the people of this country.

Now, I can see that there are times when an inspirational leader can actually elevate the people. That may happen on rare occasions. I think for a while, at least, John Kennedy did it. Roosevelt did it.

This is a part of the Presidency. There are times when the Presidency, perhaps the government itself, might tend to sink below the standards of the people of this country—in which case, people support or boost that official or those officials in a weak moment. But to exclude the people completely, as we have tended to do in recent years, removes that common sense judgment, character, safety that can preserve our country.

And it also destroys the concept of our government which did say that the government ought to be controlled by the people—and not by a powerful, secret, hidden, isolated, mistaken President.

2

"FORD HAS BEEN A DORMANT PRESIDENT," SEPT. 13, 1976

U.S. News & World Report

This was an hour-long interview conducted by editors of *U.S. News & World Report*. The interview is broad-based and touches on most of the issues that were being debated in the presidential campaign.—*Editor*

QUESTION: Governor Carter, you have described yourself as a populist. Just how do you define "populist"?

ANSWER: I tried to define it when people asked me whether my acceptance speech in New York in July was liberal or conservative. I told them I thought it was a mixture of the two: a populist speech designed to show that I derived my political support, my advice and my concern directly from people themselves, not from powerful intermediaries or representatives of special-interest groups.

"Populist" is a word, as you know, that comes from *populus*—people—and I think the people have been the origin of my own political incentives and my political strength.

QUESTION: Which of our previous Presidents would you call yourself most akin to in philosophy?

ANSWER: We've had a lot of great Presidents. My own personal favorite is Harry Truman. He revered the Presidency itself, and he used it in an aggressive fashion. The long-range concepts he had of foreign interrelationships, the courage he showed when he dealt with the firing of Gen. Douglas MacArthur during the Korean War— all these are things that I admire.

QUESTION: Do you regard President Truman as a populist?

ANSWER: I don't know, but I do think there was a cohesion within the Populist movement of different kinds of people who in the past had been excluded from having a proper voice in their own Government.

There was an aversion to inequities that had been built into the governmental structure by the powerful. In many ways Truman did represent that concern.

I lean toward letting people themselves decide their own Government and to having a guaranteed equity of treatment—a removal of the undue influence of special-interest groups—openness of Government, a closeness between the President and the people themselves.

QUESTION: Do you mean by that an activist, perhaps even an aggressive Presidency?

ANSWER: I think so.

QUESTION: What do you think will be the single most important issue influencing voters between now and November 2?

ANSWER: I don't think that issue has changed: It is the desire to restore respect for and trust of the Government within the consciousness of American people. The damage that has been done to people's attitudes toward Government has been severe in the last few years. We feel that we've lost the confidence in our Government, the sensitivity of Government to people's needs. The integrity of Government, the openness of Government have been damaged severely.

Vietnam, Cambodia, Angola, CIA revelations, Watergate—all those things have tended to destroy the pride and the respect that has been a natural feeling of people toward our own Government. We have been disconcerted, we've been alienated and embarrassed—sometimes have been ashamed of our own Government.

Our public-opinion polls show that concern about Government ranks far ahead of unemployment and inflation in voters' minds. So the campaign may depend on the question: "Which candidate can I trust to restore to my own Government the things that are important to me?"

QUESTION: Have other issues receded in importance?

ANSWER: They are mirrored in many ways, depending on the individuals, as self-assessed needs.

Some people are intensely concerned about agricultural policy. Others are concerned about unemployment, particularly those that are unemployed. There's a general concern about the creeping tendency toward Government intrusion into our private lives. There's a concern about the weakening of local government as contrasted with the Federal Government. There's concern about the gross, uncontrollable bureaucracy that's built up in Washington, the secrecy in the White House and in the Congress, the unwarranted influence of special-interest groups, the lack of a comprehensive and competent welfare system, inadequate health care, unfair tax structure.

But specific issues are just part of it. The other concern of people is whether they can trust this candidate to do something about it. Can they trust this candidate to care about them? Do they have to go through some powerful intermediary to get to the candidate and his consciousness about what their needs and their families' needs are about?

QUESTION: Are you suggesting a Jacksonian approach to an open White House? Would you go that far?

ANSWER: Not with mud-filled clodhoppers—not that kind of concept.

But I would restore, for instance, the "fireside chat" format [used by Franklin D. Roosevelt] for explaining complicated questions to the public. I would restore frequent live press conferences that have now been abandoned.

I would press for a comprehensive "sunshine" law in the Federal Government—to open decision-making meetings to the public. I would act through executive order, prior to the time a law could be passed, to initiate more openness in Government.

QUESTION: Governor, does the Carter-Mondale ticket have particular vulnerability among Roman Catholic voters?

ANSWER: I don't believe so. Among the leaders within the Catholic Church there is an open, expressed concern about the abortion issue, about my Baptist beliefs that is not mirrored among the average citizens in the country who happen to be Catholic. It's something that we discern as a potential problem, but the public-opinion-poll results now show that there's no distinguishable difference between the support for me by Protestants as contrasted with the support from Catholics.

QUESTION: What do you feel are the strongest features of the Democratic ticket in terms of voter appeal?

ANSWER: For one thing, the disaffection with the present Washington establishment, a feeling that there is a continuity present between Nixon's Administration and Ford's—not the Watergate disgrace, but that Ford is not exerting leadership to correct the deficiencies that existed when Nixon was here.

Also, there is an advantage in the youthfulness of our ticket—averaging 50 years old. I'm 51 and Mondale is 48. This gives rise to the feeling that we might be innovative.

QUESTION: You have said that you anticipated a very personal, vicious attack against you and Senator Mondale in the campaign. What is your evidence of that?

ANSWER: It's just a surmise. We should be ready for a very highly combative and hard-fought campaign.

QUESTION: On what points do you expect the attack?

ANSWER: I've noticed that there have been statements made that if I were elected, the farmers would have the decisions made for them by the Washington bureaucracy, that we would have a termination of export sales overseas, and other ridiculous things of that kind. I've made just the opposite remarks.

There have also been comments made that my promises to the American people would be grossly liberal, that the budget would be unbalanced, and that there would be no tight management of the federal spending policies—all of which I think is unjustified.

There have been statements made about Senator Mondale's liberality on some issues. I think basically his stand on the "litmus test" kind of things—concerning busing, for instance—is about the same as mine: I'm against forced busing; so is he. I'm not in favor of a constitutional amendment to try to outlaw busing, and neither is he.

QUESTION: Charges have been made that your policies are going to re-ignite inflation—

ANSWER: I don't think my policies would contribute to increased inflation.

QUESTION: Do you expect the Republicans to zero in on the inflation issue?

ANSWER: They are in an indefensible position:

We have an inflation rate of roughly 5 per cent that is going to go up between now and November. I don't think we had that kind of inflation rate for 30 years before Nixon became President.

We've got the highest unemployment levels in 25 years.

We have had in the last three budgets 160 billion dollars in deficits—greater than all the accumulated deficits that existed from World War II right on up to 1974.

QUESTION: It sounds as if you're running against Richard Nixon and not Gerald Ford. Is that your strategy?

ANSWER: I haven't seen any change in direction or an attempt to change the policies that Nixon established since Ford has been in the

White House. I think Ford has been a dormant, inactive President who has just enjoyed his domicile in the White House but has not addressed any of the problems that I see in the management of Government.

I don't think that Ford has continued the disreputable tragedy of Watergate attitudes that disgraced the White House. I don't attribute that sort of scandal to Ford at all.

But as far as just adopting what Nixon's policies were and continuing them, I don't think there's any doubt that there's been almost absolute continuity there.

QUESTION: From the point of view of geography, in which regions of the country would you say that you are weakest?

ANSWER: I would say New England and the industrial midsection of the country—in the Illinois-Indiana-Michigan area. But I would not write off any State.

QUESTION: Will you campaign in all 50 States?

ANSWER: I don't think it would be possible to go into all 50 States during this brief period of time.

In general, I'll go where I can contribute most to the Democratic ticket, including myself and candidates for Congress or Governor, U.S. Senate. And Senator Mondale will go where he can contribute the most.

QUESTION: If you win the election, Governor, should the nation expect rapid changes in policies—a quick succession of messages to Congress?

ANSWER: Yes. In some areas I would be ready for proposals immediately:

I would like to have complete authorization to reorganize the executive branch of Government, giving me as much authority as possible.

I would like to be ready to propose welfare reform.

I would seek whatever minimal authority is necessary to start a complete assessment of tax reform in a comprehensive way—and, as I've mentioned, the "sunshine" law: the openness of Government.

I think I would be ready for the first stage of implementing an adequate health-care program for the country. This would take three or four years, and I would want to be careful to phase it in a way that would be minimal in extra cost.

QUESTION: Congress willing—

ANSWER: I intend to keep all my promises. It may be that the Congress would not co-operate in some of those areas. If not, I reserve the right to go directly to the people of this country and present my case there.

There may be a danger, with so many proposals, that they will get in each other's way. But I think a compensating factor would be my inclination to capitalize on whatever mandate I get in November. The longer one waits on a controversial matter, the less chance he has of success.

QUESTION: You mentioned a reorganization of the executive branch. What do you have in mind?

ANSWER: The elimination of unnecessary agencies and departments, regulations and paper work. That is going to take a long time. I want to get the authority immediately and have a presumption of congressional support as we initiate a long, detailed study. It would take at least a year.

But there is no question we will reduce the number of agencies. We now have 100 different programs, for instance, that could come under the generic name of "welfare." I don't think we need more than one or two. Nor do we need more than one or two agencies responsible for health care.

We now have had 1,900 categorical-grant programs, compared to 150 when President Eisenhower went out of office. The multiplicity of those programs puts an inordinate load on administrative bodies at the State and local levels. That has got to be addressed.

QUESTION: Will reduction in the number of agencies reduce the cost of Government?

ANSWER: As far as the percentage of budget that goes for administrative costs, there would be a substantial savings there.

As far as a total budget is concerned, I don't think it would result in any substantial reduction. But the effectiveness of delivery services would be substantially enhanced.

QUESTION: How do you plan to cope with high unemployment if you become President?

ANSWER: My strong commitment is to take the necessary action to bring about full employment, if possible, in the private sector of our economy. I don't favor Government jobs as the principal way to alleviate the unemployment question. They cost too much at $8,000 to $10,000 per job.

The Government can help to revive construction. It can allocate research-and-development funds and establish comprehensive proposals on transportation and energy and agriculture. It can try to persuade both industry and labor to be responsible in their demands for increased prices and wages, involving them in the decision-making processes. Those kinds of things would have a cumulative effect in creating jobs within the private sector.

There are, however, a couple of areas where I would want to have federal jobs available. One is the chronic welfare recipient who is able to work full time. About 1.3 million welfare recipients have nothing wrong with them physically or mentally. I would like to have, perhaps in a welfare-reform package, a requirement that they be trained, then offered a job—and if they don't take a job, I wouldn't want to pay them any more benefits.

Another problem is unemployment among young people. We now have about a 20 to 23 per cent unemployment rate among young Americans; 40 per cent among black young Americans. I would like to pursue the concept of an approach like the CCC [Civilian Conservation Corps] program we had during the depression years, this time oriented more to the urban areas than to the woods and rural areas.

QUESTION: What is your thinking on tax reform?

ANSWER: I don't think we'll ever have comprehensive equity established within the present income-tax structure if you do it one section at a time or piecemeal, because the public has no idea what's going on. My premise would be to start from scratch rather than simply revise today's system. Many aspects of the present tax system, of course, would be part of the final result.

QUESTION: Can you indicate, at least broadly, your own approach?

ANSWER: I would have as a major goal the drastic simplification of the tax structure. It now consists of about 40,000 pages in the Tax Code. I would treat all income basically the same. I would tax income only once. I would have a truly progressive tax structure so that those who have higher incomes would pay a higher percentage of their income in taxes.

There are some things in the current system that I would certainly want to preserve: the ability to make legitimate contributions for charitable purposes, for example. But I would want to make sure the foundations that were established for that purpose don't abuse the privilege.

I'm concerned about the effect of delayed tax payments on profits overseas. I think it contributes to excessive unemployment in our nation when, for example, one of our corporations overseas makes a million dollars and reinvests it in, say, Italy because that way they don't have to pay any taxes on it. If they bring it back to this country to reinvest it—to create new jobs—they have to pay taxes. That bothers me, and my inclination would be to abolish that privilege.

On the other hand, the present right of a corporation overseas to deduct income-tax payments made to another government is a legitimate thing and ought to be continued.

QUESTION: When would you expect to present to Congress such a comprehensive tax-reform program?

ANSWER: The first part of 1978. I would want to let advocacy groups, from consumer advocates to the multinational corporations, be involved in the deliberations—probably in my presence—as well as professional analysts and economists. I don't expect to achieve any unanimity, obviously.

I would also want to be very sure that representatives from the Congress, both the House and Senate, were involved in the detailed discussions—hopefully, at the initial stages of the study. I would be the one responsible for selling the proposition or the proposal to the people and to the Congress.

QUESTION: Are you in favor of federalizing the entire welfare system?

ANSWER: No, I don't see any possibility of that. The approach that I took as Governor was to try to remove from the local governments as much as possible the financing of Statewide programs. I would take the same concept to the federal level. I don't think the property tax or the sales tax is a good base for financing the welfare system of our country.

But I wouldn't propose to put the full responsibility for welfare payments onto the Federal Government. It may be that we would freeze the State contribution and let the Federal Government assume the responsibility for financing any increase in future cost brought about by broader coverage or by inflationary trends.

But there needs to be some predictability about it. Mayors and Governors and their compatriots of the State governments should be able to predict ahead of time how much they're going to have to pay.

QUESTION: In the field of health care, what are your proposals?

ANSWER: We need a better health care-and-delivery system in this country. We're spending for every man, woman and child in our nation $550 a year. There are vast areas where health care is not available at all. We have little emphasis on preventive health care—less now than we had when I was a boy on the farm.

The crux of the problem lies in the complete confusion that exists in the delivery of health care now. We have 72 different agencies responsible for physical-health care. We have 37 agencies responsible for mental-health care. We have 10 different major departments that are involved in health care. To have any sort of good health-delivery system, you've got to have some way to have a clear assignment of responsibility for the delivery of health care to our people.

QUESTION: Where do you stand on abortion—and on the Government's role in the matter?

ANSWER: I think abortion is wrong and that the Government ought never do anything to encourage abortion. But I do not favor a constitutional amendment which would prohibit all abortions, nor one that would give States local option to ban abortions.

Government ought to do everything possible to minimize the need for abortions. We need a comprehensive national program designed to minimize abortions with better adoptive procedures, sex education and family planning.

QUESTION: On foreign policy, would you press for a summit conference with other leaders soon after you took office?

ANSWER: I would like to avoid very much travel myself during the first period of my Administration if I am elected.

I think that a summit conference after the election would be important, but I would prefer that leaders of other countries come here.

QUESTION: Do you feel that we should adopt a tougher approach in pursuing détente with the Soviet Union?

ANSWER: Yes, I think so. The Soviets would respect that approach. I would also make our commitments much more public.

I think that the stature of our nation in international councils is damaged when the President and the Secretary of State speak just as two people, when there's no bipartisan assessment or support derived from the Congress, and when it's obvious that the American people don't know what is going on: It inherently makes the Secretary of State weak.

QUESTION: In what ways would you be tougher toward the Soviet Union?

ANSWER: We should have been much more aggressive when we attended the Helsinki Conference—or should have been absent in the first place.

We now have in Eastern Europe at least a tentative endorsement by our country of the domination of that region by the Soviet Union. They didn't have that before the Helsinki accords. It was a very great diplomatic achievement for the Soviets to have our promise not to interfere in their control over Eastern Europe.

In response to our yielding on that point, there was an agreement on the Soviet Union's part that they would liberalize their policies toward human rights. They have not fulfilled those commitments.

As we sell the Russians things that they must have—food in their drought years, electronics equipment, heavy machinery—we ought to get a *quid pro quo* from the Soviets.

I think it was a mistake, personally, to attach the Jewish-migration question to the trade bill: You can't have the legislative body of a sovereign nation requiring publicly that another sovereign nation accede to a certain demand in order to get a very slight favor. But freedom for Jews to leave Russia would be a legitimate and a very strong commitment of mine as President. As we negotiate with the Soviets, they should know that if they could yield on that point it would greatly improve our relationships.

I think we could ask them to help to resolve the Middle Eastern question, not let them stoke the fires; to help us avoid a future oil embargo; to try to give us stronger assurances that they would restrain Northern Korea from any possible attack on South Korea; to yield on controversial points in the SALT II talks.

There are a lot of things that we need and would like to have from the Soviet Union to insure peace around the world, and there are a lot of materials we have that they would need more of.

QUESTION: Would you envisage moving quickly to normalize relations with Peking—perhaps involving recognition?

ANSWER: No, I don't envision that. It's an ultimate goal that's good for us to maintain.

Eventually we're going to have to recognize the existence of the People's Republic of China. But I would want to have an assurance in some way, to my satisfaction, that there would not be a military attack on Taiwan and that the Taiwanese people would be relatively independent and our commitment to them respected.

QUESTION: On the Middle East, should the United States underwrite the security of Israel as a way of bringing about a final settlement?

ANSWER: Not a commitment to send troops, no. But I would let it be known to the world, and particularly the people of Israel, that our backing for Israel in economic and military aid is absolute, that this would be a national commitment of ours. Most Americans would agree with this: to give the Israelis whatever military or economic aid they need to protect the integrity of their country, their right to exist in peace.

I would also play a more aggressive role in searching for some degree of compatibility among Middle East nations. The situation there is fluid. The relationship, for instance, among Israel, Lebanon and Syria has changed in the last few months. That fluidity might create an opportunity for success. The Soviet Union may be seeing that their allegiances or alliances in the Middle East could be more advantageous with permanent peace assured.

The framework of United Nations Resolution 242 is a general one that everybody has adopted. The interpretation of the language is obviously widely diverse, depending on the point of view. But I think the recognition of Israel as a permanent entity in the Middle East—the nonbelligerency status or declaration by their potential adversaries—is important; the willingness of Israel to cede back to other countries major portions of land acquired in the '67 war is an inevitable requirement.

Some resolution of the Palestinian question is certainly inevitable. There are some very serious problems that would have to be addressed, possibly through secret negotiations and through concerted commitments to preserve the peace. One would be control of the Golan Heights and Jerusalem.

QUESTION: In Africa, should the U.S. throw its weight behind black-majority rule in Rhodesia and even in South Africa?

ANSWER: The historic expressions of our Government in favor of majority rule ought to be continued.

The crisis in Rhodesia is much more acute than it is in South Africa. The principle is the same. There's a difference, obviously, between those two nations in that the South Africans have been there for, I think, 300 or 400 years.

QUESTION: On defense, Governor, would you make any fundamental changes in our military structure?

ANSWER: Possibly. I do favor the continuation of our three delivery systems for atomic weapons until we can negotiate some over-all reduction of weapons with the Soviet Union.

We are inferior to the Soviets in our land-based intercontinental missiles—greatly inferior. We have a rough equivalency at sea, and we are strongly superior in manned bombers. I think in general we have what is called rough equivalency. I certainly want to maintain that. But I don't think we could give up any of those three elements of international strategic defense.

As far as redeployment of forces is concerned, I don't think we have had a substantive reassessment of strategic deployment since President Truman's time. In the past, a basic presumption has been that we had to be prepared for a major land war in the Far East and in the Western Pacific. I'm not sure that that's still a good supposition.

I don't want to be more specific, but I think a reassessment of our strategic deployment of nonnuclear weapons and delivery systems is needed now.

QUESTION: Turning to the organization of your Administration: If you win in November, would you change the role of the Cabinet?

ANSWER: There would be a much heavier dependence on the Cabinet members to run their departments than we've had in the past. I would not establish a "palace guard" in the White House with the authority to run the departments in the Federal Government. I don't say that lightly. A lot of people say, "Well, I've heard that before."

When I was Governor of Georgia, we never tried to run the State government just with my personal staff. I chose the best people I could, the strongest advocates for those who received services from their department, and good managers.

I would make sure that every person I put in charge of a major department in the capital would be a good manager. I would lean, I think, toward people who've had experience—maybe as Governors, for instance—and who would be compatible with me. They should be able spokesmen for and have a strong belief in the purpose of their department. For example, I would choose someone to head up the Defense Department who believed in a strong defense.

QUESTION: Given a strong Cabinet, what role do you have in mind for the White House staff? Will it arbitrate disputes between Cabinet members?

ANSWER: I think not, except that when you have a Director, say, of the National Security Council or his successor, that would certainly be a very strong and influential person.

I would say the Appointments Secretary would be the one to provide access to me.

And the relationship that I would establish between the White House and the Office of Management and Budget would be much closer than we've known in the past. I think that would obviate the need for a large White House staff. We would make reductions in the size of the staff.

QUESTION: How do you think the style of leadership in a Carter White House would differ from that in the Ford White House?

ANSWER: I don't detect any leadership emanating from the White House at this point.

I would try to find in my own mind what improvements might be made in legislation and Government policy. I'd take on myself the responsibility for being the one to present changes to the Congress and to the people and pursue those changes aggressively once I've decided what ought to be done.

I would also involve the Congress in an intimate way, as much as they would permit me, in the evolution of new proposals.

QUESTION: It has been said that one of your faults as Governor of Georgia was an unwillingness to compromise with the State legislature. Would you anticipate similar problems in dealing with Congress?

ANSWER: Yes, sir. But there are several things that can be done. I learned a lot as Governor, and I think that's one of the things that I did learn.

QUESTION: To compromise more often?

ANSWER: When to compromise and when not to compromise. The best way to deal with it is to have engendered within the consciousness of the President and the Congress a feeling of mutual respect, as well as continuing consultations and sharing of ideas.

Along with that would come an openness to let the public know what we are doing and to restore the concept in the Congress that their constituents are also my constituents. I have just as much right and responsibility to reach to the people for support as a member of Congress does.

3

PLAYBOY INTERVIEW, NOV. 1976

Playboy, Robert Scheer

This interview is arguably the best known, most widely read, and most frequently quoted of all Carter conversations. Shortly after its publication, Carter lost 15 points in the polls. Although the interview is extensive and informative, most of the world only remembers that Carter lusted in his heart.—*Editor*

PLAYBOY: After nearly two years on the campaign trail, don't you feel a little numbed by the routine—for instance, having to give the same speech over and over?

CARTER: Sometimes. Once, when I was campaigning in the Florida primary, I made 12 speeches in one day. It was the worst day I ever had. But I generally have tried to change the order of the speech and emphasize different things. Sometimes I abbreviate and sometimes I elaborate. Of 20 different parts in a speech, I might take seven or eight and change them around. It depends on the audience—black people, Jewish people, *chicanos*—and that gives me the ability to make speeches that aren't boring to myself.

PLAYBOY: Every politician probably emphasizes different things to different audiences, but in your case, there's been a common criticism that you seem to have several faces, that you try to be all things to all people. How do you respond to that?

CARTER: I can't make myself believe these are contrivances and subterfuges I've adopted to get votes. It may be, and I can't get myself to admit it, but what I want to do is to let people know how I stand on the issues as honestly as I can.

PLAYBOY: If you feel you've been fully honest, why has the charge persisted that you're "fuzzy" on the issues?

CARTER: It started during the primaries, when most of my opponents were members of Congress. When any question on an issue came up, they would say, "I'm for the Kennedy-Corman bill on health care, period, no matter what's in it." If the question was on employment, they would say, "I'm for the Humphrey-Hawkins bill, no matter what's in it." But those bills were constantly being amended!

I'm just not able to do that. I have to understand what I'm talking about, and simplistic answers identifying my position with such-and-such a House bill are something I can't put forward. That's one reason I've been seen as fuzzy.

Another is that I'm not an ideolog and my positions are not predictable. Without any criticism of McGovern, if the question had ever come up on abortion, you could pretty well anticipate what he was going to say. If it were amnesty, you could predict what McGovern was going to say about that. But I've tried to analyze each question individually; I've taken positions that to me are fair and rational, and sometimes my answers are complicated.

The third reason is that I wasn't a very vulnerable opponent for those who ran against me. Fuzziness was the only issue Congressman Udall, Senator Church—and others that are hard to remember now—could adopt in their campaigns against me. I think the drumming of that factor into the consciousness of the American voter obviously had some impact.

PLAYBOY: Still, not everybody's sure whether you're a conservative in liberal clothing or vice versa. F.D.R., for instance, turned out to be something of a surprise to people who'd voted for him, because he hadn't seemed as progressive before he was elected as he turned out to be. Could you be a surprise that way?

CARTER: I don't believe that's going to be the case. If you analyze the Democratic Party platform, you'll see that it's a very progressive, very liberal, very socially motivated platform. What sometimes surprises people is that I carry out my promises. People ask how a peanut farmer from the South who believes in balanced budgets and tough management of Government can possibly give the country tax and welfare reform, or a national health program, or insist on equal rights for blacks and women. Well, I'm going to *do* those things. I've promised them during the campaign, so I don't think there will be many people disappointed—or surprised—when I carry out those commitments as President.

PLAYBOY: But isn't it true that you turned out to be more liberal as governor of Georgia than people who voted for you had any reason to suspect?

CARTER: I don't really think so. No. *The Atlanta Constitution,* which was the source of all information about me, categorized me during the gubernatorial campaign as an ignorant, racist, backward, ultraconservative, rednecked South Georgia peanut farmer. Its candidate, Carl Sanders, the former governor, was characterized as an enlightened, progressive, well-educated, urbane, forceful, competent public official. I never agreed with the categorization that was made of me during the campaign. I was the same person before and after I became governor. I remember keeping a check list and every time I made a promise during the campaign, I wrote it down in a notebook. I believe I carried out every promise I made. I told several people during the campaign that one of the phrases I was going to use in my inaugural speech was that the time for racial discrimination was over. I wrote and made that speech.

The ultraconservatives in Georgia—who aren't supporting me now, by the way—voted for me because of their animosity toward Carl Sanders. I was the alternative to him. They never asked me, "Are you a racist or have you been a member of the Ku Klux Klan?" because they knew I wasn't and hadn't been. And yet, despite predictions early this year by *The Atlanta Constitution* that I couldn't get a majority of the primary vote in Georgia against Wallace, I received about 85 percent of the votes. So I don't think the Georgia people have the feeling I betrayed them.

PLAYBOY: Considering what you've just said about *The Atlanta Constitution,* how do you feel about the media in general and about the job they do in covering the election issues?

CARTER: There's still a tendency on the part of some members of the press to treat the South, you know, as a suspect nation. There are a few who think that since I am a Southern governor, I must be a secret racist or there's something in a closet somewhere that's going to be revealed to show my true colors. There's been a constant probing back ten, twelve years in my background, even as early as the first primaries. Nobody probed like that into the background of Udall or Bayh or other people. But I don't object to it particularly, I just recognize it.

(The answer was broken off and, at a later session, Carter returned to the question of the press and its coverage of issues. This time he was tired, his head sunk far back into his airplane seat. The exchange occurred during one of the late primaries.)

Issues? The local media are interested, all right, but the national news media have absolutely no interest in issues *at all.* Sometimes we freeze out the national media so we can open up press conferences to local people. At least we get questions from them—on timber management, on health care, on education. But the traveling press have zero interest in any issue unless it's a matter of making a mistake. What they're looking for is a 47-second argument between me and another candidate or something like that. There's nobody in the back of this plane who would ask an issue question unless he thought he could trick me into some crazy statement.

PLAYBOY: One crazy statement you were supposed to have made was reported by Robert Shrum after he quit as your speechwriter earlier this year. He said he'd been in conversations with you when you made some slighting references to Jewish voters. What's your version of what happened?

CARTER: Shrum dreamed up eight or ten conversations that never took place and nobody in the press ever asked me if they had occurred. The press just assumed that they had. I never talked to Shrum in private except for maybe a couple of minutes. If he had told the truth, if I had said all the things he claimed I had said, I wouldn't vote for *myself.*

When a poll came out early in the primaries that said I had a small proportion of the Jewish vote, I said, "Well, this is really a disappointment to me—we've worked so hard with the Jewish voters. But my pro-Israel stand won't change, even if I don't get a single Jewish vote; I guess we'll have to depend on non-Jews to put me in office." But Shrum treated it as if it were some kind of racist disavowal of Jews. Well, that's a kind of sleazy twisting of a conversation.

PLAYBOY: While we're on the subject of the press, how do you feel about an issue that concerns the press itself—the right of journalists to keep their sources secret?

CARTER: I would do everything I could to protect the secrecy of sources for the news media.

PLAYBOY: Both the press *and* the public seem to have made an issue out of your Baptist beliefs. Why do you think this has happened?

CARTER: I'm not unique. There are a lot of people in this country who have the same religious faith. It's not a mysterious or mystical or magical thing. But for those who don't know the feeling of someone who believes in Christ, who is aware of the presence of God, there is, I presume, a quizzical attitude toward it. But it's always been something I've discussed very frankly throughout my adult life.

PLAYBOY: We've heard that you pray 25 I times a day. Is that true?

CARTER: I've never counted. I've forgotten who asked me that, but I'd say that on an eventful day, you know, it's something like that.

PLAYBOY: When you say an eventful day, do you mean you pray as a kind of pause, to control your blood pressure and relax?

CARTER: Well, yes. If something happens to me that is a little disconcerting, if I feel a trepidation, if a thought comes into my head of animosity or hatred toward someone, then I just kind of say a brief silent prayer. I don't ask for myself but just to let me understand what another's feelings might be. Going through a crowd, quite often people bring me a problem, and I pray that their needs might be met. A lot of times, I'll be in the back seat of a car and not know what kind of audience I'm going to face. I don't mean I'm terror-stricken, just that I don't know what to expect next. I'll pray then, but it's not something that's conscious or formal. It's just a part of my life.

PLAYBOY: One reason some people might be quizzical is that you have a sister, Ruth, who is a faith healer. The association of politics with faith healing is an idea many find disconcerting.

CARTER: I don't even know what political ideas Ruth has had, and for people to suggest I'm under the hold of a sister—or any other person—is a complete distortion of fact. I don't have any idea whether Ruth has supported Democrats or not, whereas the political views of my other sister, Gloria, are remarkably harmonious with mine.

PLAYBOY: So you're closer to Gloria, who has described herself as a McGovern Democrat and rides motorcycles as a hobby?

CARTER: I like them both. But in the past 20 or 25 years, I've been much closer to Gloria, because she lives next door to me and Ruth lives in North Carolina. We hardly saw Ruth more than once a year at family get-togethers. What political attitudes Ruth has had, I have not the slightest idea. But my mother and Gloria and I have been very compatible. We supported Lyndon Johnson openly during the 1964 campaign and my mother worked at the Johnson county headquarters, which was courageous, not an easy thing to do politically. She would come out of the Johnson headquarters and find her car smeared with soap and the antenna tied in a knot and ugly messages left on the front seat. When my young boys went to school, they were beaten. So Mother and Gloria and I, along with my Rosalynn, have had the same attitudes even when we were in a minority in Plains. But Ruth lives in a different world in North Carolina.

PLAYBOY: Granting that you're not as close to your religious sister as is assumed, we still wonder how *your* religious beliefs would translate into political action. For instance, would you appoint judges who would be harsh or lenient toward victimless crimes—offenses such as drug use, adultery, sodomy and homosexuality?

CARTER: Committing adultery, according to the Bible—which I believe in—is a sin. For us to hate one another, for us to have sexual intercourse outside marriage, for us to engage in homosexual activities, for us to steal, for us to lie—all these are sins. But Jesus teaches us not to judge other people. We don't assume the role of judge and say to another human being, "You're condemned because you commit sins." All Christians, all of us, acknowledge that we are sinful and the judgment comes from God, not from another human being.

As governor of Georgia, I tried to shift the emphasis of law enforcement away from victimless crimes. We lessened the penalties on the use of marijuana. We removed alcoholism as a crime, and so forth. Victimless crimes, in my opinion, should have a very low priority in terms of enforcing the laws on the books. But as to appointing judges, that would not be the basis on which I'd appoint them. I would choose people who were competent, whose judgment and integrity were sound. I think it would be inappropriate to ask them how they were going to rule on a particular question before I appointed them.

PLAYBOY: What *about* those laws on the books that govern personal behavior? Should they be enforced?

CARTER: Almost every state in the Union has laws against adultery and many of them have laws against homosexuality and sodomy. But they're often considered by police officers as not worthy of enforcing to the extent of disturbing consenting adults or breaking into a person's private home.

PLAYBOY: But, of course, that gives the police a lot of leeway to enforce them selectively. Do you think such laws should be on the books at all?

CARTER: That's a judgment for the individual states to make. I think the laws are on the books quite often because of their relationship to the Bible. Early in the nation's development, the Judaeo-Christian moral standards were accepted as a basis for civil law. But I don't think it hurts to have this kind of standard maintained as a goal. I also think it's an area that's been interpreted by the Supreme Court as one that can rightfully be retained by the individual states.

PLAYBOY: Do you think liberalization of the laws over the past decade by factors as diverse as the pill and *Playboy*—an effect some people would term permissiveness—has been a harmful development?

CARTER: Liberalization of some of the laws has been good. You can't legislate morality. We used to outlaw consumption of alcoholic beverages. We found that violation of the law led to bigger crimes and bred disrespect for the law.

PLAYBOY: We're confused. You say morality can't be legislated, yet you support certain laws because they preserve old moral standards. How do you reconcile the two positions?

CARTER: I believe people should honor civil laws. If there is a conflict between God's law and civil law, we should honor God's law. But we should be willing to accept civil punishment. Most of Christ's original followers were killed because of their belief in Christ; they violated the civil law in following God's law. Reinhold Niebuhr, a theologian who has dealt with this problem at length, says that the framework of law is a balancing of forces in a society; the law itself tends to alleviate tensions brought about by these forces. But the laws on the books are not a measure of this balance nearly as much as the degree to which the laws are enforced. So when a law is anachronistic and is carried over from a previous age, it's just not observed.

PLAYBOY: What we're getting at is how much you'd tolerate behavior that your religion considers wrong. For instance, in San Francisco, you said you considered homosexuality a sin. What does that mean in political terms?

CARTER: The issue of homosexuality always makes me nervous. It's obviously one of the major issues in San Francisco. I don't have any, you know, personal knowledge about homosexuality and I guess being a Baptist, that would contribute to a sense of being uneasy.

PLAYBOY: Does it make you uneasy to discuss it simply as a political question?

CARTER: No, it's more complicated than that. It's political, it's moral and it's strange territory for me. At home in Plains, we've had homosexuals in our community, our church. There's never been any sort of discrimination—some embarrassment but no animosity, no harassment. But to inject it into a public discussion on politics and how it conflicts with morality is a new experience for me. I've thought about it a lot, but I don't see how to handle it differently from the way I look on other sexual acts outside marriage.

PLAYBOY: We'd like to ask you a blunt question: Isn't it just these views about what's "sinful" and what's "immoral" that contribute to the feeling that you might get a call from God, or get inspired and push the wrong button? More realistically, wouldn't we expect a puritanical tone to be set in the White House if you were elected?

Carter: Harry Truman was a Baptist. Some people get very abusive about the Baptist faith. If people want to know about it, they can read the New Testament. The main thing is that we don't think we're better than anyone else. We are taught not to judge other people. But as to some of the behavior you've mentioned, I can't change the teachings of Christ. I can't change the teachings of Christ! I believe in them, and a lot of people in this country do as well. Jews believe in the Bible. They have the same commandments.

Playboy: Then you as President, in appointing Supreme Court Justices—

Carter: I think we've pursued this conversation long enough—if you have another question. . . . Look, I'll try to express my views. It's not a matter of condemnation, it's not a matter of persecution. I've been a governor for four years. Anybody can come and look at my record. I didn't run around breaking down people's doors to see if they were fornicating. This is something that's ridiculous.

Playboy: We know you didn't, but we're being so persistent because of this matter of self-righteousness, because of the moral certainty of so many of your statements. People wonder if Jimmy Carter ever is unsure. Has he ever been wrong, has he ever had a failure of moral nerve?

Carter: Well, there are a lot of things I could have done differently had I known during my early life what I now know. I would certainly have spoken out more clearly and loudly on the civil rights issue. I would have demanded that our nation never get involved initially in the Vietnam war. I would have told the country in 1972 that Watergate was a much more horrible crime than we thought at the time. It's easy to say in hindsight what you would have done if you had had information you now have.

Playboy: We were asking not so much about hindsight as about being fallible. Aren't there any examples of things you did that weren't absolutely right?

Carter: I don't mind repeating myself. There are a lot of those in my life. Not speaking out for the cessation of the war in Vietnam. The fact that I didn't crusade at a very early stage for civil rights in the South, for the one-man, one-vote ruling. It might be that now I should drop my campaign for President and start a crusade for black-majority rule in South Africa or Rhodesia. It might be that later on, we'll discover there were opportunities in our lives to do wonderful things and we didn't take advantage of them.

The fact that in 1954 I sat back and required the Warren Court to make this ruling without having crusaded myself—that was obviously a mistake on my part. But these are things you have to judge under the circumstances that prevailed when the decisions were being made. Back then, the Congress, the President, the newspaper editors, the civil libertarians all said that separate-but-equal facilities were adequate. These are opportunities overlooked, or maybe they could be characterized as absence of courage.

PLAYBOY: Since you still seem to be saying you'd have done the right thing if you'd known what you know now, is it realistic to conclude that a person running for the highest office in the land *can't* admit many mistakes or moments of self-doubt?

CARTER: I think that's a human circumstance. But if there are issues I'm avoiding because of a lack of courage, either I don't recognize them or I can't make myself recognize them.

PLAYBOY: You mentioned Vietnam. Do you feel you spoke out at an early enough stage against the war?

CARTER: No, I did not. I never spoke out publicly about withdrawing completely from Vietnam until March of 1971.

PLAYBOY: Why?

CARTER: It was the first time anybody had asked me about it. I was a farmer before then and wasn't asked about the war until I took office. There was a general feeling in this country that we ought not to be in Vietnam to start with. The American people were tremendously misled about the immediate prospects for victory, about the level of our involvement, about the relative cost in American lives. If I had known in the Sixties what I knew in the early Seventies, I think I would have spoken out more strongly. I was not in public office. When I took office as governor in 1970, I began to speak out about complete withdrawal. It was late compared with what many others had done, but I think it's accurate to say that the Congress and the people—with the exception of very small numbers of people— shared the belief that we were protecting our democratic allies.

PLAYBOY: Even without holding office, you must have had some feelings about the war. When do you recall first feeling it was wrong?

CARTER: There was an accepted feeling by me and everybody else that we ought not to be there, that we should never have gotten involved, we ought to get out.

PLAYBOY: You felt that way all through the Sixties?

CARTER: Yeah, that's right, and I might hasten to say that it was the same feeling expressed by Senators Russell and Talmadge—very conservative Southern political figures. They thought it was a serious mistake to be in Vietnam.

PLAYBOY: Your son Jack fought in that war. Did you have any qualms about it at the time?

CARTER: Well, yes, I had problems about my son fighting in the war, period. But I never make my sons' decisions for them. Jack went to war feeling it was foolish, a waste of time, much more deeply than I did. He also felt it would have been grossly unfair for him not to go when other, poorer kids had to.

PLAYBOY: You were in favor of allocating funds for the South Vietnamese in 1975 as the war was coming to a close, weren't you?

CARTER: That was when we were getting ready to evacuate our troops. The purpose of the money was to get our people out and maintain harmony between us and our Vietnamese allies, who had fought with us for 25 years. And I said yes, I would do that. But it was not a permanent thing, not to continue the war but to let us get our troops out in an orderly fashion.

PLAYBOY: How do you respond to the argument that it was the Democrats, not the Republicans, who got us into the Vietnam war?

CARTER: I think it started originally, maybe, with Eisenhower, then Kennedy, Johnson and then Nixon. It's not a partisan matter. I think Eisenhower probably first got us in there thinking that since France had failed, our country might slip in there and succeed. Kennedy thought he could escalate involvement by going beyond the mere advisory role. I guess if there was one President who made the most determined effort, conceivably, to end the war by massive force, it was certainly Johnson. And Nixon went into Cambodia and bombed it, and so forth.

It's not partisan—it's just a matter that evolved as a habit over several administrations. There was a governmental consciousness to deal in secrecy, to exclude the American people, to mislead them with false statements and sometimes outright lies. Had the American people been told the facts from the beginning by Eisenhower, Kennedy, MacNamara, Johnson, Kissinger and Nixon, I think there would have been different decisions made in our Government.

PLAYBOY: At the Democratic Convention, you praised Johnson as a President who had vastly extended human rights. Were you simply omitting any mention of Vietnam?

CARTER: It was obviously the factor that destroyed his political career and damaged his whole life. But as far as what I said at the convention, there hasn't been another President in our history—with the possible exception of Abraham Lincoln—who did so much to advance the cause of human rights.

PLAYBOY: Except for the human rights of the Vietnamese and the Americans who fought there.

CARTER: Well, I really believe that Johnson's motives were good. I think he tried to end the war even while the fighting was going on, and he was speaking about massive rehabilitation efforts, financed by our Government, to help people. I don't think he ever had any desire for permanent entrenchment of our forces in Vietnam. I think he had a mistaken notion that he was defending democracy and that what he was doing was compatible with the desires of the South Vietnamese.

PLAYBOY: Then what about the administration that *ended* the war? Don't you have to give credit to Kissinger, the Secretary of State of a Republican President, for ending a war that a Democratic President escalated?

CARTER: I think the statistics show that more bombs were dropped in Vietnam and Cambodia under Nixon and Kissinger than under Johnson. Both administrations were at fault; but I don't think the end came about as a result of Kissinger's superior diplomacy. It was the result of several factors that built up in an inexorable way: the demonstrated strength of the Viet Cong, the tremendous pressure to withdraw that came from the American people and an aroused Congress. I think Nixon and Kissinger did the proper thing in starting a phased withdrawal, but I don't consider that to be a notable diplomatic achievement by Kissinger. As we've now learned, he promised the Vietnamese things that cannot be delivered—reparations, payments, economic advantages, and so forth. Getting out of Vietnam was very good, but whether Kissinger deserved substantial diplomatic credit for it is something I doubt.

PLAYBOY: You've said you'll pardon men who refused military service because of the Vietnam war but not necessarily those who deserted while they were in the Armed Forces. Is that right?

CARTER: That's right. I would not include them. Deserters ought to be handled on a separate-case basis. There's a difference to me. I was in the Navy for a long time. Somebody who goes into the military joins a kind of mutual partnership arrangement, you know what I mean? Your life depends on other people, their lives depend on you. So I don't intend to pardon the deserters. As far as the other categories of war resisters go, to me the ones who stayed in this country and let their opposition to the war be known publicly are more heroic than those who went and hid in Sweden. But I'm not capable of judging motives, so I'm just going to declare a blanket pardon.

PLAYBOY: When?

CARTER: The first week I'm in office.

PLAYBOY: You've avoided the word amnesty and chosen to use the word pardon, but there doesn't seem to be much difference between the two in the dictionary. Could it be because amnesty is more emotionally charged and pardon a word more people will accept?

CARTER: You know I can't deny that. But my reason for distinguishing between the two is that I think that all of those poor, and often black, young men who went to Vietnam are more worthy of recognition than those who defected, and the word pardon includes those who simply avoided the war completely. But I just want to bring the defectors back to this country without punishment and, in doing so, I would like to have the support of the American people. I haven't been able to devise for private or public presentation a better way to do it.

PLAYBOY: Earlier this year, there was a report that as governor of Georgia, you had issued a resolution that seemed to support William Calley after his trial for the My Lai massacre and that you'd referred to him as a scapegoat. Was that a misreading of your position?

CARTER: Yes. There was no reason for me to mislead anybody on the Calley thing. I thought when I first read about him that Calley was a murderer. He was tried in Georgia and found to be a murderer. I said two things: One, that Calley was not typical of our American Servicemen and, two, that he was a scapegoat because his superiors should have been tried, too. The resolution I made as governor didn't have anything to do with Calley. The purpose of it, calling for solidarity with our boys in Vietnam, was to distinguish American Servicemen fighting an unpopular war. They weren't murderers, but they were equated, unfortunately, with a murderer in people's minds.

PLAYBOY: In preparing for this interview, we spoke with your mother, your son Chip and your sister Gloria. We asked them what single action would most disappoint them in a Carter Presidency. They all replied that it would be if you ever sent troops to intervene in a foreign war. In fact, Miss Lillian said she would picket the White House.

CARTER: They share my views completely.

PLAYBOY: What about more limited military action? Would you have handled the Mayaguez incident the same way President Ford did?

CARTER: Let me assess that in retrospect. It's obvious we didn't have adequate intelligence; we attacked an island when the Mayaguez crew was no longer there. There was a desire, I think, on the part of President Ford to extract maximum publicity from our effort, so that about 25 minutes after our crew was released, we went ahead and bombed the island airport. I hope I would have been capable of getting adequate intelligence, surrounded the island more quickly and isolated the crew so we wouldn't have had to attack the airport after the crew was released. These are some of the differences in the way I would have done it.

PLAYBOY: So it's a matter of degree; you would have intervened militarily, too.

CARTER: I would have done everything necessary to keep the crew from being taken to the mainland, yes.

PLAYBOY: Then would you summarize your position on foreign intervention?

CARTER: I would never intervene for the purpose of overthrowing a government. If enough were at stake for our national interest, I would use prestige, legitimate diplomatic leverage, trade mechanisms. But it would be the sort of effort that would not be embarrassing to this nation if revealed completely. I don't ever want to do anything as President that would be a contravention of the moral and ethical standards that I would exemplify in my own life as an individual or that would violate the principles or character of the American people.

PLAYBOY: Do you feel it's fair criticism that you seem to be going back to some familiar faces—such as Paul Warnke and Cyrus Vance—for foreign-policy advice? Isn't there a danger of history's repeating itself when you seek out those who were involved in our Vietnam decisions?

CARTER: I haven't heard that criticism. If you're raising it, then I respond to the new critic. These people contribute to foreign-affairs journals, they individually explore different concepts of foreign policy. I have 15 or 20 people who work with me very closely on foreign affairs. Their views are quite divergent. The fact that they may or may not have been involved in foreign-policy decisions in the past is certainly no detriment to their ability to help me now.

PLAYBOY: In some respects, your foreign policy seems similar to that established by Kissinger, Nixon and Ford. In fact, Kissinger stated that he didn't think your differences were substantial. How, precisely, does your view differ from theirs?

CARTER: As I've said in my speeches, I feel the policy of *détente* has given up too much to the Russians and gotten too little in return. I also feel Kissinger has equated his own popularity with the so-called advantages of *détente*. As I've traveled and spoken with world leaders—Helmut Schmidt of West Germany, Yitzhak Rabin of Israel, various leaders in Japan—I've discerned a deep concern on their part that the United States has abandoned a long-standing principle: to consult mutually, to share responsibility for problems. This has been a damaging thing. In addition, I believe we should have stronger bilateral relations with developing nations.

PLAYBOY: What do you mean when you say we've given up too much to the Russians?

CARTER: One example I've mentioned often is the Helsinki agreement. I never saw any reason we should be involved in the Helsinki meetings at all. We added the stature of our presence and signature to an agreement that, in effect, ratified the take-over of eastern Europe by the Soviet Union. We got very little, if anything, in return. The Russians promised they would honor democratic principles and permit the free movement of their citizens, including those who want to emigrate. The Soviet Union has not lived up to those promises and Mr. Brezhnev was able to celebrate the major achievement of his diplomatic life.

PLAYBOY: Are you charging that Kissinger was too soft on the Russians?

CARTER: Kissinger has been in the position of being almost uniquely a spokesman for our nation. I think that is a legitimate role and a proper responsibility of the President himself. Kissinger has had a kind of Lone Ranger, secret foreign-policy attitude, which almost ensures that there cannot be adequate consultation with our allies; there cannot be a long-range commitment to unchanging principles; there cannot be a coherent evolution on foreign policy; there cannot be a bipartisan approach with support and advice from Congress. This is what I would avoid as President and is one of the major defects in the Nixon-Ford foreign policy as expressed by Kissinger.

PLAYBOY: Say, do you always do your own sewing? *(This portion of the interview also took place aboard a plane. As he answered the interviewer's questions, Carter had been sewing a rip in his jacket with a needle and thread he carried with him.)*

CARTER: Uh-huh. *(He bit off the thread with his teeth.)*

PLAYBOY: Anyway, you said earlier that your foreign policy would exemplify your moral and ethical standards. Isn't there as much danger in an overly moralistic policy as in the kind that is too pragmatic?

CARTER: I've said I don't think we should intervene militarily, but I see no reason not to express our approval, at least verbally, with those nations that develop democratically. When Kissinger says, as he did recently in a speech, that Brazil is the sort of government that is most compatible with ours—well, that's the kind of thing we want to change. Brazil is not a democratic government; it's a military dictatorship. In many instances, it's highly repressive to political prisoners. Our Government should justify the character and moral principles of the American people, and our foreign policy should not short-circuit that for temporary advantage. I think in every instance we've done that it's been counterproductive. When the CIA undertakes covert activities that might be justified if they were peaceful, we always suffer when they're revealed—it always seems as if we're trying to tell other people how to act. When Kissinger and Ford warned Italy she would be excluded from NATO if the Communists assumed power, that was the best way to make sure Communists *were* elected. The Italian voters resent it. A proper posture for our country in this sort of situation is to show, through demonstration, that our own Government works properly, that democracy is advantageous, and let the Italian people make their own decisions.

PLAYBOY: And what if the Communists in Italy had been elected in greater numbers than they were? What if they had actually become a key part of the Italian government?

CARTER: I think it would be a mechanism for subversion of the strength of NATO and the cohesiveness that ought to bind European countries together. The proper posture was the one taken by Helmut Schmidt, who said that German aid to Italy would be endangered.

PLAYBOY: Don't you think that constitutes a form of intervention in the democratic processes of another nation?

CARTER: No, I don't. I think that when the democratic nations of the world express themselves frankly and forcefully and openly, that's a proper exertion of influence. We did the same thing in Portugal. Instead of going in through surreptitious means and trying to overthrow the government when it looked like the minority Communist Party was going to assume power, the NATO countries as a group made it clear to Portugal what it would lose in the way of friendship, trade opportunities, and so forth. And the Portuguese people, recognizing that possibility, decided that the Communists should not lead their government. Well, that was legitimate exertion of influence, in my opinion. It was done openly and it was a mere statement of fact.

PLAYBOY: You used the word subversion referring to communism. Hasn't the world changed since we used to throw words like that around? Aren't the west European Communist parties more independent of Moscow and more willing to respect democracy?

CARTER: Yes, the world's changed. In my speeches, I've made it clear that as far as Communist leaders in such countries as Italy, France and Portugal are concerned, I would not want to close the doors of communication, consultation and friendship to them. That would be an almost automatic forcing of the Communist leaders into the Soviet sphere of influence. I also think we should keep open our opportunities for the east European nations—even those that are completely Communist—to trade with us, understand us, have tourist exchange and give them an option from complete domination by the Soviet Union.

But again, I don't think you could expect West Germany to lend Poland two billion dollars—which was the figure in the case of Italy—when Poland is part of the Soviet government's satellite and supportive-nation group. So I think the best way to minimize totalitarian influence within the governments of Europe is to make sure the democratic forces perform properly. The major shift toward the Communists in Italy was in the local elections, when the Christian Democrats destroyed their reputation by graft and corruption. If we can make our own Government work, if we can avoid future Watergates and avoid the activities of the CIA that have been revealed, if we can minimize joblessness and inflation, this will be a good way to lessen the inclination of people in other countries to turn away from our form of government.

PLAYBOY: What about Chile? Would you agree that that was a case of the United States', through the CIA, intervening improperly?

CARTER: Yes. There's no doubt about it. Sure.

PLAYBOY: And you would stop that sort of thing?

CARTER: Absolutely. Yes, sir.

PLAYBOY: What about economic sanctions? Do you feel we should have punished the Allende government the way we did?

CARTER: That's a complicated question, because we don't know what caused the fall of the Allende government, the murder of perhaps thousands of people, the incarceration of many others. I don't have any facts as to how deeply involved we were, but my impression is that we were involved quite deeply. As I said, I wouldn't have done that if I were President. But as to whether or not we ought to have an option on the terms of our loans, repayment schedules, interest charges, the kinds of materials we sell to them—those are options I would retain depending upon the compatibility of a foreign government with our own.

PLAYBOY: To what do you attribute all those deceptions and secret maneuverings through the years? Why were they allowed to happen?

CARTER: It was a matter of people's just saying, Well, that's politics; we don't have a right to know what our Government is doing; secrecy is OK; accepting gifts is OK; excluding the American people is OK. These are the kinds of things I want to change.

PLAYBOY: It sounds as if you're saying Americans accepted indecency and lies in their Government all too easily. Doesn't that make your constant campaign theme, invoking the decency and honesty of the American people, somewhat naïve and ingenuous?

CARTER: I say that the American people are basically decent and honest and want a truthful Government. Obviously, I know there are people in this country, out of 214,000,000, who are murderers. There are people, maybe, who don't want a decent Government. Maybe there are people who prefer lies to truth. But I don't think it's simplistic to say that our Government hasn't measured up to the ethical and moral standards of the people of this country. We've had better governments in the past and I think our people, as I've said many times, are just as strong, courageous and intelligent as they were 200 years ago. I think we still have the same inner strength they had then.

PLAYBOY: Even though a lot of people support that feeling, many others think it makes you sound like an evangelist. And that makes it all the more confusing when they read about your hanging out with people so different from you in lifestyle and beliefs. Your publicized friendship with journalist Hunter Thompson, who makes no secret of his affinity for drugs and other craziness, is a good example.

CARTER: Well, in the first place, I'm a human being. I'm not a packaged article that you can put in a little box and say, "Here's a Southern Baptist, an ignorant Georgia peanut farmer who doesn't have the right to enjoy music, who has no flexibility in his mind, who can't understand the sensitivities of an interpersonal relationship. He's gotta be predictable. He's gotta be for Calley and for the war. He's gotta be a liar. He's gotta be a racist."

You know, that's the sort of stereotype people tend to assume, and I hope it doesn't apply to me. And I don't see any mystery about having a friendship with Hunter Thompson. I guess it's something that's part of my character and it becomes a curiosity for those who see some mystery about someone of my background being elected President. I'm just a human being like everybody else. I have different interests, different understandings of the world around me, different relationships with different kinds of people. I have a broad range of friends: sometimes very serious, sometimes very formal, sometimes lighthearted, sometimes intense, sometimes casual.

PLAYBOY: So when you find yourself at a rock concert or in some other situation that seems at odds with your rural, religious background, you never feel a sense of estrangement?

CARTER: None. No. I feel at home with 'em.

PLAYBOY: How did you get to feel this way without going through culture shock?

CARTER: I have three sons, who now range from 23 to 29, and the oldest of them were very influenced by Bob Dylan in their attitudes toward civil rights, criminal justice and the Vietnam war. This was about the period of time I was entering politics. I've been fairly close to my sons and their taste in music influenced my taste, and I was able to see the impact of Bob Dylan's attitudes on young people. And I was both gratified by and involved emotionally in those changes of attitudes.

Later, when I became governor, I was acquainted with some of the people at Capricorn Records in Macon—Otis Redding and others. It was they who began to meld the white and black music industries, and that was quite a sociological change for our region. So as I began to travel around Georgia, I made contact a few days every month or two with Capricorn Records, just to stay in touch with people in the state, and got to know all the Allman Brothers, Dicky Betts and others. Later on, I met Charlie Daniels and the Marshall Tucker Band.

Then I decided to run for President. I didn't have any money and didn't have any political base, so I had to depend substantially on the friends I already had. One of my potential sources for fund raising and for recruiting young volunteers was the group of recording stars I already knew. So we began to have concerts and I got to know them even better.

Of course, I've also been close to the country-music folks in Georgia, as well as the Atlanta Symphony Orchestra. The first large contribution I got—$1000—was from Robert Shaw, the music director of the orchestra. We've been over at the Grand Ole Opry a few times and gotten to know people like Chubby Jackson and Tom T. Hall.

PLAYBOY: There's been a lot of publicity about your relationship with Dylan, whom you quoted in your acceptance speech at the Democratic Convention. How did that come about?

CARTER: A number of years ago, my second son, Chip, who was working full time in our farming business, took a week off during Christmas. He and a couple of his friends drove all the way to New York— just to see Bob Dylan. There had been a heavy snowstorm and the boys had to park several miles from Dylan's home. It was after Dylan was injured, when he was in seclusion. Apparently, Dylan came to the door with two of his kids and shook hands with Chip. By the time Chip got to the nearest phone, a couple of miles away, and called us at home, he was nearly incoherent. Rosalynnn couldn't understand what Chip was talking about, so she screamed, "Jimmy, come here quick! Something's happened to Chip!"

We finally deciphered that he had shaken Dylan's hand and was just, you know, very carried away with it. So when I read that Dylan was going on tour again, I wrote him a little personal note and asked him to come visit me at the governor's mansion. I think he checked with Phil Walden of Capricorn Records and Bill Graham to find out what kind of guy *is* this, and he was assured I didn't want to use him, I was just interested in his music.

The night he came, we had a chance to talk about his music and about changing times and pent-up emotions in young people. He said he didn't have any inclination to change the world, that he wasn't crusading and that his personal feelings were apparently compatible with the yearnings of an entire generation. We also discussed Israel, which he had a strong interest in. But that's my only contact with Bob Dylan, that night.

PLAYBOY: That brings us back to the reason so many people find it hard to get a handle on you: On the one hand, your association with youth culture, civil rights and other liberal movements; and on the other, your apparent conservatism on many issues. Would you care to put it in a nutshell for us?

CARTER: I'll try. On human rights, civil rights, environmental quality, I consider myself to be very liberal. On the management of government, on openness of government, on strengthening individual liberties and local levels of government I consider myself a conservative. And I don't see that the two attitudes are incompatible.

PLAYBOY: Then let's explore a few more issues. Not everyone is sure, for instance what you mean by your call for tax reform. Does it mean that the burden will shift to corporations and upper-income groups and away from the middle- and lower-income groups, or are you talking merely about a simplified tax code?

CARTER: It would involve both. One change I'm calling for is simplification, and the other involves shifting the income-tax burden away from the lower-income families. But what I'm really talking about is total, comprehensive tax reform for the first time since the income tax was approved back in 1913, I think it was.

It's not possible to give you a definitive statement on tax reform any time soon. It's going to take at least a year before we can come up with a new tax structure. But there are some general provisions that would be instituted that aren't there now. The income-tax code, which now comprises 40,000 pages, will be greatly simplified. Income should be taxed only once. We should have a true progressive income tax, so that the higher the income, the higher the percentage of taxation. I see no reason why capital gains should be taxed at half the rate of income from manual labor. I would be committed to a great reduction in tax incentives, loopholes or whatever you want to call them, which are used as mechanisms to solve transient economic problems; they ought to be on a basis of annual appropriation or a time limit, rather than be built into the tax structure.

In any case, these are five or six things that would be dramatic departures from what we presently have and they should tell you what side of the issue I stand on.

PLAYBOY: Would one of those be increasing taxes for corporations, especially the overseas and domestic profits of multinational corporations?

CARTER: No, I don't think so. Obviously, there have been provisions written into the law that favor certain corporations, including those that have overseas investments; I would remove those incentives. Tax laws also benefit those who have the best lobbying efforts, those who have the most influence in Washington, and the larger the corporations are, on the average, the smaller proportion they pay in taxes. Small businesses quite often pay the flat maximum rate, 48 percent, while some larger corporations pay as little as five or six percent. That ought to be changed.

But as far as increasing over-all corporate taxes above the 50 percent level, I wouldn't favor that. We also have the circumstance of multinational corporations' depending on bribery as a mechanism for determining the outcome of a sale. I think bribery in international affairs ought to be considered a crime and punishable by imprisonment.

PLAYBOY: Would you sympathize with the anticorporate attitude that many voters feel?

CARTER: Well, I'm not particularly anticorporate, but I'd say I'm more oriented to consumer protection. One of the things I've established throughout the campaign is the need to break up the sweetheart arrangement between regulatory agencies and the industries they regulate. Another is the need for rigid and enthusiastic enforcement of the antitrust laws.

PLAYBOY: To take another issue, you favor a comprehensive Federal health-care system. Why don't you just support the Kennedy-Corman bill, which provides for precisely that?

CARTER: As a general philosophy, wherever the private sector can perform a function as effectively and efficiently as the Government, I would prefer to keep it within the private sector. So I would like the insurance aspect of the health program to be carried out by employer/employee contribution. There would be contributions from the general fund for those who are indigent. I would also have a very heavy emphasis on preventive health care, since I believe most of the major afflictions that beset people can be prevented or minimized. And I favor the use to a greater degree of nonphysicians, such as nurses, physicians' assistants, and so forth. Some of these things are in conflict with the provisions of the Kennedy-Corman bill.

PLAYBOY: Let us ask you about one last stand: abortion.

CARTER: I think abortion is wrong and I will do everything I can as President to minimize the need for abortions—within the framework of the decision of the Supreme Court, which I can't change. Georgia had a more conservative approach to abortion, which I personally favored, but the Supreme Court ruling suits me all right. I signed a Georgia law as governor that was compatible with the Supreme Court decision.

PLAYBOY: You think it's wrong, but the ruling suits you? What would we tell a woman who said her vote would depend on how you stood on abortion?

CARTER: If a woman's major purpose in life is to have unrestricted abortions, then she ought *not* to vote for me. But she wouldn't have anyone to vote for.

PLAYBOY: There seem to have been relatively few women in important staff positions in your campaign. Is that accurate?

CARTER: Women have been in charge of our entire campaign effort in Georgia and in New York State outside New York City. Also in Nebraska, Kansas, a third of the state of Florida and other areas.

PLAYBOY: But whenever we hear about a meeting of top staff members they almost always seem to be white males. Is that a failing in your organization?

CARTER: I don't know about a failing. The three people with whom I consult regularly—in addition to my wife—are white males: Hamilton Jordan, Jody Powell and Charles Kirbo. But we *do* have a lot of women involved in the campaign. We are now setting up a policy committee to run a nationwide effort to coordinate Democratic races and 50 percent of the members of this committee will be women. But Jody has been my press secretary since 1970, and Hamilton and Kirbo were my major advisors in 1966. It's such an extremely stable staff that there's been no turnover at all in the past five or six years. But we've made a lot of progress, I think, in including women, and I think you'll see more.

PLAYBOY: You mention very frequently how much you count on your wife's advice. Isn't there a strain during the campaign, with the two of you separated so much of the time?

CARTER: Well, when I was in the Navy, I was at sea most of the time and I'd see her maybe one or two nights a week. Now, when I'm home in Plains, I see her almost every night. And if I'm elected President, I'll see her *every* night. So there is obviously a time to be together and a time to be separated. If you're apart three or four days and then meet again, it's almost—for me, it's a very exciting reunion. I'll have been away from Rosalynnn for a few days and if I see her across an airport lobby, or across a street, I get just as excited as I did when I was, you know, 30 years younger.

We have a very close, very intimate sharing of our lives and we've had a tremendous magnification of our life's purposes in politics. Before 1966, she and I were both very shy. It was almost a painful thing to approach a stranger or make a speech. It's been a mutual change we've gone through, because we both felt it was worth while; so no matter what the outcome of the election, the relationship between Rosalynnn and me will be very precious.

PLAYBOY: Did you both have the usual share of troubles adjusting to marriage?

CARTER: We did at first. We've come to understand each other much better. I was by far the dominant person in the marriage at the beginning, but not anymore. She's just as strong, if not stronger than I am. She's fully equal to me in every way in our relationship, in making business decisions, and she makes most of the decisions about family affairs. And I think it was a struggle for her to achieve this degree of independence and equality in our personal relationship. So, to summarize, years ago we had a lot of quarrels—none serious, particularly—but now we don't.

PLAYBOY: A lot of marriages are foundering these days. Why is yours so successful?

CARTER: Well, I really love Rosalynnn more now than I did when I married her. And I have loved no other women except her. I had gone out with all kinds of girls, sometimes fairly steadily, but I just never cared about them. Rosalynnn had been a friend of my sister's and was three years younger than I, which is a tremendous chasm in the high school years. She was just one of those insignificant little girls around the house. Then, when I was 21 and home from the Navy on leave, I took her out to a movie. Nothing extraordinary happened, but the next morning I told my mother, "That's the girl I want to marry." It's the best thing that ever happened to me.

We also share a religious faith, and the two or three times in our married life when we've had a serious crisis, I think that's what sustained our marriage and helped us overcome our difficulty. Our children, too, have been a factor binding Rosalynnn and me together. After the boys, Amy came along late and it's been especially delightful for me, maybe because she's a little girl.

PLAYBOY: This is a tough question to ask, but because it's been such a factor in American political life, we wonder if you've ever discussed with Rosalynnn the possibility of being assassinated. And, assuming you have, how do you deal with it in your own mind?

CARTER: Well, in the first place, I'm not afraid of death. In the second place, it's the same commitment I made when I volunteered to go into the submarine force. I accepted a certain degree of danger when I made the original decision, then I didn't worry about it anymore. It wasn't something that preyed on my mind; it wasn't something I had to reassess every five minutes. There is a certain element of danger in running for President, borne out by statistics on the number of Presidents who have been attacked, but I have to say frankly that it's something I never worry about.

PLAYBOY: Your first answer was that you don't fear death. Why not?

CARTER: It's part of my religious belief. I just look at death as not a threat. It's inevitable, and I have an assurance of eternal life. There is no feeling on my part that I *have* to be President, or that I *have* to live, or that I'm immune to danger. It's just that the termination of my physical life is relatively insignificant in my concept of over-all existence. I don't say that in a mysterious way; I recognize the possibility of assassination. But I guess everybody recognizes the possibility of other forms of death—automobile accidents, airplane accidents, cancer. I just don't worry.

PLAYBOY: There's been some evidence that Johnson and Nixon both seemed to have gone a bit crazy while they were in the White House. Do you ever wonder if the pressures of the office might make *anyone* mentally unstable?

CARTER: I really don't have the feeling that being in the White House is what caused Nixon's or Johnson's problems. Other Presidents have served without developing mental problems—Roosevelt, Truman, Eisenhower, Kennedy, for instance. As far as I've been able to discern, President Ford approaches—or avoids—the duties of the White House with equanimity and self-assurance.

I think the ability to accept oneself and to feel secure and confident, to avoid any degree of paranoia, to face reality, these factors are fairly independent of whether or not one is President. The same factors would be important if someone were chief of police, or a schoolteacher, or a magazine editor. The pressure is greater on a President, obviously, than some of the jobs I've described, but I think the ability to accommodate pressure is a personal thing.

PLAYBOY: We noticed your crack about President Ford's avoiding the duties of the White House. Do you agree with Senator Mondale's assessment, when he said shortly after the nomination that Ford isn't intelligent enough to be a good President?

CARTER: Well, if you leave Mondale out of it, I personally think that President Ford is adequately intelligent to be President.

PLAYBOY: And what about your Presidency, if you're elected—will you have a dramatic first 1000 days?

CARTER: I would hope that my Administration wouldn't be terminated at the end of 1000 days, as was the case with one administration. I'm beginning to meet with key leaders of Congress to evolve specific legislation to implement the Democratic platform commitment. If I'm elected, there will be no delay in moving aggressively on a broad front to carry out the promises I've made to the American people. I intend to stick to everything I've promised.

PLAYBOY: Thanks for all the time you've given us. Incidentally, do you have any problems with appearing in *Playboy?* Do you think you'll be criticized?

CARTER: I don't object to that at all. I don't believe I'll be criticized.

(At the final session, which took place in the living room of Carter's home in Plains, the allotted time was up. A press aide indicated that there were other appointments for which Carter was already late, and the aide opened the front door while amenities were exchanged. As the interviewer and the Playboy *editor stood at the door, recording equipment in their arms, a final, seemingly*

casual question was tossed off. Carter then delivered a long, softly spoken monolog that grew in intensity as he made his final points. One of the journalists signaled to Carter that they were still taping, to which Carter nodded his assent.)

PLAYBOY: Do you feel you've reassured people with this interview, people who are uneasy about your religious beliefs, who wonder if you're going to make a rigid, unbending President?

CARTER: I don't know if you've been to Sunday school here yet; some of the press has attended. I teach there about every three or four weeks. It's getting to be a real problem because we don't have room to put everybody now when I teach. I don't know if we're going to have to issue passes or what. It almost destroys the worship aspect of it. But we had a good class last Sunday. It's a good way to learn what I believe and what the Baptists believe.

One thing the Baptists believe in is complete autonomy. I don't accept any domination of my life by the Baptist Church, none. Every Baptist church is individual and autonomous. We don't accept domination of our church from the Southern Baptist Convention. The reason the Baptist Church was formed in this country was because of our belief in absolute and total separation of church and state. These basic tenets make us almost unique. We don't believe in any hierarchy in church. We don't have bishops. Any officers chosen by the church are defined as servants, not bosses. They're supposed to do the dirty work, make sure the church is clean and painted and that sort of thing. So it's a very good, democratic structure.

When my sons were small, we went to church and they went, too. But when they got old enough to make their own decisions, they decided when to go and they varied in their devoutness. Amy really looks forward to going to church, because she gets to see all her cousins at Sunday school. I never knew anything except going to church. My wife and I were born and raised in innocent times. The normal thing to do was to go to church.

What Christ taught about most was pride, that one person should never think he was any better than anybody else. One of the most vivid stories Christ told in one of his parables was about two people who went into a church. One was an official of the church, a Pharisee, and he said, "Lord, I thank you that I'm not like all those other people. I keep all your commandments, I give a tenth of everything I own. I'm here to give thanks for making me more acceptable in your sight." The other guy was despised by the nation, and he went in, prostrated himself on the floor and said, "Lord, have mercy on me, a sinner. I'm not worthy to lift my eyes to heaven." Christ asked the disciples which of the two had justified his life. The answer was obviously the one who was humble.

The thing that's drummed into us all the time is not to be proud, not to be better than anyone else, not to look down on people but to make ourselves acceptable in God's eyes through our own actions and recognize the simple truth that we're saved by grace. It's just a free gift through faith in Christ. This gives us a mechanism by which we can relate permanently to God. I'm not speaking for other people, but it gives me a sense of peace and equanimity and assurance.

I try not to commit a deliberate sin. I recognize that I'm going to do it anyhow, because I'm human and I'm tempted. And Christ set some almost impossible standards for us. Christ said, "I tell you that anyone who looks on a woman with lust has in his heart already committed adultery."

I've looked on a lot of women with lust. I've committed adultery in my heart many times. This is something that God recognizes I will do—and I have done it—and God forgives me for it. But that doesn't mean that I condemn someone who not only looks on a woman with lust but who leaves his wife and shacks up with somebody out of wedlock.

Christ says, Don't consider yourself better than someone else because one guy screws a whole bunch of women while the other guy is loyal to his wife. The guy who's loyal to his wife ought not to be condescending or proud because of the relative degree of sinfulness. One thing that Paul Tillich said was that religion is a search for the truth about man's existence and his relationship with God and his fellow man; and that once you stop searching and think you've got it made—at that point, you lose your religion. Constant reassessment, searching in one's heart—it gives me a feeling of confidence.

I don't inject these beliefs in my answers to your secular questions.

(Carter clenched his fist and gestured sharply.)

But I don't think I would *ever* take on the same frame of mind that Nixon or Johnson did—lying, cheating and distorting the truth. Not taking into consideration my hope for my strength of character, I think that my religious beliefs alone would prevent that from happening to me. I have that confidence. I hope it's justified.

4

EXCLUSIVE INTERVIEW WITH PRESIDENT-ELECT CARTER, NOV. 15, 1976

U.S. News & World Report

This is one of a flurry of interviews conducted shortly after Carter was elected president.—*Editor*

QUESTION: Governor Carter, what is your interpretation of what the voters were saying in electing you President?

CARTER: I believe the voters were saying they wanted new leadership that would give our nation new ideas, new goals, new vision, and a restoration of trust and pride in our Government.

In domestic affairs, I think the voters were demanding economic policies that will halt inflation and put our people back to work.

In foreign affairs, they were demanding an end to secrecy and the return to a foreign policy that reflects the generosity, the decency, the strength and the common sense of the American people.

QUESTION: Do you view the close vote as being a signal to go slow on sweeping change?

CARTER: I believe that the defeat of an incumbent President and the election of a new President who comes from outside Washington indicates that our people want new policies and new directions from their Government.

I don't think our people want "sweeping" change. They do want prudent, responsible, imaginative and efficient programs that are understood by the public and that can effectively address the serious social and economic problems we face.

QUESTION: What do you view as our biggest domestic problem?

CARTER: The nation's biggest domestic problem is the economy. Our first priority must be to strengthen the economic recovery and restore basic health to our economy through a balanced attack on both inflation and unemployment. Only when the economy is sound can we meet our other national priorities.

QUESTION: How do you propose to deal with that problem?

CARTER: Any immediate action to strengthen the economic recovery must await a clarification of what exactly has happened to the 10 to 15 billion dollars in the fiscal 1977 budget that has been budgeted, appropriated, but not spent by the present Administration. We must also carefully examine the economic statistics and indicators in the next month or two to determine the extent to which the recovery continues to falter.

If the decline continues, consideration of a tax reduction for low and middle-income citizens may be in order. We must act swiftly against unemployment and inflation. These are twin evils that must be addressed simultaneously. We must find ways to increase employment without increasing inflation, through the use of incentives to the private sector to hire and train the unemployed and through employment programs carefully targeted to areas of greatest need. The only true long-term solution to our economic problems is through jobs in the private sector.

QUESTION: Are you confident that you can make good on your promise to reorganize the Federal Government and make its agencies and employees more responsive to the people?

CARTER: I do not underestimate the difficulties involved in reorganizing the executive branch of our Federal Government, but I am confident the job can be done. As I did when Governor of Georgia, I will work with leaders from many different areas—including Congress, the civil service, business and labor, universities and minority groups—to design a comprehensive plan for reorganization.

QUESTION: How long is all this going to take?

CARTER: It may take a year or more to develop the best possible plan; if so, that time is well spent. Once we have our blueprint, we must implement it effectively and forcefully. Nothing as complex as the reorganization of our massive federal bureaucracy will be achieved overnight. I envision the reorganization process as one that will continue throughout my time as President.

QUESTION: Will you make a number of legislative proposals in the early weeks of your term? Or do you envision a more deliberate series of requests after study by task forces?

CARTER: I will devote a good deal of my time during the transition period to setting legislative priorities. As I've said, our economic problems are a matter of urgent concern to me, and if new legislation is needed to provide jobs or to combat inflation, that legislation would receive higher priority.

In general, however, I think the American people are more concerned with having well-considered, effective proposals and decisions than they are with seeing a flurry of legislative actions in a new President's first weeks in office.

QUESTION: Do you anticipate trouble with the new Congress?

CARTER: I will make every effort to know the members of Congress personally, to understand their political concerns and the problems of their constituents and to work with them harmoniously for the good of the country. I will consult with members of both parties as programs are developed—particularly in the area of foreign policy. We may not always agree, but we must always try to work together with mutual respect and understanding.

QUESTION: Suppose Congress balks at your key proposals—will you take your case directly to the people?

CARTER: As I said during my campaign, if one of my major proposals was blocked by Congress, I would not hesitate to go directly to the people to rally their support. But I intend to use consultation and cooperation to avoid such a situation whenever possible.

QUESTION: In foreign affairs, what will be your first priority? Will you be making any early trips abroad to meet other leaders or will you be inviting them to the United States?

CARTER: My first priority will be to consult closely with leaders of Congress of both parties and with my advisers and with other foreign-affairs experts on the basic premises and long-term goals of American foreign policy. We must have well-considered, agreed-upon goals, and we must communicate them to the American people, if our foreign policy is to have the public understanding and support that are essential to its success.

I will also give high priority to consultation with our allies so we and they can have the best possible understanding of one another's views and concerns. I have no plans for an early trip abroad.

QUESTION: With the White House and Congress both under control of the Democrats, what future do you see ahead for the Republican Party and what role will it play during your Administration?

CARTER: The Republican Party continues to reflect the political views of millions of Americans. I expect to include Republicans in my Administration. I will seek the advice of Republican leaders in Congress, in the business world and elsewhere, and I hope that a great many Republicans will support my goals and programs. I recognize and respect the role of the G.O.P. as the "loyal opposition" in both foreign and domestic matters.

However, I hope to re-establish a basic bipartisanship in our foreign policy. I will try never to lose sight of the fact that partisan divisions are always secondary to our common devotion to this country and the well-being of its people.

QUESTION: What do you think the American people want from a new President?

CARTER: Most immediately, I think the American people want swift, decisive action on the specific problems facing our country—jobs, reduced inflation, welfare reform, tax reform, Government reorganization, a sound foreign policy, better schools and health care, and other specific programs, which Senator Mondale and I discussed throughout the campaign.

Americans also want to be told the truth, even when it is unpleasant. We have always responded well to a challenge.

Only when our leaders have lost faith in that basic toughness of spirit and willingness to sacrifice have we been disappointed or embarrassed. But there is something else, something less tangible, that our people want. They want to be proud of our Government again. They want to trust their Government again. They want to be inspired by their leaders again. They want a new spirit of optimism and trust and confidence. They want a Government that is both competent and compassionate.

As a citizen, those are the things I've always wanted from my President. As President, those are the goals I will try to meet.

5

"I LOOK FORWARD TO THE JOB," JAN. 3, 1977

Time, Murray Gart, Hugh Sidey, Stanley Cloud & Bonnie Angelo

QUESTION: Has your view of the presidency changed from the view you had as a candidate?

CARTER: I think the overall thing is that I've learned a lot about the Government and seen the need to address myself to broad policy issues and foreign affairs and defense matters, and the coordination among Cabinet officers, rather than the details that have sometimes preoccupied previous Presidents.

QUESTION: How about the presidency itself? The pressures of the job?

CARTER: As far as the prospect of actually being President, I look forward to that with anticipation, with a growing sense of confidence, because I know I have a good team to work with me and the good will of the American people. I think almost all of them want me to succeed.

QUESTION: Have you had any second thoughts about your desire to conduct am "open" presidency?

CARTER: No, I've not changed my mind about that. In whatever way I can be open, I'll do it—with frequent press conferences, fireside chats to explain complicated issues, perhaps with town-hall-type forums around the country, where I answer questions from the public. I think, on occasion, I might very well have Cabinet meetings open for a limited number of news people to come in.

I would have a fairly steady stream of visitors—just average Americans whom we've met during the campaign from around the country—to come in and spend a night with us at the White House and eat supper with us, so that we could have that interrelationship.

QUESTION: In your dealings with Congress, might you establish a procedure somewhat similar to the question period in the British Parliament, in which a Cabinet officer—or even you yourself—would go before Congress to answer questions?

CARTER: Yes, I would like to see this done—to have Cabinet officers go there. I would reserve judgment on whether I should go myself. But it's a possibility.

QUESTION: What about a role for your wife Rosalynn in the Administration?

CARTER: She's already announced that she's going to help organize a commission on mental health. She would certainly be interested in the comprehensive health care program. I'll let her decide what sort of projects she wants to become involved in. But she and other members of my family will probably travel a good bit, both within this country and in foreign countries. I'll use her as an extension of myself.

QUESTION: How large a role will your Vice President play?

CARTER: There's no doubt in my mind that Fritz Mondale will play a major role in governing. He'll be my chief staff person, and his office will be near mine in the White House. He ought to get the same CIA briefings, the same foreign affairs dispatches that I look at, and he'll be a constant adviser to me and constant partner with me in making decisions.

QUESTION: Do you expect to ask the American people to make any sacrifices, given the economic and energy situations in the country now?

CARTER: I hope to evolve, within the first 90 days of my Administration, an overall energy policy. This might very well have, as a major component, the conservation of energy. In economic matters as well as energy matters, on occasion, I would certainly feel free, without embarrassment, to call on the American people to make a sacrifice. I think they would respond well.

QUESTION: What sort of energy program do you have in mind?

CARTER: One person, Mr. Schlesinger, will be in charge of the whole energy field. He will be located in the White House, as an assistant to me. It's imperative that we should know what our goals are in conservation and in research and development priorities, and this will be the first major undertaking of the Administration. I hope, too, to establish a separate Department of Energy.

QUESTION: Is your goal self-sufficiency for the U.S.?

CARTER: No. I think that's something that we can't ever hope to achieve and I don't see any reason for it. We can't become self-sufficient in zinc, or molybdenum, or bauxite or oil. But we can have an adequate assured supply from overseas, and an adequate reserve supply in this country, an adequate conservation program so that we don't waste fuel any further. And we must make a shift toward coal, whose quantity is almost unlimited.

QUESTION: Doesn't a conservation program suggest major changes in American life, like smaller cars and less travel and smaller houses?

CARTER: I think it would encompass all those things, yes.

QUESTION: Do you favor a federal job freeze?

CARTER: That's certainly a possibility. In different departments, perhaps many departments, you can freeze the hiring. I don't intend to fire anyone because of reorganization. I don't think that's fair to the civil service employees. But I would reserve the right not to fill all vacancies as they occur, to reduce the total number of employees in certain areas of Government and to transfer people to more productive jobs with no loss in pay or seniority.

QUESTION: In the economic area, will you give priority to tax cuts or to job-creation legislation?

CARTER: My first preference would be to enhance job opportunities, preferably on a continuing basis—and not just a quick, temporary, or transient effort toward employment. There are several job programs already evolved by Commerce, and the Administration structures are in place. They would be immediately available for expansion. There's a limit on what we can do in the job-enhancement area. Whatever we can't do in stimulating jobs I would make up with some form of tax reduction. I don't know yet the full level of economic stimulus to recommend. Perhaps I'll decide before January 1.

QUESTION: Which is the greater evil now, inflation or unemployment?

CARTER: The greater urgency now is to address the unemployment question. We've got so many people out of work, and we've got so much unused industrial capacity, that I think if we carefully target employment opportunities around the country, we can decrease unemployment substantially before we start becoming equally concerned about inflation.

QUESTION: Which would be more important, stimulating the private sector or enlarging the public sector?

CARTER: I think the private sector. But you have to remember how tightly they're interrelated. Public money can ultimately be used to stimulate the private sector. An illustrative point would be in the housing field, where Government action to encourage the building of homes can be done with a minimum expenditure of public funds, but a maximum amount of benefits.

QUESTION: Do you have plans for a major housing program?

CARTER: I think that would be a part of the immediate proposal that I would make to Congress.

QUESTION: Mostly low-cost housing?

CARTER: No, I think not mostly. There would be guarantees of loans by private and corporate agencies; construction of multifamily dwellings, as under the 202 program for senior citizens; some restoration of funds for rehabilitating existing homes. Perhaps some interest subsidy. And I'll do everything I can to hold down interest rates. Perhaps we could modify, through the Government mortgage programs, the scheduled rate of repayment, so that a family that wants to buy a home could make lower monthly payments now, and higher ones later.

QUESTION: What about welfare reform?

CARTER: Our proposals will be forthcoming in 1977. I haven't decided on the specific formula, but there would be both federal and state participation.

QUESTION: With the greater burden on the federal?

CARTER: I think so; I don't have time now to put together a comprehensive welfare or tax or health program, but it will all be done very expeditiously. I would guess all those would be forthcoming this year.

QUESTION: When would you expect the U.S. to have a national health insurance plan?

CARTER: It'll probably take at least four years to fully implement a comprehensive health program for our citizens. And it will be phased in, year by year. The first step has got to be the reorganization of the federal agencies that now handle roughly 300 different health programs.

QUESTION: What changes do you plan for the CIA and the rest of the intelligence community?

CARTER: I wouldn't make any precipitous changes in the intelligence community's functions until I know more about them. My knowledge of the intelligence community outside the CIA is very limited so far.

QUESTION: Are you leaning toward a kind of intelligence czar?

CARTER: Well, President Ford's executive order set up the Director of Central Intelligence as a kind of czar. There are several intelligence agencies, as you know, and I haven't decided whether to change the present arrangement.

QUESTION: Are you thinking about changing the structure and the responsibilities of the FBI?

CARTER: I think the FBI director has got to be more directly responsible to the Attorney General. I would like to see a top person in the Department of Justice responsible for the control of crime, maybe the Deputy Attorney General, or some other top official, coordinating the efforts of the FBI, the LEAA [Law Enforcement Assistance Administration] program, the U.S. Attorneys around the nation, and perhaps a crime division. I'd like to pursue aggressively the control of crime. I'd like to remove the FBI completely from politics, maximize its professional status.

QUESTION: That amounts to a war on crime, doesn't it?

CARTER: That's right. The control of crime now is divided up under too many different entities. I would like to bring more of a responsibility for drug control, for instance, under the FBI than there has been in the past. These responsibilities have been scattered around the Government and are not nearly so effective as they would be if they fell under a comprehensive and enlightened and aggressive leader.

QUESTION: Turning to foreign affairs: many leaders around the world have been asking what you mean by morality in foreign policy. Can you describe your feelings about your foreign policy?

CARTER: I'd like to go out of office with people being able to say that I always told the truth. I'd like to continue to play a leading role in the search for an enhancement of human rights. I'd like to do everything I can as President to ensure world peace, a reduction in the arms race. I don't mean to preach to other countries. I'm not going to try to set a standard on the type of government the other nations should have.

QUESTION: Do you expect to travel widely?

CARTER: No, not as a main thing. I hope that I can speak in such a way that the rest of the world will know that I accurately speak for the

American people. I think it's important that during this next year I meet and get to know personally the leaders of many nations around the world. I can't say that I'll not travel at all, but I'd like to hold it to a minimum. I would certainly welcome an opportunity to have other foreign leaders come to this country to meet with me. The order of sequence of my meeting with foreign leaders is something on which [Secretary of State–designate] Cy Vance has been doing a great deal of work.

QUESTION: What do you hope to get done first?

CARTER: I think the Panama treaty ought to be resolved quite rapidly. That's almost uniquely our responsibility. In the Rhodesia question, I would like to see Britain retain the leadership role there. I want to establish a feeling within South Korea and within Japan that we won't do anything abrupt that will disturb them or upset their belief that we are still going to play a legitimate role in the western Pacific. I've spent long hours talking to Cyrus Vance about our general approach [on Turkey, Greece and Cyprus].

QUESTION: What about the Soviet Union? Do you give high priority to the SALT agreements?

CARTER: Yes. I think the basis [for the next agreement] would be the Vladivostok terms, perhaps expanded to some degree. [During their meeting at Vladivostok in November 1974, President Ford and Leonid Brezhnev reached a tentative agreement on the limitation of strategic offensive weapons.] This would be a satisfactory beginning [for negotiation]. I don't want to say that I'd adopt everything in the Vladivostok agreement. I would like to conclude this [new SALT agreement] before [the interim agreement expires in October].

QUESTION: Would this involve a meeting with Brezhnev?

CARTER: If necessary. I would guess that Mr. Brezhnev and I would meet during this coming year, probably before September. My own preference would be [to hold the meetings] in this country, but that would depend on a mutual decision between us. But I think that to get into discussions on the present SALT talks, we would lay the groundwork for much more drastic reductions in common nuclear capabilities.

QUESTION: Would you want to include any destruction of existing nuclear armaments?

CARTER: Yes. I would like to set that as a goal. The exchange that has taken place already between Secretary Brezhnev and myself has been to explore the possibility of a freeze on the number of missiles, the number of warheads, [leading to] some limits for this next SALT agreement below those that were established at Vladivostok. And then I would like to see a careful amount of mutual reduction in total numbers of atomic weapons between us and the Soviet Union, and I'd like to encourage, as much as I can, other nations to follow suit. In addition, I would like to see the termination of all tests of nuclear weapons. And I might add that there has been some indication that the Soviets agree with this proposal and have even put forward the possibility of on-site inspection.

QUESTION: What sort of communication have you had with Brezhnev?

CARTER: Indirectly, I've had messages from him to the Soviet ambassador here. I've also had messages through Averell Harriman when he was over there a few months ago. [Brezhnev] did write to congratulate me on my election, and I responded to thank him.

I've tried to be very cautious about acting as though I was already the President, so I've not met with any ambassadors or any foreign leaders, although I've had a lot of invitations. And I don't believe any President could possibly have been more gracious or more firm in his commitment to an orderly transition than President Ford has been. I really do appreciate it, and it's been a great service to the country, I believe. He could have just been polite about it, but he's been very forceful in directing his Cabinet to cooperate fully.

QUESTION: On the Israeli-Arab crisis, the Soviet view seems to be that the Geneva conference should be resumed as soon as possible. Do you agree?

CARTER: I don't yet know to what extent the U.S. should play a role in initiating a date [for such a conference]. I think the first step should be for me to meet with Mr. Rabin [the Israeli Prime Minister], Mr. Sadat [of Egypt], Mr. Assad [of Syria] and others—and then to decide what public proposal we might make to initiate any peace talks. Whether it would be appropriate to try to have exploratory meetings before the Israeli elections, I don't really know yet.

QUESTION: On South Africa, you have said you support majority rule. What do you mean by that?

CARTER: I think it means that basically a one-man, one-vote provision should prevail, with mutual respect for majority and minority elements in the society. And this should be our ultimate goal. How rapidly it can be achieved is still to be determined, and I hope it can be achieved by peaceful means.

QUESTION: What are your thoughts about the relationship between your Administration and the new government in Peking?

CARTER: I don't know yet if there is any urgency about resolving the differences that exist between the mainland and Taiwan. I would go into that very cautiously. We have a defense pact with Taiwan, the Republic of China, and we see the need to have good relationships with the People's Republic. I don't really know to what degree [Taipei and Peking] want to accommodate our commitments and at the same time search for a way to resolve their differences.

QUESTION: Would you hope to continue the personal relationship between the President of the U.S. and the Chairman of the People's Republic?

CARTER: Yes, I would hope so. I would certainly consider it one of my major responsibilities to pursue and continue the peaceful relationships we have with China [Taiwan] and the People's Republic.

QUESTION: A European statesman predicted recently that Communists will join the Italian government in 1977 and the French government in 1978. How much does this matter to the U.S.?

CARTER: It matters a great deal. And concerns me very much, depending on the degree of Communist participation in the government, and the loss of the respect and confidence of the citizens of those nations in the democratic processes that we prefer over Communism. Another factor is the degree of allegiance that might be shown by Communist leaders toward the Soviet Union and away from our own nation and from NATO. I think the best way to minimize the Communist influence in Italy and France is to make the democratic processes work, and to restore the confidence of the citizens in the government.

QUESTION: What are your thoughts about yourself now, less than a month before the Inaugural?

CARTER: I hope I can live up to the expectations of the American people. I've had a rapid learning process. You asked my wife whether we could be satisfied to live in Plains and not try to stretch ourselves beyond Plains. Well, I think we've managed to stretch ourselves a little.

PART 2

THE PRESIDENTIAL YEARS

6

ASK PRESIDENT CARTER, MAR. 5, 1977

Public Papers of the Presidents, Walter Cronkite, et al.

This conversation with the "American people" took the form of a call-in radio program conducted early in the Carter administration. The program was moderated by Walter Cronkite and broadcast March 5, 1977, on the CBS Radio Network. This interview has been edited and condensed. —*Editor*

WALTER CRONKITE: Good day. President Carter and I are in the so-called Oval Office of the White House. We are in a couple of wing-backed chairs in front of a coffee table and in front of the fireplace. Across from us is the desk at which the President spends much of his day working; over to our left the large doors opening out into the beautiful Rose Garden of the White House, on a very nice spring-like day here in Washington.

This is a unique occasion, in the sense that it marks a new approach to communication between the President and the people of the United States. It is indeed historic—unique, historic—and we must also say an experiment since the President has never taken part before in this sort of broadcast.

Mr. President, we are very pleased that you've accepted our CBS News invitation and are giving us this time to let the Nation "Ask President Carter."

THE PRESIDENT: Thank you, Walter.

I'm glad to have a chance to let people have direct access to me, and in the process of answering 50 to 100 questions this afternoon in an unrehearsed way, not knowing what's going to come next, I think the people will learn something and I know I will learn a lot about

---

Reprinted from *Public Papers of the Presidents,* Jimmy Carter.

what is of interest to them. Also, I believe that if there are tens of thousands of folks who want to get through and can't do it, in listening to the other questions that are asked, they are likely to get an answer to their questions. I am looking forward to the 2 hours. And whenever you are ready, I am.

MR. CRONKITE: All right, Mr. President, we're ready here. Let's take our [first] caller. It's Pete Belloni of Denver, Colorado.

MR. BELLONI: Good afternoon, Mr. President.

THE PRESIDENT: Good afternoon.

MR. BELLONI: How are you?

THE PRESIDENT: Fine.

MR. BELLONI: Good. Mr. President, your proposal of increasing the gasoline tax by 25 cents a gallon, won't that put quite a burden on the people of this country who are already financially strapped with higher taxes and fuel bills?

THE PRESIDENT: Well, Mr. Belloni, I've never proposed any such thing and don't know where the story originated.

MR. BELLONI: It was in the paper last week, the Rocky Mountain News.

THE PRESIDENT: I don't believe the story was attributed to me in any way, because I've never commented on that at all and have never even insinuated to anyone that I was going to raise the gasoline tax by 25 cents.

MR. BELLONI: Have you heard about it, though?

THE PRESIDENT: I had one news question about it and responded the same way I am to you, that I don't know anything about the proposal and have no intention of doing it. I might say that on April 20 I will—if plans go the way we have them now—make a speech to the Joint Session of the Congress, probably in the evening, and explain for the first time in our country what our comprehensive energy policy is. We don't have one at this moment. And we've been working on it ever since—even before I became President. So, April 20 we will try to spell out an approach to the energy problem that will involve all aspects of it—oil, coal, solar energy, obviously nuclear power, hydroelectric, pricing, mandatory efficiency, conservation, voluntary and so forth. This may or may not involve any changes in the price structure, but I certainly have not considered and have no intention of any such increases you've talked about this afternoon.

MR. BELLONI: Yes, sir, Mr. President.

Whoever brought out the story—do they know who did it or anything or how it leaked out or anything?

THE PRESIDENT: Well, it didn't leak anywhere from the White House because that's not a decision that has been made in the White House.

MR. BELLONI: I see. Well, thank you very much, Mr. President. It's been an honor.

THE PRESIDENT: Thank you, Pete. I've enjoyed talking to you.

MR. CRONKITE: Thank you, Mr. Belloni.

The next question, Mr. President, is from Mark Fendrick of Brooklyn, New York. Mr. Fendrick, go ahead.

MR. FENDRICK: Good afternoon, Mr. President. What I'd like to ask is in relationship to the attempts for returning to a normal relationship with Cuba. Now in the paper the last couple of days here in New York there's been talk about the Yankees baseball team going to Cuba.

Do you think that this is a possibility in the near future, and do you think that normal relations to Cuba are possible with, again in the near future?

THE PRESIDENT: Well, there are varying degrees of relationships with Cuba. As you know, we have had some discussions with them in the past; for instance, on the antihijacking agreement which expires this spring. And we now have no visitation rights by American citizens to go to Vietnam, to North Korea, to Cuba, and one or two other nations.

We do have a procedure already in effect whereby a limited number of Americans can go into Cuba without using a passport because of a prior agreement with the Cuban Government.

I would like to do what I can to ease tensions with Cuba. It's only 90 miles, as you know, from the Florida coast. And I don't know yet what we will do. Before any full normalization of relationships can take place, though, Cuba would have to make some fairly substantial changes in their attitude. I would like to insist, for instance, that they not interfere in the internal affairs of countries in this hemisphere, and that they decrease their military involvement in Africa, and that they reinforce a commitment to human rights by releasing political prisoners that have been in jail now in Cuba for 17 or 18 years, things of that kind.

But I think before we can reach that point we'll have to have discussions with them. And I do intend to see discussions initiated with Cuba quite early on reestablishing the antihijacking agreement, arriving at a fishing agreement between us and Cuba, since our 200-mile limits do overlap between Florida and Cuba, and I would not be averse in the future to seeing our visitation rights permitted as well.

MR. FENDRICK: In relationship, though, to the Yankees playing an exhibition game there, I've noticed that Secretary Vance has backed this idea. Do you think that that's a possibility this season?

THE PRESIDENT: It's a possibility, yes.

MR. FENDRICK: Okay. Thank you, Mr. President.

MR. CRONKITE: Mr. President, may I ask, it seemed that Secretary Vance indicated just the last day or so that there would be no preconditions in discussions with Cuba. Are you now saying that there will be?

THE PRESIDENT: No. The preconditions that I describe would be prior to full normalization of relationships, the establishment of embassies in both our countries, the complete freedom of trade between the two countries.

But you couldn't possibly arrive at a solution to some of those questions without discussions. So, we will begin discussions with Cuba if they approve the idea fairly shortly on the items that I have described—increased visitation of Americans to and from Cuba, the fishing rights question that has to be resolved for the protection of our own fishermen, and also the antihijacking agreement which has been in effect in the past, but is about to expire.

MR. CRONKITE: This is "Ask President Carter" on the CBS Radio Network. The next call, Mr. President, is from Miss Cheryl Clark of Paris, Kentucky. Miss Clark?

MISS CLARK: Mr. President, Miss Clark, a student at the University of Kentucky.

THE PRESIDENT: Yes?

MISS CLARK: Let me ask, do you consider it possible for government to create jobs similar to the WPA and the CCC in the Depression years in order to reduce unemployment, or do you want the Humphrey-Hawkins bill?

THE PRESIDENT: Well, the first major proposal that I made to the Congress, which was worked out with the congressional leaders even before I was inaugurated, was to put the American people back to work or to start that process. I think this is one of the primary responsibilities that I have as President.

We've asked for a so-called stimulation package to our economy over the next 2 years—this one and next year—of about $31 billion, a major portion of which is either reducing people's taxes or providing direct jobs. The jobs can be provided in a number of ways, including the one that you described for young people, similar to the CCC program we had during the Depression years back in the thirties.

In addition to that, we have approved, as far as my administration is concerned, a substantial amount of money for public works projects; that is, to build libraries, schools, and other facilities in communities and let the Federal Government help to pay for it. This work would be done by those who are employed by private contractors, and the same thing would apply in the insulation of homes, in building recreation areas, and employment in local and State government, perhaps in mental institutions, health programs, teachers' aides, also in the training of, primarily, young people to hold a full-time job in the private sector. And the total cost of this, as I said, is about $31 billion.

I think this is the best approach to it.

The Humphrey-Hawkins bill is pretty much a philosophical kind of expression of our Government's commitment to full employment. The Humphrey-Hawkins bill has been constantly modified. It's never gotten out of committee, either in the House or Senate. And I think some of the things that we propose this year are a substitute for some of the provisions of the Humphrey-Hawkins bill.

I do feel, in closing, that most of the job opportunities ought to be generated permanently and in the private sector of our free enterprise system, and not in Government itself. And that would be the result, I hope, of this 2-year effort to stimulate an economy which is very dormant now and where the employment rate and the inflation rate is excessively high.

MISS CLARK: Okay. Thank you very much, Mr. President—

THE PRESIDENT: Thank you, Cheryl.

MISS CLARK: —for public confidence in Government interests.

THE PRESIDENT: Thank you.

MISS CLARK: Goodbye.

THE PRESIDENT: Bye.

MR. CRONKITE: Mrs. Esther Thomas of Villanova, Pennsylvania, Mr. President, is on the phone. Go ahead, Mrs. Thomas.

MRS. THOMAS: Thank you.

Good afternoon, Mr. President. First, I'd like to say as a mother of an American officer in the United States Army, a career officer, I hope you go into history books as the first Democratic President that did not solve our Nation's financial and unemployment problems by going to war.

Now for my question. How can we, as middle-class earners, expect legislation or reforms that would remove tax loopholes the rich or affluent use as deductions, when all laws and legislation are made by the rich? There are no poor people, no poor or no lower-class wage earners in either the House or the Senate.

THE PRESIDENT: Well, Mrs. Thomas, I think, you may have noticed during the campaign that I made an issue of this almost constantly, and in my acceptance speech, at the Democratic Convention, said that I thought the income tax system of this country was a disgrace.

MRS. THOMAS: Yes.

THE PRESIDENT: I haven't changed my opinion about that, and I have initiated a comprehensive analysis of the income tax structure. And before the end of September we will propose to the American people and the Congress, in a highly publicized way, basic reforms in income tax structure. In the stimulation package that I mentioned earlier this afternoon, we have one provision in there that helps people like yourselves. It increases the personal exemption for a family up to $3,000, and this is a permanent change and also greatly simplifies the income tax forms which, as you noticed for 1976 calendar year that you are filling out now, are very complicated.

MRS. THOMAS: And how.

THE PRESIDENT: Now this average for a family, for instance, that makes $10,000 a year, this tax reduction or refund will amount to about 30 percent of the taxes paid, and the permanent reduction that will be in effect from now on will amount to about 20-percent tax reduction for that $10,000-a-year family.

We anticipate in September eliminating a great number of the loopholes that do benefit the rich and the powerful, and any of those savings that are derived from that will be passed along to the low- and middle-income families like, perhaps, yourself.

MRS. THOMAS: Thank you. And may I say, as a registered Republican, I'm behind you 100 percent. And I'm sure there are a lot of us out here.

THE PRESIDENT: Thank you, ma'am. I really appreciate that.

MRS. THOMAS: Thank you. Bye-bye.

MR. CRONKITE: What about Mrs. Thomas' question about the Congress being loaded in the upper-middle classes and upper classes and not enough representation from the lower classes. Do you think that's true?

THE PRESIDENT: Well, I think once a Congressman gets in office now, with a fairly substantial salary, they are obviously in the upper class. So is a President, by the way. I guess, so is an anchorman for CBS.

But I think that to the extent that Government officials like myself and the Members of Congress make an extra effort to stay in touch with people, to let folks like Mrs. Thomas ask us questions and to scrutinize who pays the bills for my family within the White House and so forth, that's a good way to restore confidence in us. Also, I believe that the campaigns which come every 2 years for the Members of Congress keep them in touch with poor or working people. I know my own campaign for the last 2 years, joined by my wife and all my sons and their wives, my mother quite often, and my sister and my aunt, we learned a lot about people in other parts of the country outside of Georgia during the 2-year period. So, the campaign process, as part of our constitutional system, I believe, is a good guarantee that, to a substantial degree, public officials stay in touch with folks back home.

Now, the problem is, Walter, in a case like income tax, over a period of years the laws change. And the ones who demand the changes are those who are powerful and who are influential and who can hire lobbyists, or who can pay for their own private lawyer and who can form a cohesive approach to Congress and put tremendous pressure on the Congress to meet a permanent or a transient, temporary need. Once a need is passed, that special privilege in the law stays there.

The average American family with $10,000, $15,000, sometimes $25,000 a year, has no organization. They don't have any lobbyists. And the only way for them to understand what goes on in a very complicated income tax law is for somebody like the President to take the initiative and present to the American people, in a comprehensive way, all at once, these are the things that are unfair, these are the things that can be changed to make it fair, so that the American people can be marshaled to exert their influence and their interest in the tax laws.

A person who has a special privilege, they focus their attention and their influence on that one tiny part of the law, and the average American has no idea what's going on. But if I can get the whole American tax-paying body, toward the end of September, to join with me and to demand from the Congress that we make the laws simple and fair, then in that instance, I think, we can overcome this deterioration which, in my opinion, has taken place ever since 1913 or whenever it was that the income tax laws went into effect.

And that's why I am so interested in having the American people not only believe that I am acting for them but let them understand what's going on. That's the reason for this radio broadcast.

MR. CRONKITE: The next questioner, Ronald Fouse, Centerville, Georgia. Mr. President, Mr. Fouse.

MR. FOUSE: Good afternoon, Mr. President.

THE PRESIDENT: Good afternoon, Mr. Fouse. I came through Centerville the last time I was home.

MR. FOUSE: Yes. You come through the Air Force Base I work at every time you come down.

THE PRESIDENT: Very fine. Go ahead with your question.

MR. FOUSE: Yes, sir. Now that you pardoned the draft evaders and you propose to pardon the junkies and deserters, do you propose to do anything for the veterans such as myself that served the country with loyalty?

THE PRESIDENT: Well, I thought I might get a friendlier question from Georgia, but I'll try to answer your question.

I don't intend to pardon any more people from the Vietnam era. I promised the American people when I was running for office that I would pardon the ones who violated the selective service laws. I don't have any apology to make about it, and think I made the right decision. But the deserters and others who have committed crimes against military law or civilian law will not be pardoned by me on any sort of blanket basis. My preference is to let the Defense Department handle those cases by categories or by individual cases.

We have moved, I think, already to help, as you said, loyal and patriotic veterans like yourself. And I have appointed a very fine young man to head up the Veterans Administration now, Max Cleland, who is a veteran of the Vietnam war. This is kind of a new generation of leadership, and within the economic package that I presented to Congress, we have a heavy emphasis on training and job opportunities for veterans.

So, I hope in the future that we can have a restoration in our country of appreciation for veterans who did go to the Vietnam war, who have not been thanked or appreciated enough in the past, and a much more sensitive Veterans Administration toward the Vietnam veterans who have not had as many benefits as veterans of previous wars that were more popular.

But I don't have any apology to make for what I have done, but you need not be concerned about an extension of pardons on a blanket basis in the future from me.

MR. FOUSE: Okay, sir. Thank you very much.

THE PRESIDENT: Thank you.

MR. CRONKITE: Mr. President, there seems to be increasing talk of a bonus for Vietnam veterans. Is that in your thinking at all?

THE PRESIDENT: No, sir.

MR. CRONKITE: Let's do move on. We want to get as many questioners in as possible today.

Mike McGrath of Warsaw, Indiana, has won the lottery to get on the air here. Mr. McGrath, go ahead with your question to President Carter.

MR. MCGRATH: Yes, sir. Mr. President, sir, are you there?

THE PRESIDENT: Yes, sir. Go right ahead, Mike.

MR. MCGRATH: Okay. There is a little quotation there—I was awfully proud to serve in the Vietnam war there. I was aboard the U.S.S. *Constellation* there in North Vietnam, there.

THE PRESIDENT: Yes.

MR. MCGRATH: But at any rate, is that there tax rebate supposed to be for $50 or what?

THE PRESIDENT: I think it'll be more than $50 for some people, Mike, depending on what your income is.

MR. MCGRATH: Oh.

THE PRESIDENT: The ones that make above $25 or $30,000 a year don't get any rebate, according to the latest action of the Congress. And that means that a little bit more would be available to those at the lower levels of income.

In addition to that, there's a special provision for allocation of funds to veterans like yourself.

And in addition, we have a tax reduction that's permanent, by giving a higher personal exemption of $3,000 for a married couple. I think the latest version is $2,400 for a single person. So, you'll get about an equivalent of a 30-percent reduction in your income taxes for 1976 if you are at the $10,000 or so level.

MR. MCGRATH: Mine might be a little lower than that.

THE PRESIDENT: If you have a real high income, like you seem to have, you might get a little bit lower. But it won't be lower than $50 in the tax rebate unless you are well above the $25,000 level. And in addition, as I said, you'll get the permanent reduction in your income taxes brought about by the higher personal exemption.

That'll stay on the books even after the stimulation package has gone.

MR. McGRATH: Oh, okay.

THE PRESIDENT: Pretty good deal for you, I think.

MR. McGRATH: I think so.

Another thing, though, was somebody told me at the factory where I work at, the Peabody American Brands plant, somebody told me that there GI bill was supposed to have been reactivated or something. Is there anything to that at all?

THE PRESIDENT: Mike, I don't know about the latest version of that. But if you'll listen in on the radio program for the next 10 or 15 minutes, I'll get the answer for you and give it to you in a few minutes.

MR. McGRATH: That is fine. Thank you, Mr. President.

THE PRESIDENT: Thank you, Mike.

MR. CRONKITE: I might note that the President has a plan for just that. If he doesn't have the answer here, he's got a couple of aides standing by to see if they can get them. It is Saturday afternoon. A lot of Government offices are closed, but he's going to do the best he can to get them for you.

THE PRESIDENT: I might say, Walter, that if I can't find the answer before we go off the air, I will call Mike personally and give him the answer, if I can.

MR. CRONKITE: The next call is from Mrs. Helen Heller of Vineland, New Jersey.

MRS. HELLER: Good afternoon, Mr. President.

THE PRESIDENT: Good afternoon, Mrs. Heller.

MRS. HELLER: Thank you for this opportunity to talk to you.

My question concerns the medicare program. Does HEW have any plan to reevaluate this program with the possibility of extending benefits to senior citizens so as to reimburse them for things like needed dental care, eyeglasses, and/or medications? The cost of these items are so often beyond our fixed social security income, and yet they're vital necessities to us.

THE PRESIDENT: Yes, ma'am. Those things are all under consideration. We are now in the process of reorganizing the internal structure of the Department of Health, Education, and Welfare, so that we can put the financing of health care under one administrator.

This will help a great deal to cut down on the cost of those items for people like yourself. Also, we are freezing the amount of money that you have to pay for medicare this coming year, although the price of health care has gone up about 15 percent a year the last few years. We are trying to prevent your monthly payments from going up for this coming year.

MRS. HELLER: That is good.

THE PRESIDENT: Additionally, we have introduced into the Congress a bill that would hold down hospital costs and try to prevent health care costs from going up faster than other parts of our economy. There's been a great deal of maladministration or poor administration of the health costs.

I hope that over a period of years—and it's not going to come easily—that we can have a comprehensive health care plan in our country. It will be very expensive, but the first step has got to be to bring some order out of chaos in the administration of the health problems we have already got, and to help poorer people like, perhaps, yourself—I don't know what your income is—be able to prevent rapidly increasing costs of programs like medicare.

So, we are at least freezing your medicare costs, if the Congress goes along with our proposal, and over a period of years we'll try to expand the coverage of the health care services for all citizens like you.

MRS. HELLER: Well, thank you very much, Mr. President.

THE PRESIDENT: Thank you, ma'am.

MR. CRONKITE: The next caller is Miss Phyllis Dupere of Rehoboth, Massachusetts. Miss Dupere, the President is on the line.

MISS DUPERE: Hello, Mr. President.

THE PRESIDENT: Good afternoon, Phyllis.

MISS DUPERE: I'm a recent graduate from college and I majored in science. And my question is about the space shuttle program. If you had the opportunity to go on one of the missions, would you go, and why or why not?

MR. CRONKITE: You are talking about a space mission, Miss Dupere?

MISS DUPERE: The shuttle program.

THE PRESIDENT: Oh, I see. Miss Dupere, I'm probably too old to do that. I don't know if I could start now and train and get ready to go. When I was a younger person I was always very eager to do the most advanced and sometimes quite dangerous things. As soon as our country had the idea of having atomic power to propel submarines, I was one of the first ones to volunteer and was one of the very earliest submarine officers to go into the atomic power program. And I am thinking about, in the next few weeks, going with Admiral Rickover out on one of our atomic submarines to ride on that as a President, as part of my duty to learn about things of that kind.

But I can't tell you that I'm ready to go on the space shuttle. I think I just don't have the time to get ready for it. I might say that my sons would like very much to do it. But not me.

MISS DUPERE: You think your daughter would?

THE PRESIDENT: I think perhaps she would, yes. She is a very innovative young lady and is always trying for new things, and I think she's competent to be a pilot in a space shuttle in the future or to be a Member of Congress or even to be President. Yes, ma'am.

MISS DUPERE: Okay, thank you. Goodbye.

MR. CRONKITE: You know, Mr. President, with that shirtsleeve environment, so-called, with the shuttle, they're holding out a little hope that some of us fellows may get a chance to go along.

THE PRESIDENT: I'm interested in that program, by the way. I think that it's going to be a much cheaper means by which we can perform our very valuable flights in space and still return the costly vehicle back to Earth. I'm very interested in that.

MR. CRONKITE: It's going to mean the utilization of space. We are getting past the exploration stage, I think, now.

THE PRESIDENT: It is. We are using it now. I think, as you probably know, with the space satellite photography we not only guarantee the security of our country but we do a great deal of analysis for crop conditions, topographical mapping to see how far it is between certain places, highway planning. And this is a good way, too, by the way, from either a high-flying airplane or space to analyze waste of energy to see where we are not insulating adequately, and so forth.

So, for all those reasons, even things that are very common, like growing crops or mining or building highways or cutting down on heat losses, we are already using space vehicles for those purposes.

MR. CRONKITE: Mrs. Phyllis Rogers of Albuquerque, New Mexico, is on the phone, Mr. President. Mrs. Rogers?

MRS. ROGERS: Good afternoon, President Carter.

THE PRESIDENT: Good afternoon, Mrs. Rogers.

MRS. ROGERS: Thank you again for the invitation to the Inauguration.

THE PRESIDENT: Did you come?

MRS. ROGERS: Two questions: Would it be possible to eliminate the word "drug" from drug store advertising? Also, when new drugs are invented, they always use the word "drug." Why not use the terminology "medication"? Maybe it would discourage drug abusers. What do you think?

THE PRESIDENT: I think that's a good idea. I was talking yesterday, just coincidentally, Mrs. Rogers, to Dr. Peter Bourne, who is now the head of my entire drug control effort, and he will be working with foreign countries, including your neighbor of Mexico, and with the Congress and others, to try to hold down the abuse of drugs, and as you know, this applies not only to the illegal drugs like heroin and cocaine and marihuana, and others, but it also applies to some of the medications that you've described.

The barbiturates, for instance—there is a developing question about whether they are necessary at all, and Dr. Bourne pointed out to me that the number one drug that causes death is heroin, and the second is barbiturates, which is a medication that's used quite frequently by medical doctors.

So, the two are mixed in the people's minds, and I think that "medication," as you have suggested, is a better word. I am not sure if you could name the dispensers of that, though, "medication stores." They might object to that. Maybe there's a better word. Maybe "pharmacy" would be best. But I don't have any authority over what they name it. But that's a good idea, to separate the two, the illegal drugs from the legal medications would be a good distinction.

MRS. ROGERS: Thank you. And the other question is, we are very concerned about the solar energy program here in the State of New Mexico.

THE PRESIDENT: Yes.

MRS. ROGERS: And we're hoping it will go through for us. Can you comment?

THE PRESIDENT: I don't know what the decision will be. I don't intend to get involved in the decision personally. I would like to see the research and development programs for solar energy be decided on a merit basis and where the installations are best.

I would say, though, that New Mexico has a head start on many of the places around the country because of the long history of research and development and because of your climate. But I think we will have several places around the country where we will be doing an increasing amount of research and development on solar energy in the future.

MRS. ROGERS: We love you, President Carter, and thank you very much.

THE PRESIDENT: Thank you very, very much yourself.

I've just gotten an answer, by the way, that I'd like to give, Walter, if I can, to Mike McGrath from Warsaw, Indiana, regarding the GI bill.

President Ford had recommended terminating benefits under the GI bill for all persons who entered military service after January 1, 1977. He wanted to cut the period of eligibility for veterans who had entered military service before this time from 10 years to 8 years.

During the campaign I came out against these actions and supported strengthening of the GI bill and to hold to the 10-year period of eligibility. In the budget that I just put into the Congress, I added the extra 2 years of benefits. So the 10-year period will remain for Vietnam veterans for the GI bill.

So, the answer, I think, is a good one for Mike, and I hope that he is still on the air to listen to it.

MR. CRONKITE: Mrs. Opal Dehart of Trinity, North Carolina, is on the phone, Mr. President.

THE PRESIDENT: Good afternoon, Mrs. Dehart.

MRS. DEHART: Good afternoon, President Carter. I'm proud to have the opportunity to speak with you.

THE PRESIDENT: Well, it's nice to talk to folks from North Carolina. You got a question for me?

MRS. DEHART: Well, I really had more of a favor to make than a request. My father has terminal cancer. He found out a month ago. He's a hard-working man all his life, never made much money and doesn't have much now and for several years I have been reading about vitamin B17, Laetrile.

And I feel that the people in this country should be permitted to use this treatment in this country. I realize that the AMA says it's not been proved safe, but for a terminal patient, who is not going to live and has a chance to live with it, I don't see how it could be dangerous. And hospital insurance does not cover treatment not authorized by the AMA, and most hard-working people in this country cannot afford treatment that's not paid under insurance benefits.

And if a person has money available to leave the country for treatment in one of the 17 countries where the cancer specialists use this successfully, they have a chance of recovery. And a lot of people even from my area have done this.

What I want to say is that we need your help and the Government's help in taking this vitamin out, that it's made available to the American people.

THE PRESIDENT: All right. Mrs. Dehart, I might let someone from the Department of HEW give you a call Monday and talk to you about it further. And you didn't ask me a question, but I have heard about the controversy. I know that in some of our neighboring countries, I think Mexico, you can buy the Laetrile and be treated with it.

MRS. DEHART: That's right.

THE PRESIDENT: Why don't you let me have someone call you Monday, if you don't mind. It wouldn't help much if I called you, because I'm not a medical doctor and I'm not familiar with it. Would that suit you okay?

MRS. DEHART: Yes, sir, it would. I just wanted you to be aware and maybe, sir, something could be done. There's an investigation needed. I know that right now it is banned because of the 1953 ban from the State of California.

THE PRESIDENT: Yes, ma'am.

MRS. DEHART: That's a little outdated. It's not been tested, and the doctors who signed the papers at the time had not tested it. They went on somebody else's word—

MR. CRONKITE: Thank you, Mrs. Dehart. I know the President is going to have you called on that. It is a matter that concerns a lot of people in the U.S.—

THE PRESIDENT: Walter, I might say one of the things that concern the medical profession in permitting the use of a drug that might not be harmful and may not do any good either, is that sometimes it causes people not to seek treatment because they are depending on a worthless drug. I'm not trying to make a judgment on this one, but I know that's a concern to us.

MR. CRONKITE: Mr. O. B. Parris of Vinemont, Alabama, on the phone, Mr. President. Mr. Parris?

MR. PARRIS: Yes, Mr. President, I'm Red Parris with Gulf Oil. I'm a jobber for Gulf Oil Company here in Cullman [County], Alabama; also with Goodly Construction Company.

I was wondering how you feel on the vertical divestiture of the oil companies—vertical and horizontal divestiture of the oil companies.

THE PRESIDENT: The position that I took during the campaign, Mr. Parris, is the same one that I have now, I think, as a general proposition, vertical integration of major industries is not contrary to the best interests of the American people, provided you have a continued and adequate competition.

I am concerned on two ends of the vertical integration process. One is that there be an insured competition for leasing rights. I think it would be a mistake for us to require a different company to drill for oil, to extract the oil from the ground, to pump the oil to a refinery, to do the refining, and then to distribute it, and then to wholesale it, and then to retail it.

If different companies had to do all those processes, I think that the price of the final product, like gasoline, would be greatly increased because of inefficiency.

MR. PARRIS: I do, too.

THE PRESIDENT: I think at the wholesale and retail level, though, there have been occasions that I've witnessed when there has been an inadequate amount of competition. And sometimes small and independent service station operators have been forced to shift toward the majors, and this particularly did occur in the initial stages of the 1973 embargo period.

I have a concern also about horizontal investments. When the major oil companies acquire over a period of time a controlling interest in, say, coal mining operations, it means quite often that there's not a heavy enough emphasis placed on increasing coal production.

So, at the wholesale and retail level, I have some concern.

And in the horizontal investments by oil companies, like in coal or uranium, I have some concern unless I am convinced that there is adequate competition there. I would be in favor of considering divestiture, but my first preference would be to insure competition through the antitrust laws and disclosure of profits at the individual levels of the vertical integration, rather than divestiture itself.

MR. PARRIS: Thank you very much.

THE PRESIDENT: Thank you, Mr. Parris.

MR. CRONKITE: Mr. President, let's take another call. It is from Mr. Phillip Roche Tooele of—or it's Mr. Phillip Roche of Tooele, Utah.

THE PRESIDENT: Very good.

MR. CRONKITE: Let's go through this once more, Mr. President. We might as well spend the afternoon with this. Mr. Roche of Tooele, Utah.

MR. ROCHE: That's Tooele.

MR. CRONKITE: All right, thank you, sir. It is Roche, though, isn't it?

MR. ROCHE: It is Roche.

THE PRESIDENT: Phillip, go ahead with your question.

MR. ROCHE: Mr. President, are you familiar with the sick leave portion of the 1976 income tax revision?

THE PRESIDENT: What was the first part of that? I heard the 1976 income tax revision. What's the first part?

MR. ROCHE: The sick leave portion of the 1976 income tax revision.

THE PRESIDENT: Yes, I am fairly familiar with it.

MR. ROCHE: Well, my question is this, Mr. President, of those that can't qualify for their Federal medical retirement now, could they possibly be given their jobs back?

THE PRESIDENT: I don't know.

MR. ROCHE: The 1976 income tax revision changed the agreement to which these people retired at. And by changing the agreements, people making $300 or $400 a month are going to have to come up with $400, $500, $600 for their 1976 income tax, due to the retroactive clause in the sick leave portion.

THE PRESIDENT: Mr. Roche, perhaps Walter could answer that question. I don't know. But I'll have my staff see if I can get the answer. If I can't give it to you on this program, I'll give you a call Monday and try to answer your question.

MRS. ROCHE: That would be great, but, Mr. President—

THE PRESIDENT: Yes, ma'am.

MRS. ROCHE: If we would be allowed, the truly disabled ones were allowed up to $100 a week tax deduction, if they were truly disabled, even though they are truly disabled now, this new revision has taken away that exclusion.

MR. CRONKITE: I gather that is Mrs. Roche, it it?

MR. ROCHE: That's the boss.

MR. CRONKITE: Well, I tell you, the President is going to look up this question for you. It's a rather complicated one. He is going to see if he can get an answer for you and get back to you. The question is almost as difficult as pronouncing Tooele—

MR. ROCHE: Tooele.

MR. CRONKITE: —Utah.
 Thank you very much, Roches; glad to talk to both of you.

THE PRESIDENT: I'll call you back personally on Monday and talk to you about it.

MR. CRONKITE: Now, Mr. Charles Stone, Mr. President, of Dallas, Texas. I can pronounce both of those names, Stone and Dallas.

MR. STONE: Two questions, sir. Having recently completed figuring the income tax for my fiancee and myself, the tax difference was $1,000 between single and married. When and what action do you plan to take?
 Also, in the news you recently stated that the cost of a new home is out of reach to most Americans. Is there anything that can be done about the price or the interest rates?

THE PRESIDENT: Mr. Stone, the only thing that I know of that can cut down on the price of interest rates would be to control inflation. And we have been working for the last 6 weeks on a comprehensive approach so that we will know in Washington and so that the American people can be informed about all the things that we do that cause an increase in interest rates.
 In addition, for low-income families or middle-income families, we are trying to stimulate housing construction by helping with the repayment of your mortgage on a monthly basis.
 I hope to increase the amount of guaranteed loans for people like yourselves, and I hope that this will be of help to you in the years to come.
 We've increased the authorization for home construction by between $8 billion and $9 billion which is an awful lot of money. Of course, that extends over 40 years in the future.
 To answer your first question, I would like to see in a tax reform package a removal as much as possible of any sort of tax advantage for either single people or married people. This is a complicated question, and I don't know how to deal with it.
 We have now in some parts of the income tax laws a fairly substantial reward for people who live in the same house but who are not married, and I would like to remove that, but at the same time let people who are single and who live alone, not as married people, not be punished.
 So, that's one of the complicated questions that has always been a matter of debate, both in the States' and National Legislatures.

I don't know how to give you the answer yet. But there is a great disparity now.

MR. STONE: Yes, sir, you will have an answer, I believe you said in September, in your tax package.

THE PRESIDENT: I hope so. We're going to address that issue, and I hope we can come up with a reasonable answer. We are going to complete the study of this entire tax code, which is enormously complicated, as you know, and the deadline that I have established and the Secretary of the Treasury, Mike Blumenthal, is the lead Cabinet officer on it, has agreed we can complete this study and make our recommendations to the people and to the Congress by September 30. Yes.

MR. STONE: Thank you, sir.

THE PRESIDENT: Good luck to you.

MR. CRONKITE: Mr. President, did I understand you to say there you would penalize unmarrieds living together?

THE PRESIDENT: No, I just don't think there ought to be an advantage between married people and the unmarried people who share the same household. I'd like to remove, if possible, any advantage one way or the other, Walter.

MR. CRONKITE: The next call, Mr. President, is from the Reverend James Baker, Ridgeland, South Carolina. Reverend Mr. Baker.

REVEREND BAKER: Good afternoon, Mr. President.

THE PRESIDENT: Good afternoon.

REVEREND BAKER: First, sir, I would like to commend you for the efforts you have made to restore ethics and morality in Government. I think you have taken a splendid action in that direction. And I wonder if more cannot be done to protect the consumer from shoddy merchandise or warranties that are not honored and similar unconscionable profit actions on the part of a minority in our country, either through the Federal Trade Commission or a consumer protection bureau sort of setup.

THE PRESIDENT: If I don't do that, Reverend Baker, before I go out of office, I will consider my administration being a failure. You are absolutely right.

In many instances the regulatory agencies in Washington have been staffed and led by men and women whose primary interest is not to the consumer at all, but to the industries being regulated.

REVEREND BAKER: Yes, sir.

THE PRESIDENT: So far we've not been able to get passed the legislation for establishing a consumer protection agency and the consumers' interests quite often are supposed to be protected by a little tiny group of people in many dozens, even hundreds of agencies scattered throughout the city of Washington.

So, I'm in favor of establishment of the consumer protection agency itself to focus the consumer's interest in one agency as much as possible. This agency would be quite small. I think the budget would be in the neighborhood of $11 million a year for the entire nationwide coverage, and it would let you and I and other people know where to go to register a complaint. And it would also have a group of people there whose only interest would be to protect people like you from being cheated.

So, I am strongly in favor of that. And I believe that before the next year or two goes by, we'll have the new agency in operation, and I wish that you would examine every one of my appointments in these regulatory agencies that have taken place now and that will take place over the next 4 years, and I believe, in every instance, you'll see that the people that I do appoint have their obligation to the consumer. That's the way it should have been in the past.

REVEREND BAKER: Thank you. Since you're interested in the small consumer, you see, the consumer with a small complaint is not able to hire an attorney, naturally, to handle it for him, where a consumer, you know, has a $25 or $50 complaint. He has nowhere to turn unless he has an agency that can handle it for him. Many of these are poor people.

THE PRESIDENT: You're right. I favor, in certain instances, the right, the increased right of consumers to file class action suits, law suits, where a thousand customers who have been cheated can get together and get some relief from unfair trade practices. And also, on occasion, the consumers ought to have an increased right to have legal standing in court.

I think that within the Government itself, quite often the consumers have not been treated fairly. That's why I believe it is better to have a separate agency for consumer protection itself.

REVEREND BAKER: Thank you, sir. You have the prayers of the American public for a successful term of office.

THE PRESIDENT: Thank you, Mr. Baker.

MR. CRONKITE: Mr. President, when do you expect to send legislation or a proposal for legislation to establish a consumer agency up to the Hill?

THE PRESIDENT: The legislation, Walter, as you know, made a lot of progress last year. My own inclination is to support the legislation that was already considered by Congress, and I believe that with the support of the White House, instead of the opposition that was the case under the previous administration, that it will be passed.

MR. CRONKITE: Will you support the present legislation as it is now up at the Hill then?

THE PRESIDENT: Yes. I wouldn't want to say I would support it in any language that is put in it, but if I can approve the basic language, I am strongly in favor of the agency, yes.

MR. CRONKITE: The next caller is John Melfi of Johnson City, New York.

MR. MELFI: Good afternoon, Mr. President.

THE PRESIDENT: Good afternoon, John.

MR. MELFI: I know we have a foreign aid policy to help countries in need, but why do we spend so much on this when we have so much poverty, unemployment, et cetera, in our own country?

THE PRESIDENT: Well, John, I am going to take a position that's not very popular, politically speaking. We only spend about 3/10 of one percent of our gross national product on foreign aid, which is about half the proportion that is allotted to this purpose by other countries like France, Germany, and so forth.

I don't particularly want to increase this greatly, but I would like for it to be predictable. Also, in the past, we've not had foreign aid used in an effective way. As one of my friends has said quite often, I'm not in favor of taxing the poor people in our rich country and sending the money to the rich people in poor countries, and quite often that has been done in the past.

We have also a need, in my opinion, to support the lending institutions, the International Monetary Fund, the World Bank—they give aid to other countries in the form of loans, sometimes low-interest loans. But instead of just handing gifts out that are kind of bad, as a basic philosophy, and also that are abused, I would favor contributing to the capital stock of these international or regional lending agencies. I believe we will get a lot better return on our money, and I might say that my own experience in this first 6 weeks has been that the International Monetary Fund, for instance, and the World Bank are quite strict on a nation that makes a loan.

They make them work hard toward balancing their budget. Quite often they require them to clean up corruption. They make them assess very carefully their trade policies.

So, I believe that the lending procedure in foreign aid is much better than the gift procedure, and when direct grants are made, we ought to do more than we have in the past to get the grants to people who actually need it.

Within those changes, I think that our present level of foreign aid is about right, John.

MR. MELFI: Okay. Thank you, Mr. President. Best of luck to you in the future, and I hope you are here for another 8 years.

THE PRESIDENT: Thank you very much.

I might say, Walter, there's a Mr. Otto Flaig of Milwaukee, Wisconsin. His telephone number, unfortunately for him today, is 242-1611, and ever since 6 o'clock this morning he has been getting calls from people who want to talk to me. He has requested me to announce that people please dial the 1 and then the 900 before they dial the 242-1611, so his phone will quit ringing.

MR. CRONKITE: I assume those calls could only get to him from the Milwaukee area, and if they once dial the 900, it won't get through to him at all.

THE PRESIDENT: That's true. I'd like to ask people—I guess there are other folks around the country that got the same last seven numbers. So, everybody ought to remember to dial the 900 before the 2.

MR. CRONKITE: I wonder if that gentleman in Milwaukee is giving them any answers. Maybe he is giving them quite satisfactory solutions to their problems.

THE PRESIDENT: I am sure he is getting a lot of questions. His answers are probably better than mine.

MR. CRONKITE: We have a call from Lapeer, Michigan, from Ms. Colleen Muir, I believe it is.

Muir, is it?

MS. MUIR: Muir.

MR. CRONKITE: She's 16 years old, I am told, Mr. President.

Go ahead, Ms. Muir.

MS. MUIR: Good afternoon, Mr. President, and thank you for this opportunity to talk to you.

THE PRESIDENT: Thank you, Colleen.

MS. MUIR: I was wondering, since the volunteer draft program isn't working too well, that you would put a draft system into effect; and, if you would, would you draft women the same as men as the equal rights amendment infers?

THE PRESIDENT: Well, Colleen, we don't have any plans now to put in a draft system. So far we are still getting by with the voluntary armed forces.

The major problem has been in the reserves. We are about 800,000 people short, I believe, now in reserve recruitment. The regular armed forces are holding their own.

But if I see it is necessary in the future to initiate a draft, then I would certainly recommend to the Congress that this be done.

I would like to combine it with a much more comprehensive public service opportunity where people might go into jobs like the Peace Corps or VISTA, teachers' aides or mental institutions and so forth, along with military training as well.

I would make it much more all-inclusive than it has been in the past. I would not, for instance, exclude college students. And if it becomes necessary for national security, the likelihood is that women would be included as well. But I'd like to draw a distinction between military service and other service that would benefit our country just as much in a time of need or crisis.

But I might reemphasize that at this time we have no intention of going to a draft.

MS. MUIR: Okay, thank you.

MR. CRONKITE: Thank you, Ms. Muir.

The next question is from Samuel Rankin of Billings, Montana, Mr. President.

MR. RANKIN: Good afternoon, Mr. President.

THE PRESIDENT: Good afternoon, Sam.

MR. RANKIN: I have a two-part question. The first is broken into two minor economic questions. I hope that this has not been covered previously. If it has, maybe you would like to add some things that possibly you didn't get to add in the previous questions.

I would like your commitment and your comments on a resolution in the public's favor that would alleviate the painfully high cost of medical care in the U.S. And I know also that these two are related—a total commitment to the lowering of the transfer payments, which I believe are your 46 percent of the income derived by the Government from corporate and individual taxes.

THE PRESIDENT: Mr. Rankin, I don't know any way to answer your question very well at this point. I might say that these are two questions that we're working on simultaneously. The income tax changes are part of the transfer of payments. Also, the welfare system in its entirety needs to be reformed.

By the first of May, Joe Califano, who is the new Secretary of HEW, working with literally hundreds of different people, will come up for me and for the Congress with a comprehensive reform of the welfare system. It will be, I would say, next year before we can complete an adequate analysis of the health care system as a whole.

Now, we are trying now to hold down the cost of both medicine, treatment, and also hospital care. But I can't answer your question yet.

MR. RANKIN: All right.

THE PRESIDENT: The first part of the answer, though, will be forthcoming May 1 with a welfare reform package; the second part, September 30, with income tax revision proposals. And the comprehensive health care would probably have to wait until next year. There's just so much we can do the first year, Sam.

MR. RANKIN: I appreciate that.

THE PRESIDENT: I'm sorry.

MR. RANKIN: Then, the second part of my question, Mr. President, with many of our young people so involved in the past and presently with Vietnam, I would like to respectfully suggest that possibly you appoint a young person, preferably a Vietnam veteran, to accompany the mission headed by Leonard Woodcock and including my State's most distinguished Member of the Senate, Senator Mansfield, going to Vietnam in the near future. I believe this would help many of us, myself included, who felt hesitant in going to Vietnam and would now like to feel that we are helping rebuild that country.

And I respectfully request that my name be on that list if and when you do decide to include a young member.

My wife wants me to be sure and say that if you are ever in Billings, Montana, that we would more than like to have you stay at our home.

THE PRESIDENT: That's a very nice invitation for me. My roommate at the Naval Academy back in ancient days was from Butte, Montana. His name was Blue Middleton, and I hear a lot about Montana from him. And, of course, Senator Mike Mansfield is one of the most distinguished Members of Congress that has ever served in our country.

The five members who will go to Vietnam have already been chosen. Leonard Woodcock will be the chairman. As you have said, Mike

Mansfield would go. A woman, Marian Edelman, will also be on the trip, and a professional diplomat will go along, and also one Member of the House of Representatives as well.

Unfortunately, we won't have a veteran of the Vietnam war. I thought about this, Sam, and I also thought about sending a member of an MIA family.

MR. RANKIN: Right.

THE PRESIDENT: But my judgment was that we probably ought not to get people there who are so deeply and emotionally involved in the process. We've been encouraged so far—nobody can predict what is going to happen in the future—at the response of the Vietnamese Government.

I think they want to reestablish relationships with our own country. They need help in exploring for oil and in other ways. They need to trade with the outside world and not be completely dependent upon the Communist countries, like China and Russia.

Of course, we want to get an accounting for the more than 2,500 Americans who still are not completely accounted for in Vietnam. So you have a good suggestion. But I have already chosen the five people, and they are now getting ready to go.

They'll arrive in Vietnam, if the plans go through, I think, the 16th of March. So it is well underway.

MR. RANKIN: I think your proposal, your counterpoint to mine, was well taken. I can understand, you know, your thinking behind choosing someone who isn't necessarily a Vietnam veteran.

MR. CRONKITE: The next call is from Louis Lawson of Richmond, Virginia.

Mr. Lawson?

MR. RUSSELL LAWSON: Mr. Cronkite, President Carter, my name is Russell. You may call me Russell. Unfortunately, I had two questions before Mr. Cronkite asked me to limit it to one. But I have one that is really uppermost in my mind.

I was wondering if you feel if there is any inequity in passing laws which encourage the hiring of members of minority groups and women while passing such laws implies resisting hiring equally qualified white males?

THE PRESIDENT: Yes, I don't like that concept, either. I think most of the laws that have been passed have been designed very narrowly to insure that there is no continued discrimination against somebody because they are in a minority group or women. Now, the courts have interpreted this to mean that if a company, for instance, has historically excluded men and women from the labor force, from their own labor force, that they have to go back and take corrective action.

But I think all of the laws with which I am familiar on equal employment opportunities just guarantee that now and in the future there won't be discrimination and that if there has been a history of discrimination, that it be corrected.

MR. LAWSON: I hope that is true. I have been unemployed for a while. I feel I am the victim of this kind of system.

I want to say though before I go, that I'm really impressed by your desire to involve Americans more closely in the Government, and I am so pleased to have had the chance to talk to you.

Thank you, Mr. President.

THE PRESIDENT: Thank you.

I might say we have a question we can answer, I think, now, for the man and his wife in Utah about the exclusion for disabled people.

This was removed from the income tax law in the 1976 act; that is, sick pay exclusion for anyone except the permanently disabled. The Congress gave as its reason, it sounded like a good reason, that such sick persons could deduct their medical expenses from the income tax and would therefore get a double benefit.

When anybody in our society, even if it is an afflicted person or disabled person, has a special exclusion, then other people have to pay their taxes for them. This is one of the things that will be assessed this year, and we may or may not put the double credit back for permanently disabled, but my guess is it would not be put back in.

MR. CRONKITE: Let me remind you that these calls are not being screened in any way for content. There is no censorship at all of the calls into us here in the Oval Office of the White House.

Gerald Anderson, Denver, Colorado, is the next caller.

MR. ANDERSON: Hello, Mr. President.

THE PRESIDENT: Hi, Gerald.

MR. ANDERSON: I'm wondering what is the justification with you trying to reduce the Federal budget, the justification behind the $12,000 pay increase for Congress? How can you lower the budget by giving them $12,000 a year and us $50 back?

THE PRESIDENT: Gerald, that is a hard question for me to answer.

MR. ANDERSON: I'm sure it is. That's why I thought I would throw it at you.

THE PRESIDENT: I think you probably know that there is a law that was passed by Congress and the previous Presidents, before I came into office, that said that a commission would recommend pay levels for the Congress and for others like the Federal judges and Cabinet officers and unless the Congress voted no, that the pay raises would go into effect. In other words, if the Congress does nothing, the pay raises go into effect.

And that's what occurred. That law has been on the books for quite a while.

MR. ANDERSON: Well, right, what I am getting at, though, is with you trying to lower the budget, why did you not try to do something to stop that or if there was anything that could be done to stop it? Why couldn't in some way they be convinced that it was against, you know, the fiscal matters of the country to give them this increase?

THE PRESIDENT: Well, I might say that I think that the salary increases were justified. One of the things that President Ford asked me to do before I was inaugurated, while he was still in office, was to add my support to the increase in salaries. I agreed not to object to the increase, provided there was a strict law on ethics tied to it to limit the outside income of Congress Members and to remove the conflicts of interest that exist between, with them and also with people serving in the executive branch of Government.

I do think the law ought to be changed, Gerald, to make sure that in the future, if any sort of salary increase goes into effect, that it not go into effect until after the following general election. I think this would help a great deal to make all of us more careful about it, and it would mean that if the Congress doesn't veto an increase, that they would not get an increase in salary until after they had to face the voters again in the next general election.

With that change, I would be in favor of continuing the law as it is.

MR. ANDERSON: So, there was no way you could have stopped this increase?

THE PRESIDENT: That's correct. I didn't have any authority over it. I have to say to you, I could have made speeches around the country against it, but it was not my inclination to do so.

MR. ANDERSON: Don't you feel that with the Congress people receiving this excessive amount of money, compared to the average working person, that it puts them out of touch with reality as far as what the average person has to go through to live in this country?

THE PRESIDENT: Well, I can't say that you are exactly right on that, no. I have seen, from my own experience, that it costs a Member of

Congress an enormous amount of extra money to maintain close contacts with the people back home. Quite often to finance and to own a house, say, in Colorado, where you live, and also to buy and to own or to rent an extremely expensive house here in Washington. Also, the Congress Member, in order to stay in office and to build up seniority to serve you and the other people around Denver better, has to run for office every 2 years. Now, there are also Members of Congress who have no trouble raising money for a political campaign. Others have to spend a lot of their own money in a political campaign.

If you compare, say, a Member of Congress who has to do that with a Federal judge who lives in Denver full time, who doesn't have to run for office, who gets the same amount of pay, and who doesn't have the constant political world to live in and to deal with all kinds of complicated and very controversial questions like a Congressman does, all in the open, I think the Congressmen deserve just as much salary as a Federal judge.

So, it cuts both ways. I think, Gerald, that in fairness to the Members of Congress—I've never been in Congress as you know—there are some extraordinary expenses that a Member of Congress has that an average person, even a public servant like a Federal judge, does not have.

But I believe that the one change that I described to you ought to be made; that is, to let future salary increases go into effect only after the next general election.

MR. CRONKITE: It is also true, Mr. President, isn't it, that the Members of Congress, members of the judiciary and the executive branch who are entitled to these raises, had not had one for a very long time and had fallen far behind the general cost-of-living increases?

THE PRESIDENT: I think the last raise went into effect about 8 years ago.

I might say, Walter, that I made a mistake a while ago. I got my decimal point wrong on the shortage in the reserve figures because of not having a draft. The total reserve is about 800,000 and the shortage is about 10 percent of that, 70,000 or 80,000. Somebody just called in and said that I said the shortage was 800,000. And I'm sorry I made that mistake.

MR. CRONKITE: An officer in the reserve I would guess.

THE PRESIDENT: I guess.

MR. CRONKITE: Let's go to the next telephone call, from Walter Lipman of Spring Valley, New York.

MR. LIPMAN: Good afternoon, Mr. President.

THE PRESIDENT: Good afternoon.

MR. LIPMAN: I am rather amazed at being able to get hold of you.

This question is something that a bunch of friends of mine and I bandied back and forth and swore would never get on the air, but anyhow, Mr. President, it seems, well, at least to me and my friends, that the term "drug addict" is more a function of one's social station than anything else. Many famous people, such as Sigmund Freud and Sir Arthur Conan Doyle, who wrote Sherlock Holmes, and Dr. William Halsted, who was one of the founders of the Johns Hopkins Medical School, were quite heavy users of drugs such as cocaine and morphine, yet they were considered leaders of society in their day.

Now, in this light, doesn't the prosecution of drug users and their habits by the Drug Enforcement Administration seem capricious, arbitrary, and rather unjust?

THE PRESIDENT: No, it doesn't, Walter, not to me. I established a drug treatment program in Georgia while I was in office there as Governor. In July of 1972, I believe it was, we had 11 deaths in the Atlanta area from heroin overdose, primarily among young people. We put in a drug treatment program and kind of opened the whole question up to public awareness in October, and the following 12 months we had zero heroin deaths.

I've been in our treatment centers throughout the State of Georgia. In fact, my sons have worked in those treatment centers. I've seen literally hundreds of young people's lives almost completely destroyed by addiction to heroin, in particular.

I think that a question like morphine would be a different one altogether. Morphine is a drug that's, as you know, administered legally—or as a previous caller said, a medication that is administered legally.

But I would do all I can, and am moving as aggressively as possible, to stamp out the traffic in drugs like cocaine or heroin. I believe they are a devastating affliction on our society and ought to be eliminated as much as we can.

MR. LIPMAN: Mr. President, do you know the drug origin of heroin?

THE PRESIDENT: Yes, I know it comes from poppies.

MR. LIPMAN: No, but the purpose of this—

MR. CRONKITE: Mr. Lipman, thank you very much for your call, but we're running a little short of time. We do want to get in as many calls as possible.

MR. CRONKITE: The next call is from John Raymond Lau of Yorktown Heights, New York, Mr. President. Mr. Lau?

MR. LAU: Yes, how are you doing, Mr. President?

THE PRESIDENT: Fine.

MR. LAU: I would like to know what your opinion is of the French-English Concorde, and with the elections in France this week, do you feel that rejection of the Concorde would bring the power to the French Communist Party?

And also I'd like to say that many French citizens are counting on the SST to keep France from going the Communist way. So, what is your opinion on that, Mr. President?

THE PRESIDENT: Okay. Our Government has already expressed its opinion, Mr. Lau. The previous administration authorized the Concorde to come into our country for a 16-month trial period, and a couple of weeks ago I made a statement that I agreed with that decision and thought the Concorde ought to be given a chance to fulfill its trial itself. As you know, under the Federal law I have authority over Dulles Airport.

MR. LAU: Right.

THE PRESIDENT: And so did President Ford. We're permitting the test flights to come into Dulles, and we're very carefully monitoring environmental consequences of the SST flights, including primarily noise.

The Kennedy Airport in New York is not under my control at all. I have nothing to do with it, no authority over it. The New York Port Authority has that decision to make, and I understand on March the 10th they are going to make a decision whether the Concorde can come in for test flights or not. I don't know what their decision will be.

I talked to President Giscard from France yesterday about the Concorde, and I also talked to Governor Hugh Carey to let Governor Carey know, as President Giscard had asked me to, that the French people consider this a very important issue. My own statement to President Giscard is that we are not concerned about the SST flights because of commercial competition. About 6 years ago our own Congress decided not to go into the SST-building business.

MR. LAU: Yes, I remember.

THE PRESIDENT: And the whole problem in our country is noise and environmental quality maintenance. Now, I might say one other thing. I think that the noise standards in our country are going to be stricter and stricter in the future, and not more and more lenient, and the same noise standards ought to apply to an airplane, whether it's a Concorde or a Lockheed or an airplane of some other kind, or any sort of American commercial plane.

So, I think we can establish strict environmental laws. I think they ought to apply to the SST flying, of course, at subsonic speeds, and our own commercial planes the same. But it is the environmental question that will exclude the Concorde, if it is excluded, and not any sort of animosity toward the French people. Nor is it any commercial competition between us and France on SST flights.

MR. LAU: Okay, Thank you, Mr. President.

MR. CRONKITE: And your next caller, Mr. President, is Mr. Kerry Kimble of Fulton, Missouri. Mr. Kimble?

MR. KIMBLE: Yes. Mr. President, my question covers the war powers resolution. And do you feel that it infringes upon your power as Commander in Chief in the limiting or getting the approval from Congress to continue the use of American forces in a certain situation past the 60 days?

THE PRESIDENT: Mr. Kimble, it is a reduction, obviously, in the authority that the President has had prior to the Vietnam war. But I think it's an appropriate reduction. My own attitude toward government is that I would never see our Nation approach a time of war with any sort of predictability about it without discussing it thoroughly and frequently with the Congress and also letting the American people know what is going on.

Although we did get involved in the Vietnam war, and even fought extensively in Cambodia without telling the American people, and sometimes lying to them, I would never have that inclination. So, I have no hesitancy about communicating with Congress, consulting with them and also letting the American people know what we do before we start any combat operation. And I think with that process we can minimize greatly the chances that we will get involved in combat anywhere in the world.

MR. KIMBLE: Sir, you would accept their approval for your actions on that?

THE PRESIDENT: Yes. There is, I think, a provision that in a time of crisis, where an unanticipated attack might be launched against our country's security, that I could act, but to continue any sort of military operation, I would have to get the Congress approval. I have no doubt that that is the right thing to do.

MR. CRONKITE: Thank you, Mr. Kimble.

The next call is from Mr. Johnnie Strickland of Fayetteville, North Carolina.

MR. STRICKLAND: Good afternoon, Mr. President.

THE PRESIDENT: Good afternoon.

MR. STRICKLAND: I am John Strickland from Fayetteville, North Carolina. And I want to thank you for this opportunity to talk with you, and I would like to know what your sentiments are on the Panama Canal 1904 treaty, and changing it.

THE PRESIDENT: Okay. It is good to hear from you, Mr. Strickland. My sister lives in Fayetteville, as you may know. I am glad to answer your question.

We are now negotiating with Panama as effectively as we can. As you may or may not know, the treaty, signed when Theodore Roosevelt was President, gave Panama sovereignty over the Panama Canal Zone itself. It gave us control over the Panama Canal Zone as though we had sovereignty. So, we've always had a legal sharing of responsibility over the Panama Canal Zone.

As far as sovereignty is concerned, I don't have any hang-up about that. I would hope that after that—and expect that after the year 2000, that we would have an assured capacity or capability of our country with Panama guaranteeing that the Panama Canal would be open and of use to our own Nation and to other countries.

So, the subject of the negotiation now—it has been going on quite a while—is to phase out our military operations in the Panama Canal Zone, but to guarantee that even after the year 2000 that we would still be able to keep the Panama Canal open to the use of American and other ships.

MR. STRICKLAND: I understand, and I certainly hope that we are not too lenient, because we have lots of money invested in the Canal Zone. And I really think the Canal Zone belongs to us a whole lot more than most people think it does.

MR. CRONKITE: Thank you, Mr. Strickland.

Mr. President, we have just about run out of time. I am just curious, Mr. President, before we close this off today, what you thought of the questions you got in this first experiment in meeting the people through a telephone call-in broadcast.

THE PRESIDENT: Walter, I liked it. The questions that come in from people all over the country are the kind that you would never get in a press conference. And I think it's very good for me to understand directly from the American people what they are concerned about and questions that have never been asked of me and reported through the news media.

So, my inclination would be to do this again in the future. And I'll wait and see how the American people react to it, to see whether or not I have done a good job to make it worth their while.

But I want to thank you for being here with me this afternoon. The 2 hours passed very quickly, and I've enjoyed it and learned a lot from it.

MR. CRONKITE: I think they did, indeed, and we'd be glad to sign you up again, Mr. President.

THE PRESIDENT: Good deal.

MR. CRONKITE: We have run out of time. We thank you for your time and the cooperation of your entire staff in making this broadcast possible.

We regret such a small number of those who wanted to talk with you actually did call in and many of you who did call and didn't get through to the President, we apologize for that.

Our special thanks to all of you who were interested in this new broadcast idea and for President Carter and me in the Oval Office of the White House, good afternoon.

I am Walter Cronkite, CBS News.

NOTE: The program began at 2 p.m. It was videotaped for television broadcast at 5 p.m. on the same day on the Public Broadcasting Service.

7

THE PRESIDENT TALKS TOUGH, JUNE 6, 1977

U.S. News & World Report

QUESTION: Mr. President, your plan to withdraw American troops from Korea is at the top of the news. What are the benefits to be gained from such a withdrawal—weighed against the impact it might have on the Japanese, the Koreans themselves, and also the Chinese?

THE PRESIDENT: We've been in Korea more than 25 years with a substantial ground-troop implacement. My own belief, shared with many advisers, is that a very careful and predictable and orderly withdrawal over the next four or five years will leave the military balance in the Korean peninsula unchanged.

We will maintain adequate air and naval support, intelligence support on the ground, some troops in Korea to handle the Air Force requirements. This will be combined with a building up of the strength of the South Korean ground forces.

It will also be accomplished with continuing close consultation not only with President Park in the Republic of Korea but also with Prime Minister Fukuda in Japan and also with our friends in New Zealand, Australia and other places in the Pacific. We have kept the People's Republic of China and the Soviet officials also informed, and with a heavy emphasis there that our commitment to South Korea is unchanged.

It's a firm military and political commitment. I think that this would add to the stability of the Korea peninsula. There comes a time when continued presence of ground troops is not advisable, and the time has just arrived.

Let me say one other thing: They've got a dynamic, growing, strong, varied economy brought about in part by our own military and economic aid but primarily because of the resourcefulness of the South Korean people. And I think their ground troops, combined with our own air and naval forces, will be more than adequate to protect them in case of any warlike intentions on the part of their northern neighbors.

QUESTION: Would withdrawal of U.S. troops carry the implication that you would be ready to use tactical nuclear weapons if necessary to protect South Korea in the event of invasion?

THE PRESIDENT: I think anyone recognizes that the first nation to use atomic weapons would be taking a very profound step toward the self-condemnation of the whole world.

However, in areas where nuclear weapons are deployed in the Western Pacific and also in Europe and to defend our own homeland, their very deployment implies a possibility of their use, if necessary.

I think the combination of our overwhelming strategic cover with atomic weapons, plus the conventional military alliance that I've described to you, is adequate, but I can't say that the two are necessarily tied together in my own plans.

QUESTION: Another area in the news is Africa, and on that subject many people are asking: Is U.N. Ambassador Andrew Young speaking for the President?

THE PRESIDENT: The answer is "Yes." I don't think there's been any time when Secretary [of State] Cy Vance and Andrew Young and myself had any disagreement on the thrust of our policy or statements in Africa.

If there's one overwhelming impression that's growing on me, it's the long-range strategic need—looking 10, 15, 20 years in the future—for a close friendship and mutual trust, social and political alliance with the developing nations of the world.

Our approach has been very well evoked by Ambassador Young, and he works very closely and intimately with me and the Secretary of State. He has a great sensitivity about the yearnings, the frustrations and, in the past, even the animosities and hatred of many developing nations' people toward our own country. I think he's made great strides in repairing that damage that had been done. And he also gives us a very clear understanding of the opportunities there.

So I consider him to be a very valuable and a very compatible spokesman for us.

QUESTION: Some critics of U.S. policy in Africa contend that your Administration is moving too fast in an area where the problems are very deep-rooted—

THE PRESIDENT: I believe that the actions that we've planned and discussed in Zimbabwe—that is, Rhodesia—and in Namibia—formerly South-West Africa—have been evolved in a completely compatible way, not only with the African neighboring nations but also with our friends and allies in Europe; and also, I might say, within the United Nations. These policies are not abrupt, they're not ill-conceived, and I don't think we have moved too fast.

As a matter of fact, I think the progress has been too slow. We see the possibility of war in the southern part of Africa as being ever-present. I think to the extent that we are staunch in our support and our co-operation with the allies and friends who only want peace in southern Africa, I think this is a good basis for our foreign policy.

QUESTION: Switching to the Middle East: Are you worried that the Israeli election outcome might harm peace negotiations?

THE PRESIDENT: I think it would be good to repeat what I said last week-end [May 22] at Notre Dame as an answer to the question, because it was very carefully devised by me to express accurately what our nation feels: that our friendship for Israel is based on two principles. One is a respect for human freedom, and the other one a common commitment to find a permanent and lasting peace in the Middle East.

Secondly, that this is a time, because of the moderate attitude of the nations in the Middle East, particularly now among the Arab nations, for progress; that the premise of the negotiations so far, and we presume in the future, is the United Nations resolutions, particularly 242, and that a change in the leadership in the United States and Israel should not be interpreted as a change in those basic commitments.

I don't know what the new Government might do in Israel. It hasn't been put together yet. As you know, the identity of a Prime Minister in Israel is not the final definition of what a Government's policies might be, because the Government must be put together with minority leadership, with a great deal of negotiation and compromise and public discussion. But our presumption is that the Government of Israel will continue to join with us and the Arab countries in seeking a permanent solution in the Middle East to their problems there, based on the United Nations resolutions that have been espoused time and again by the nations involved.

QUESTION: But what if the new Israeli Government refuses to consider returning lands captured from the Arab nations?

THE PRESIDENT: I really would rather not presuppose what an unformed Government will do. I don't believe that any responsible Government leader in Israel has ever disavowed Israel's commitment to the United Nations resolution that I described to you.

If Israel should disavow those commitments, which have been the basis for the hopes for peace for years, then that would be a very profound change, and I think the consequences of it can't be accurately predicted. But my hope is and my belief is that this will not occur.

QUESTION: Have you heard any rumblings of Arab impatience or threats of another oil embargo to pressure us to crack the whip on speedier peace talks?

THE PRESIDENT: No, I haven't. I think any nation that made a threat of that sort would be taking a counterproductive action. The American people would not respond well to any overt or implied threats.

I met this week, as you know, with Crown Prince Fahd of Saudi Arabia. My experience as President so far with the Saudi Arabians has been one of the most pleasant things that I've witnessed since I've been in this office. They have gone out of their way to be supportive and friendly to us, and they've been highly responsible in every action they've taken. And I don't anticipate any problems in this area.

QUESTION: Another foreign-affairs topic that is heating up is Panama. Do you stand by your campaign pledge that you would never surrender effective control of the Panama Canal?

THE PRESIDENT: What we've maintained, and what I said in the campaign, is that the Panama Canal itself has got to be protected. It's got to be protected for international and peaceful use, and the United States feels a responsibility for that open, free use.

As I pointed out many times during the campaign, the original treaty when signed gave Panama sovereignty over the Panama Canal Zone. It gave us control over the Panama Canal Zone as though we had sovereignty. So there's always been a sharing under the treaty itself for that responsibility.

But this has been the most difficult negotiating point with Panama since we began: What would happen after the year 2000 to give us and the world assurance that the Panama Canal Zone would be adequately protected and kept open? On that point, my position wouldn't be changed. I think if the United States adopted any contrary position it would be almost impossible to get a treaty ratified.

The period within which we would turn over control of some of the properties to the Panamanians, the sharing of the responsibility of operation of the canal, the permanent protection of the Canal Zone itself—these things are now getting negotiated, but I think we are making good progress.

QUESTION: Yet there are a good many Senators who would vote against any change in the *status quo*—

THE PRESIDENT: Yes, it's always a problem. I think, though, that the common purpose is to have the Panama Canal protected and open for free use by world shipping interests. And I think there is a potential threat to the canal if we don't act in good faith concerning the demands for increased control over the Canal Zone by the Panamanians.

We have had obviously no threat from the Panamanian Government of attacks on the canal if we don't work out an agreement. But I would really hate to see sabotage result from any lack of sensitivity on our part in the desire to work out this question in a peaceful way.

We're going to protect the rights of our own country, of the world shipping needs, and of the maintenance and the security of the canal itself. Those are the overriding questions for us, and I believe in the good judgment of the Senate, although I do know that there will be some who don't want any change and will never support any change. I think we can make change in the present arrangement and meet the goals that I described.

QUESTION: A final area in foreign affairs that's of major interest, of course, is our relationship with the Soviet Union. Are you satisfied that we are making some forward movement, particularly on limiting nuclear arms?

THE PRESIDENT: The differences between us and the Soviet Union are still wide and very significant. We have made progress. The recent discussions between Foreign Minister Gromyko and Secretary of State Vance have been productive in setting a framework that might lead to future agreement.

We have a determination to reduce substantially the world's dependence on atomic weapons. So far, the Soviets have been unwilling or reluctant to join us in this commitment. They still feel threatened potentially from our nuclear forces, and they've not been nearly so forthcoming as I would like to see them in reducing present levels prohibiting the research or deployment of new kinds of ICBM's and other formidable weapons, or prior notification of test trials, or a limit on the number of test firings per year, and comprehensive test ban.

But we're going to be persistent. It's going to be a very slow process. There have been agreements made between Secretary Vance and Mr. Gromyko to meet at least twice more before the middle of September. We have laid the groundwork for progress.

The attitude of the Soviets on this mission, as contrasted with the one to Moscow, was very encouraging. But I wouldn't want to underestimate the substance of the differences that still exist.

QUESTION: Mr. President, despite the steps you've taken to reassure business people about your Administration, many still have doubts about you. Do you feel this criticism is unfair?

THE PRESIDENT: I haven't detected the criticism. We spelled out a program before I became President, and we are carefully and methodically carrying it out. It has been sound in its inception, and I think it's still sound.

The Congress has already taken action on parts of the program—the extension of some parts of the tax measures that were in effect already. I just signed an over-all tax-simplification-and-reduction measure that adds about 5 billion dollars a year to the incomes of low and middle-income families. We've had a substantial public-works program put into effect.

I think the economy is in a strong position at this time—not because of any particular action that we took but just because of a restoration of consumer confidence.

QUESTION: And yet business people keep complaining of the uncertainty about what to expect from Washington. They cite the energy program, environmental controls, tax reform. One result is that there's a delay of capital spending in some areas. What else can you do to reassure the business community?

THE PRESIDENT: It's hard to answer your question without agreeing with the premise.

I think that the accuracy that is demanded requires a recognition that both our public and private institutions that measure business-investment intentions show confidence in the future. I think McGraw-Hill recently published a report saying that business-investment intentions were up 18 per cent for the next year compared to this one, which means more than a 10 per cent increase even after you discount inflation.

The unemployment rate has dropped 1 percentage point. There is a heavy inclination on the part of consumers to spend, as contrasted to a heavy saving inclination in the past. So I don't know what else we can do.

There obviously are some causes for uncertainty about the future. We're now addressing problems that have been delayed too long: a comprehensive approach to the energy problem, the welfare problem, the Social Security problem, Tax Code problems. And in a time of consideration of these measures by the President and the Congress, it's obvious that no one knows for sure what's going to happen.

But I think the fact that they are long overdue and are being addressed at least now is a step in the right direction. I don't have any intention to change our policies, though, to accommodate any expressions of concern which I think are largely imaginative.

QUESTION: Inflation obviously is a problem, and there is concern around the country about congressional spending. Are you going to confront Congress on spending?

THE PRESIDENT: Inflation concerns me very much. As for Congress, so far my relations with Congress have been very gratifying—I think constructive. We've got some potential problems ahead.

We've laid down budget spending proposals which I think are adequate. In some very popular areas, the present indications are that Congress will exceed the budget proposals that I put forward in the area of labor and education, veterans, farm programs, public-works projects. These have a very serious effect in the coming fiscal year, but the cumulative effect over a four-year period is even more of concern to me.

Of course, my first inclination is to try to induce the Congress to be reticent in their increases in the budget beyond a level that I think is appropriate. If we can't work out the differences between us, then I would have to take action, including the possibility of a presidential veto. But my hope is that Congress will not take this action. So far they haven't.

QUESTION: Business people seem to want tax changes to encourage increased investment in plants and equipment. Do you favor that approach?

THE PRESIDENT: Yes, I do. There are several elements of an effective tax-reform package. One is simplicity. Another one is equity or fairness. And I think it's accurate to say that part of that will be the retention of more income both by business and by individual families.

QUESTION: How would you allow business to keep more income?

THE PRESIDENT: Well, we haven't worked out the details of the tax-reform package yet. But I think if you examine my own campaign promises during the last two years, I don't know of any of those from which I have any intention to depart.

QUESTION: That includes ending the double taxation of corporate dividends?

THE PRESIDENT: That's one of the goals that we've set for ourselves, yes.

QUESTION: How about cutting corporate-tax rates?

THE PRESIDENT: I'm not sure that can be done. We will certainly eliminate substantial portions of the present deductions, tax exemptions and tax credits, and have a larger proportion of the private and corporate income to tax. This would probably result in a reduction in the rates for both private taxpayers and also corporate taxpayers. But the level of those has not yet been determined.

QUESTION: Do you see more of a shifting of the tax load from the poor to the rich?

THE PRESIDENT: I think inevitably, as present societal trends are realized, there are going to be more and more people in the lower ends of the taxpayer spectrum who won't pay any taxes. The two tax measures that were passed this year have both contributed to that.

But I think in general the scale is tipped too much now on the working family, particularly when you include the payroll taxes. So my guess is that there would be a more progressive break in the future as a result of our tax-reform effort this year.

QUESTION: What happens to the great wedge of middle-class people? Are they going to get a break out of this? Are they bearing an excessive tax burden now?

THE PRESIDENT: I think they are bearing too much of the burden. We have studied in some depth—and the studies are available to the public—the present burden of taxation on different persons, depending upon their income level. These studies show that when you pass the $50,000-income level, there's a leveling off of the tax rate, and that those who earn a very high income quite often have a great-enough degree of flexibility to avoid paying taxes much more than the lower-income groups who derive their income from taxable income.

So I would guess that because of this there would be a shift away from the very-low-income families and toward some of the very-high-income families. I would expect that the average working family would have their tax burden reduced.

QUESTION: Do you favor indexing tax rates as a way of preventing inflation from pushing people into higher tax brackets?

THE PRESIDENT: No, I've never expressed support for that idea. I have seen the advantages expressed, and also some disadvantages. I think, without indexing, the Government has the flexibility to determine when to reduce tax rates and when not to.

I don't think there has been any period when tax reductions were withheld over any particular period of time. No matter what the income levels have been, really almost without regard to the prosperity of our nation or an increase in gross national product for a year, there's been a fairly stable percentage of all income that is actually paid in taxes.

We've now got a little bit too much, in my opinion, of the total income being collected and spent by the Federal Government. I would hope that the rate of growth in all Government spending could be reduced and Government spending held at no more than, say, 21 per cent of the gross national product. Now it would be a little bit above that figure.

QUESTION: If you go to a more progressive income tax that hits upper brackets harder, wouldn't that offset the benefits from your proposal to eliminate double taxation of dividends?

THE PRESIDENT: I can't answer a question that specific at this time because we've only begun to make the analysis on which our decision will be based. But, obviously, if you eliminate double taxation, which is one of our goals, there would probably be some compensatory action taken so that you wouldn't have the heaviest tax deduction among very rich people.

As I said earlier: Simplification, a reduced tax rate, more accurately maintained progressivity would be elements that we would try to have as generic goals. The elimination of double taxation is one of those specifics.

QUESTION: Mr. President, when you talk to your economic advisers about the business outlook, do you still hear that the rest of '77 looks pretty good but there are danger signs for '78?

THE PRESIDENT: Yes, this has been pretty well the prediction since even before I was President. Our over-all incentive package has been designed accordingly.

Most of the programs in public-service jobs and public-works programs, in training slots, tax reductions for business and private individuals have been designed to take effect in the latter part of 1977 and during fiscal '78. So I think that the prediction, which may or may not come true, that the economy might slow down after the passage of the next four or five months is still one that we are prepared to address.

I think that the only error made was last fall when we had over an 8 per cent unemployment rate and a GNP growth of about 3 per cent. We thought that this spring would be a time of great economic dormancy. But the growth there was very gratifying—much more than we had thought. So the immediate stimulation was not needed. But we still have instituted the stimulation that we anticipated for.

QUESTION: Where is this 10 per cent annual rate of inflation coming from?

THE PRESIDENT: A lot of it comes from food-price increases brought about by one of the worst winters we've ever had in our country, a shortage of feed and a very high price for feed that goes into the price of cattle. That's a major factor, as well as the destruction of some of our fruit crops and vegetable crops during the winter period, the rapidly increasing results and threat of the drought in the Middle and Far West. I think there's also been an unanticipated increase in the price of energy products.

So all of these factors are there. I'd say the one that's been the most difficult to anticipate and the one that's been a surprise has been the price of food.

QUESTION: Are you anticipating something less than 10 per cent inflation by the end of the year?

THE PRESIDENT: Yes. Our projections are—and I think all of our economic advisers believe—that the rate of inflation will not be nearly that high in the latter part of this year.

QUESTION: If it does continue to run high, would you foresee any possibility of seeking standby price and wage controls?

THE PRESIDENT: No, I see no possibility.

QUESTION: Have your advisers talked about the danger of slower economic growth next year?

THE PRESIDENT: Well, as a matter of fact, they haven't expressed this alarm to me. It's just always a possibility.

Our primary hope was that we could reduce the unemployment rate to 7 per cent by the end of the year—we've already achieved that goal—and at the same time control inflation. I've never had any of my own economic advisers who advocated the separation of the two items. I don't think you can address one without the other.

A tight constraint on the budget, as low a deficit as we can possibly realize in meeting the needs of our people, stability in Government programs—these kinds of things are ever-present with us. We've put forward a very comprehensive list of things that can be done short of wage and price controls to hold down the inflation rate.

I think we've got a well-balanced approach at this point. But if we do have a problem in the fall or next year, I think we have enough flexibility to address it. In my opinion, looking back on our actions so far, I don't see anything I would want to change.

QUESTION: Regarding your energy program, Mr. President, what is the minimum action you will insist on from Congress?

THE PRESIDENT: I'm going to insist on the program that we put forward, which I think is minimum. We tried to, first of all, evolve adequate and achievable goals for 1985 in the amount of energy that we produce, consume and import. And then we fashioned, as best we could, proposals to Congress to reach those goals.

The only point on which I would yield is if the Congress came forth with a patently superior approach to reach those same goals in the same time frame. I believe it's the most challenging and difficult and important domestic decision that the Congress will ever make in our lifetime. It's always a problem, when you put forward a comprehensive proposal, to defend it against those who don't like the varied aspects of it but who don't put forward acceptable or effective alternatives.

The Congress has been very responsive. The Speaker set up a unique committee under Congressman Ashley [Representative Thomas L. Ashley of Ohio], and Senator Byrd [Majority Leader Robert C. Byrd of West Virginia] assigned this difficult question to minimum number of committees. They both have committed themselves to keep it at the top of their priority in the legislative process. They are acting with expedition to establish a new Department of Energy, which is a good prerequisite and a necessary one.

QUESTION: Then you're not discouraged about prospects of your energy program—

THE PRESIDENT: I'm not discouraged at all about it.

I think when the Congress goes through the process of having special-interest witnesses deplore the varied aspects of what we have put forward and then start addressing the potential alternatives to what we've put forward, there will be an increasing degree of responsibility on the part of the Congress to take the necessary action.

The objections are divided into two parts: one, a claim that we called for great sacrifice and then came through with a program that demanded very little sacrifice; and the other criticism comes from those who said that the sacrifices that we demanded were too burdensome to bear.

I think it's a well-balanced program. It's fair. It has a heavy emphasis on increasing production. The proposal is also, in my opinion, adequate.

QUESTION: Apparently you're not reconciled to losing your most controversial energy proposal, which calls for a standby gasoline tax—

THE PRESIDENT: No. I'm not reconciled to any changes in our proposal.

QUESTION: Will small foreign cars be eligible for rebates as part of the move to discourage buying of big gas guzzlers?

THE PRESIDENT: Possibly. That would have to be negotiated, however. They can get the rebate under our proposal.

This is a very complicated subject. The concept was put forward and adopted that there should be a limitation to assure that American labor and industry will not be disadvantaged. The Special Trade Representative has been instructed to negotiate an outcome equitable to all parties.

QUESTION: If you really want to cut down on the use of gas and oil, why don't you go to rationing?

THE PRESIDENT: We don't think that's needed at this time. It's much better to approach it from a voluntary point of view. I think the price of energy is going to increase in the future regardless of what we do, whether we ration or not.

I think that there's a need to provide or to maintain—it's already there—a standby authority to ration fuel in case of a national emergency. We're prepared to impose rationing if that ever becomes necessary, but I don't anticipate that having to be done.

QUESTION: A final subject, Mr. President. You charged your Cabinet with making sure that they declared war on excessive regulation and paper work. When are you expecting them to show you some results?

THE PRESIDENT: The program is to be completed by the end of September. The Cabinet officers have been making an assessment of what they could do. It's a long, tedious process to distinguish between regulations that were initiated by executive order, which can be immediately revoked, and those that were required by congressional action.

QUESTION: And reorganization of the bureaucracy—are you still convinced it can be done?

THE PRESIDENT: I have seen with an increasingly vivid perspective the need for the reorganization of the federal bureaucracy. And I think the people and the Congress are ready for it. We asked for four-year authorization, and the Congress gave us a three-year authorization. But if we do good the first three years, I don't have any doubt that we can get an extension.

QUESTION: Are you saying it's going to be an eight-year job for you?

THE PRESIDENT: No, I haven't said that.

8

ABC NEWS INTERVIEW, AUG. 10, 1977

Public Papers of the Presidents, Harry Reasoner & Sam Donaldson

Carter discusses energy, The Strategic Arms Limitation Treaty, foreign policy, the Middle East, Bert Lance, and congressional relations. It should be noted that this early in his administration Carter is enjoying considerable personal popularity.—*Editor*

MR. REASONER: Mr. President, I suppose in 2 or 3 years before your election you were identified as a man who wanted the Presidency as much as any candidate in this century. Now that you've had it for 7 months or so, was it worth it? Are you having any fun?

THE PRESIDENT: Yes. So far, I've enjoyed it. It's been a pleasant life at the White House. I think it's brought our family back together after being divided all over the country for the last 2 or 3 years. I've been pleasantly surprised at the degree of cooperation and harmony that's evolved between me and the Congress after a shaky start. And we are now slowly but steadily putting into effect the campaign promises that I made on Government reorganization, welfare reform, energy policy, a new Energy Department, and so forth.

So, it's been a pleasant life the first 7 months, but I have to say that we've still got a long way to go. I'm learning. It's my first experience in serving in the Federal Government. But I think, in general, it's been pleasant.

MR. REASONER: As you know, Louis Harris' organization, for ABC, has taken a poll on the first 6 months of the administration and on how people feel about you. 1,515 people were talked to. Suppose

From *Public Papers of the Presidents,* Jimmy Carter.

you'd been one of the 1,515. What kind of marks would you give yourself as a leader and as a person for the first months?

THE PRESIDENT: Well, I think the major feeling that I have is that my own administration has fairly accurately represented what the American people both are and also want our country to be. I've tried to open up the White House and my own decisionmaking process to the public. I've learned from them. And I think that there has been a restoration of the confidence of people in the Government, not because of me but because there's such a deep desire on the part of our people to trust Washington, the Congress, the President, the White House for a change, after the war in Vietnam and the CIA and Watergate revelations.

So, I think to the extent that I've accurately represented what the people wanted our Government to do, it's been a good administration. Many people are impatient, perhaps overly so. We've made some good progress already in economic affairs, but everybody expected perhaps a much more rapid improvement.

When I took over, the unemployment rate was about 8 percent, and now it's, I think, 6.9 percent, which is some improvement. And the economic stimulus package, which is just now being approved by Congress and has been signed into law by me and is now being implemented, I think, will have an additional beneficial effect. I've been disappointed in the inflation rate, but it's this way all over the world almost.

So, I think as far as the tone of the Government and the attitude of our people toward the Government, the marks would be fairly high. As far as tangible results in this first 6 months on economy, they've been somewhat disappointing, but I think the slow progress is there. And we have not had any major breakthrough in foreign affairs, although we have a very coherent program that we are pursuing. We are tenacious and determined to improve the situation in southern Africa and in the Middle East, with the Soviets on SALT and test bans against atomic weapons. Our nonproliferation program has been a shock to some other nations but is making progress. And I think that in the organization of Government, our first budget is now being prepared using zero-base budgeting. So far, the progress has been good.

So, specific—too early to say. Tone, trust—pretty good.

MR. DONALDSON: You've retained a very high percentage of popularity. I think, except for the abnormal situation of Lyndon Johnson, at this point in your Presidency, you have more popularity than any recent President. And yet, that seems to be on a personal level; a lot of people don't like your programs and your initiatives.

My question really is: Down the road somewhere, does this line of Jimmy Carter—personally very popular—but President Carter's programs—not so popular—intersect? And what happens then?

THE PRESIDENT: I don't really believe there's that basic conflict between what I am, what I stand for, what I said during the campaign on the one hand, and our actual programs on the other. It's kind of a shock to certain elements in our society to come forward finally with an energy policy. The oil companies are mounting a massive advertising campaign saying that the Government ought to give them more money for additional exploration, which really translates into profits at the expense of consumers. This creates some confusion during the debate phase in Congress, for instance.

Nobody has attempted for a long time to completely revise the welfare system or to bring some renewed stability to the social security program. We've established a new Department of Energy. And we are addressing the basic question of tax reform and so forth. All these changes that will be coming forward with congressional action upset some very powerful and influential elements in our society.

But I think that after a period of 2 or 3 years, the difference between what I am and what the people perceived me to be during the campaign and what my programs actually are as they wind their way through the Congress—that difference will be narrowed and people will see that there's no difference.

MR. DONALDSON: You mentioned energy, and you are quite correct—some interest groups, of course, are chewing away at the program. Perhaps Russell Long will in the Senate. But I had in mind the total American people. They don't want to pay a gasoline tax apparently, and they don't want to conserve in the tough ways. Did you miscalculate the mood of this country?

THE PRESIDENT: No. I think that the mood of the people is there— very supportive of a comprehensive and strict and profound energy policy designed, first of all, to conserve energy, to put the increased cost of energy equal to what it actually is worth, but to return those revenues back to the people directly in tax reductions or better programs, better insulated homes, more efficient automobiles, research and development in solar energy, and so forth. I think when the whole program is passed, they'll begin to see that although oil and gas is going to cost more—and by the way, the oil and gas companies will make more profits than they are now—the benefits to be derived from that will be long-range.

There's a growing awareness that our increasing imports of foreign oil is hurting our economy. It creates inflation. It means that we import more than we export. And this has got to be turned around.

But there's no way to have a popular energy program. I think it's accurate to say that on generalities, the people are strongly in favor of a new, very tough energy conservation program. When you get down to specifics, where they have to cut a little themselves, perhaps they're not so much in favor of it.

But I think the shift toward coal, the savings in oil and gas consumption, the better insulation of homes, more efficient automobiles—these things are bound to come. And when they finally arrive, the people will, I think, favor them.

MR. REASONER: Mr. President, at a news conference a couple of weeks ago you said, very understandably, that if you had made some mistakes, you didn't propose to list them. [*Laughter*] If we mentioned a couple of things some people think have been mistakes, maybe you'd have some comment.

THE PRESIDENT: I'll try.

MR. REASONER: In foreign affairs, the suggestion has been made that both in the SALT talks and in the Mideast that you have tended to perhaps be too open, that you have come out with what might seem to be an inflexible American program and just—it's sitting up there for everyone else to shoot at. Have you changed your attitude on how to do this kind of thing since you've taken office?

THE PRESIDENT: No. I think it's best for the American people to know the reason why we have not had a Middle Eastern settlement in 30 years or maybe 2,000 years and to understand not only our own Nation's positions in seeking a compromise or an agreement that might lead to permanent peace but also to understand, as best we can, the difference of opinion that exists between Israel and Egypt and Jordan and Syria and some of the other nations in the Mideast. I think the American people ought to understand and know the facts.

To the extent that there is an open debate in the Congress, in the news media, among the people themselves, I'll feel much more secure, when we take a strong position, that I have the backing of the Congress and the American people—that we ought not to evolve a complicated position in a sensitive area like the Middle East in secret and then spring it on people or negotiate privately.

No one can expect miracles. As I say, this is something that's been sought after for generations—this peace in the Middle East. We may or may not be successful, but we're going to continue to try in a very determined and tenacious way. And I'm going to continue to go public with the American position.

In the SALT talks, we've developed a comprehensive proposal to present to the Soviets. We are doing it both privately and, to some degree, publicly. We want a complete end of testing of nuclear explosives, both military and peaceful explosives.

We have put into effect a new policy on nonproliferation to try to prevent nations that don't presently have atomic explosives from developing them. This has upset some of our allies in Europe who want to sell factories and machines that can make explosive material. But I think we ought to be tenacious about it.

And I think it's good to let the American people know the facts behind the controversies and the debates. Obviously, when these kinds of debates are made public, it creates an image of confusion and a lack of a comprehensive policy, and it shows that our Nation is not a dictator for other countries.

We have to put forward ideas, and maybe over a period of time we'll have some progress. I think we will. But I've never had any doubt that the American people ought to be as thoroughly informed as possible and also involved in the decisionmaking process.

MR. REASONER: Keeping on the Middle East for just one minute, a number of Israeli leaders in private say that you have made drastic changes in America's attitude toward Israel and that they regard you with considerable trepidation. Are you aware of that feeling, and do you think there is justification for it?

THE PRESIDENT: Yes, I'm aware of that feeling and also many other feelings. There's no single attitude among all Jews in the world or all Israeli citizens. To the extent that Israeli leaders genuinely want a peace settlement, I think that they have to agree that there will be an acceptance of genuine peace on the part of the Arabs, an adjustment of boundaries in the Middle East which are secure for the Israelis and also satisfy the minimum requirements of the Arab neighbors and the United Nations resolutions, and some solution to the question of the enormous numbers of Palestinian refugees who have been forced out of their homes and who want to have some fair treatment.

These three basic elements are there. And we are trying not only to put forward our own ideas but to search among the different disputing nations for some common basis on which they can reach agreement. We can only act as an intermediary to the extent that the different countries trust us.

So, we've tried to be fair. We've tried to be open when possible. We've kept confidences when they have been given to us in confidence. And I don't know that we can reach a final solution. We are hopeful that we can, and I think world opinion is very powerful on disputing nations when there is a consensus about what ought to be done.

So, we'll continue to labor at it, taking slings and arrows from all directions, criticisms, publicly in nations when privately the leaders say we are willing to do this when we come out publicly for the same position. Quite often for domestic political consumption there's an adamant, very disputive, and antagonistic attitude taken on the part of some leaders. But we are willing to accept this consequence. I don't know how to guarantee an ultimate success, but I am willing to accept the criticism that comes from all parties as we struggle for success.

MR. DONALDSON: Mr. President, you talked a moment ago about one of your accomplishments. You said very proudly that the restoration of confidence in government was high.

THE PRESIDENT: Yes.

MR. DONALDSON: And all the polls show that people give you high marks for integrity. Against this background, what are you going to do about the problem of Bert Lance?

THE PRESIDENT: Well, the inquiry that's going on now by the Comptroller of the Currency concerning Bert Lance's banking practices before he came into the Government, I think, is a healthy circumstance.

When allegations are made in the news media or from private sources, it's incumbent on the Government to investigate those. Bert Lance is cooperating with the Comptroller. I have confidence in both the Government officials in the Treasury Department and also in Bert Lance. And as I've said before, I don't know the details and don't want to become involved in the details of what went on in 1975 or prior to that time. But I have confidence that both the Comptroller and Bert will make the facts known to the public and let the situation be judged accordingly.

MR. DONALDSON: But I think you have a higher problem than perhaps past Presidents because you had a higher standard. The question is not illegality. As I understand it, most of these investigations are not dealing on the question of illegality, but simply propriety of a man who might have been able to do something that is common practice in the banking field and yet personally benefit, whereas, the ordinary citizen—and you ran against people who didn't pay their fair share—wouldn't benefit. Don't you have to hold Mr. Lance to that higher standard?

THE PRESIDENT: Yes, I think so. And I believe that Bert would agree that a high standard has to be maintained. I'm not aware of any improprieties that have been proven against Bert Lance. Allegations or accusations have been made against me, Bert Lance, and many others. But I have complete confidence that when all the facts are known that the situation will be judged by the American public to have been handled properly.

MR. DONALDSON: You know, one more question on this subject. Harry Truman, whom you admire greatly, had one failing that many people found as a failing. He stuck by his friends too long.

Now, at some point aren't you going to have to make a hard decision as to the good of your administration, maintaining the integrity that people have in your administration, versus a friend?

THE PRESIDENT: I don't have any qualms about that. I believe that if anything should be proven concerning Bert Lance that's either improper or illegal, that Bert would immediately take the initiative to either resign or step aside or offer to.

I don't have any concern about Bert Lance and his attitude toward me, my administration, his responsibility to the people. As I said before, though, it's something that ought to be decided between the Comptroller and Bert with a thorough investigation. All the facts ought to be and will be made public, and then a decision will be made accordingly. But—

MR. DONALDSON: But the buck stops there.

THE PRESIDENT: That's right. Well, I am ultimately responsible and don't hesitate to accept that responsibility. But I have enough confidence in Bert Lance to know that if any improprieties do exist, that he would take the initiative to step aside. So far, no improprieties have been proven.

MR. REASONER: There are a lot of ways that friends can get you glory or get you in trouble besides improprieties. How do you feel these days about Andrew Young?

THE PRESIDENT: The same as I've always felt. I think that there is now and will be a growing realization of the value of Andrew Young to our country—both his work in the United Nations and also his work among the developing countries of the world, who in the past have been turned away from us almost unanimously.

There has been a time in years gone by when in the very crucial international organizations we couldn't get 20 percent of the other nations to support our positions even when we thought we had the right positions.

Now I think there's a growing feeling among those small and poor and weak countries that they can trust us for a change, that there's someone in our Government who can listen to them with an open mind, represent the best interests of the United States, and still represent their best interests as well.

Andrew Young is intelligent, courageous, articulate, accurately represents the position that I and the Secretary of State and others have evolved for our own country and is building up trust in our country among the nations who didn't trust us before.

He's a great national treasure, in my opinion, and he has my complete confidence and I think I have his complete confidence.

I might say that there has never been any difference of opinion on basic issues among Andrew Young, the Secretary of State and the National Security Council or myself.

MR. REASONER: Mr. President, you've been sleeping in the White House for nearly 7 months now. You campaigned sort of against the White House and Washington and the establishment and the bureaucracy.

Have you changed your attitude about that? There was a comic strip the other day that said that you were going Washington, you are now an insider. [*Laughter*]

THE PRESIDENT: Well, I feel more and more like an insider. I think the thing that's made me naturally come to that sense of my position has been the increasingly good relationship between the White House and the Congress.

I've been deeply grateful at the spirit of cooperation and harmony that has evolved because of the leadership in the House and the Senate—I might say, on many occasions both Republican and Democratic leadership.

We face some tough decisions in the future that's going to require bipartisan support—Middle East questions; normalizing relations with China, if they want normal relations; how to deal with the Panama Canal treaty, which has been attempted for 13 years and which is now approaching a final conclusion; how to evolve our Nation's position on the matter of nuclear weapons or comprehensive test bans; the degree of commitment to different aspects of defense capability. All these matters involving defense and foreign affairs have got to be based on a bipartisan support.

But I feel part of the Washington Government now, not in an embarrassed way, but in a natural way. And I believe that there's been a restoration of harmony and cooperation and mutual purpose between the White House and Republicans and Democrats in the Congress, which is very healthy for our country.

MR. DONALDSON: Mr. President, the day before you took the oath of office I asked you if you thought you were just going to be an ordinary President or whether you had a chance for greatness, and you said you thought you had a chance for greatness.

THE PRESIDENT: A chance.

MR. DONALDSON: Now after 6 months of looking at the problems and finding that the bureaucracy doesn't move as rapidly as you might have thought and the Congress doesn't roll over as you might have suspected, what's your estimate?

THE PRESIDENT: Well, that's hard to say. I think it's primarily dependent on both the support that I can maintain among the people of the country and the Congress for the next 3 1/2 years. A 6- or 7-month period is brief in the historical trends that relate to problems that have been there for generations. And if all of our programs are adopted, then I think this administration will be a great one.

But we're going to have a lot of failures and a lot of frustrations, and I think the American people have got to realize that the Government can't provide magic answers for difficult questions and problems. But I think history would have to decide that 20 years from now, looking backward, rather than for me to decide after just 6 months of experience in Washington.

We've got some great ideas and goals. I think the American people have seen a substantial rebuilding of pride in our country. I think that all the polls and my own relations with American people have indicated that there's a renewed sense that our country stands for something that's clean and decent and open, that the American people have more of a participation in the decisionmaking process.

I think there's a general feeling that when we make a mistake, that the mistake is not concealed but is instantly revealed. I think the frequent news conferences and the frankness with which we've discussed formerly secret issues has been constructive.

But as far as whether greatness or mediocrity will result from this administration, it's just too early to say.

MR. REASONER: Mr. President, one final question. We're sort of taking a poll, too. How would you rate Sam Donaldson as a White House correspondent? [*Laughter*]

THE PRESIDENT: I tell you, it's too early to say. [*Laughter*] Maybe history will reveal whether Sam has been adequate or below average or great. But after just 7 months, I've not been able to decide. I've put a lot of time in thinking about this question—[*laughter*]—but so far the answer has escaped me.

MR. DONALDSON: You've wasted your time, thank you. You owe about $10,000 back to the American people. [*Laughter*]

MR. REASONER: Thank you, Mr. President.

THE PRESIDENT: Thank you very much, Harry, Sam.

NOTE: The interview began at 11:30 a.m. on August 10 at the Pond House in Plains, Ga. The transcript was released on August 14 when portions of the interview were broadcast on an ABC News television program at 10:30 p.m.

9

Interview with the President, Dec. 28, 1977

White House Press Release, Barbara Walters, Robert McNeil, Tom Brokaw & Bob Schieffer

From a White House News Release, Dec. 28, 1977. Representatives from the three major networks and public television question the president about the Middle East, energy, the SALT negotiations, the Federal Reserve Board, the economy, the national health program, the Panama Canal Treaty, and other issues.—*Editor*

THE PRESIDENT: This year we have had fireside chats and television programs and telephone call-in shows and press conferences twice a month and meetings with editors from almost every State in the Nation, and I have been very pleased to stay in touch with the American people.

Tonight we have four distinguished news reporters from the four major networks in our country. And I want to welcome you here as another opportunity for me to speak to the American people with tough interrogations from those who understand our country very well.

I understand Mr. Brokaw has the first question.

QUESTION: Mr. President, there are a number of subjects that we want to cover tonight, including some news developments that are going on even as we speak. I want to begin, however, with the question about the trip you leave on tomorrow. It was originally postponed because you did not yet have the energy bill passed. It still has not been passed.

My question is this: Aren't you playing into the twin themes of your critics who complain that your energy bill has not been passed; that you have failed on the major domestic priority of your Administration; and that your foreign policy has no real definition because this trip seems to have no urgent theme to it?

THE PRESIDENT: The only major legislation that did not pass the Congress this year, which I was expecting to pass, was energy. Speaker of the House Tip O'Neill said it was the most productive session since the first term of Franklin Roosevelt. I will let him be the judge of that.

The energy legislation, I think, will be the first item on the agenda when the Congress reconvenes in January. And there is no doubt that wherever I go on this trip, to Eastern Europe, to Western Europe, to the Mideast, to India, what our Nation does with energy will be a prime question.

We are the leader of the world. We are one of the major oil producers. We are the greatest consumer, and until Congress does take action on the energy proposal that I put forth last April, and which the House of Representatives passed in August, that cloud will hang over the determination and leadership qualities of our country.

So I am disappointed about that. As far as the trip is concerned, it is carefully planned. We began working on this trip last March, and the nations that we will visit are important to us both domestically and in our foreign relations.

Poland, in Eastern Europe, a Communist government with close ties to the Soviet Union but also friendships with us, heavy trade with the Western nations, is relatively willing to give people their religious freedom and other freedoms. We will have a good meeting, I think, in Poland.

We go from there to Iran, very close military ally of ours, strong trade partners of ours with whom we share many political responsibilities.

And then we go to India, the biggest democracy in the world, one that in recent years has turned perhaps excessively toward the Soviet Union, but under the new leadership of Prime Minister Desai is moving back toward us and assuming a good role of, I would say, neutrality. And we have a strong friendship with India. It is a strong country.

They are almost self-sufficient now. They have food surpluses.

We come back from there to Saudi Arabia, our major supplier of imported oil, a nation that has worked closely with us in foreign affairs in many parts of the world; from there back to France, our historic ally, keystone in Europe.

I will have long discussions with President Giscard there, and then go back to Brussels to strengthen our relationships with the European Community and with NATO.

So every stop will be productive for us. I will be taking the word and the goodwill and the sense of importance of the American people toward them in learning about those countries in the process.

But energy will be the tie that will bind us together on this trip, and I hope that this will demonstrate to the American people and to the Congress the necessity for rapid action on one of the most controversial and divisive issues that the Congress has ever faced, and that is to give our country for the first time a comprehensive energy policy.

QUESTION: Mr. President, I know we will all want to get back to just how you plan to go about getting that energy policy. But while we are on foreign policy, I would like to ask you about the Middle East. President Sadat, I think everyone agrees, made a spectacular gesture that opened up a whole new era here. Do you feel that the Israelis have as yet made a comparable gesture? Have they been flexible in your view?

THE PRESIDENT: Both President Sadat and Prime Minister Begin have been bold and courageous. We have been dealing with the Mideast question as a Nation for decades, in a leadership role at least within the last two Administrations. We see the complexity of the questions and the obstacles to progress. When I first became President, we spelled out the basic issues, withdrawal from occupied territories, secure borders, the establishment of real peace, the recognition of Israel's right to be there and dealing with the Palestinian question.

We are now in a role of supporter. We encourage them to continue with their fruitful negotiations. We try to resolve difficulties, to give advice and counsel when we are requested to do it. This is a better role for us. In the past, we have been in the unenviable position and sometimes unpleasant position, sometimes nonproductive position as mediator among parties who wouldn't even speak to each other. So I think that the progress that has been made in the last month and a half has been remarkable and has been much greater than I had anticipated. And I know Sadat and Begin well and personally and favorably.

If any two leaders on earth have the strength and the determination and the courage to make progress toward peace in the most difficult region that I have ever known, it is Prime Minister Begin and President Sadat. There is no reason for us to be discouraged about it. We will help in every way we can to let their progress be fruitful. I think that President Sadat and Prime Minister Begin could have reached a fairly quick solution of just the Egyptian-Israeli problem in the Sinai region. But this is not what they want.

They both want to resolve the other questions, what is real peace, will Israel be recognized as a permanent neighbor to the countries that surround them. Can the Palestinian question, the West Bank, the Gaza Strip be addressed successfully. Knowing how difficult these questions are, I have nothing but congratulations for them on what they have achieved so far.

QUESTION: You are going to see King Hussein of Jordan in Tehran. President Sadat said in an interview that was broadcast on public television last night that King Hussein had told him he was fully behind his efforts in public; until now, King Hussein's opinion has been relatively mysterious. Do you have any information that would make you agree with Mr. Sadat and are you going to discuss that with King Hussein and urge him to support the Sadat initiative when you see him?

THE PRESIDENT: I don't intend to put any pressure on King Hussein, I couldn't if I wanted to, to immediately begin to negotiate with Israel and Egypt as a partner. If he wants to do it, we would certainly welcome that. What I will try to learn, however, is what role Jordan is willing to play in the resolution of the Palestinian–West Bank problem, at what point he thinks it would be advisable for him to enter the negotiations personally as a government leader, and what we can do to get him to give his open support and encouragement to both Begin and Sadat as a struggle to resolve the differences between them.

I think King Hussein has, indeed in his private discussions with Secretary Vance and in his personal communications to me, shown a very positive attitude and in his travels around the Middle East to visit with other leaders, some who don't encourage the talks like President Assad, those who are very hopeful for progress, like those in Saudi Arabia, I think he has shown a constructive attitude already. But it helps me to understand on a current basis, the remaining problems and in what way they can be brought in to achieve a comprehensive peace.

I think they all trust our country, our motives are good. We have never misled them. We have been honest and as a person, as a country that carries messages from one to another, and I think that this puts us in a position to exert legitimate influence. But what we have always hoped for is direct negotiations or discussions, communications among the leaders involved with our offering good offices when we are requested to do it.

QUESTION: Mr. President, the chief stumbling block right now does seem to be what we might call the right of return of the Palestinians to the West Bank and the Gaza. You have in the past come out against an independent nation per se in the West Bank, but you have always talked about the legitimate rights of the Palestinians and you have been in favor of some kind of an entity, although people are still obscure about what that means, an entity perhaps linked to Jordan.

Would you, in light of the development, now clarify your views for us today, tell us if they have changed and if they have not, is it because the United States has decided to be neutral on this subject?

THE PRESIDENT: Well, you have described my position very well. We do favor a homeland or an entity wherein the Palestinians can live in peace. I think Prime Minister Begin has taken a long step forward in offering to President Sadat and indirectly to the Palestinians, self-rule.

President Sadat so far is insisting that the so-called Palestinian entity be an independent nation. My own preference is that they not be an independent nation but be tied in some way with the surrounding countries, making a choice, for instance, between Israel and Jordan.

President Sadat has not yet agreed to that position of ours. Prime Minister Begin has offered that the citizens who live in the West Bank area or the Gaza Strip be given an option to be either Israeli citizens or Jordanian citizens, to actually run for the Knesset as candidates and to vote in the elections, both national Israeli and Jordan or local elections in the occupied territories once they are released.

But we don't have any real choice. I have expressed an opinion, but if Israel should negotiate with the surrounding countries a different solution, we would certainly support it.

But my own personal opinion is that permanent peace can best be maintained if there is not a fairly radical, new independent nation in the heart of the Middle Eastern area.

QUESTION: In view of the deadlock now, however, have you tried to convince either side of your opinion? You have had conversations with both.

THE PRESIDENT: I have expressed this opinion to President Assad, to King Hussein, to President Sadat, to Crown Prince Fahad, and also to Prime Minister Begin, and privately, and of course they have heard my statements publicly.

Our preference is not to have an independent nation there, but we are perfectly willing to accept any reasonable solution that the parties themselves might evolve.

QUESTION: If I could just get back to the question I asked you, I take it that you would not pass judgment in public at least at this point on whether the Israelis had been flexible enough in the negotiating so far. Do you think that the position that they put forward—Mr. Begin said today that there would always be Israeli troops on the West Bank and that all who wanted peace will have to know that. Is that a realistic negotiating position?

THE PRESIDENT: Yes. It certainly is a realistic negotiating position.

QUESTION: Would Sadat ever accept that?

THE PRESIDENT: I don't know. There is a great deal of flexibility there; the number of military outposts; the length of time when this interim solution might be in effect. I think Prime Minister Begin said it would be reassessed at the end of five years.

The degree of participation of the governments of Israel and Jordan in a possible administrative arrangement, all these questions could add a tone of progress or a possibility for resolution of what seems to be insurmountable obstacles.

So I think that Prime Minister Begin already has shown a great deal of flexibility. Obviously President Sadat and King Hussein and others would have to accept (or reject) whatever proposal is put forward (i.e., President Sadat and King Hussein, not the President of the United States, would have to make that decision).

But the length of time when the interim agreement would be in effect would be negotiable and the exact relationship between the new self-rule government as far as its autonomy is concerned, its dependence or subservience to the Jordanians or Israelis, all of these things are still to be negotiated. I think there is enough flexibility at this point.

QUESTION: Could I just ask one follow-up on that? Has either Egypt or Israel, or both, asked the United States formally yet to provide guarantees for any agreement that is made?

THE PRESIDENT: In my private conversations with some of them, they have expressed to me that if a guarantee arrangement between ourselves and Israel should be worked out, that it would be acceptable to the Arab leaders. But we have never discussed this between ourselves and Israel in any definitive form.

My preference would be that our involvement would be minimized after an agreement has been reached. But if it became a matter of having the negotiations break down completely, our having some limited role as mutually accepted among those parties involved, then we would consider that very, very favorably.

QUESTION: Mr. President, if we may move along in another area of foreign policy for just a moment, there now seems to be some signals coming out of Geneva, and even from friends of this Administration, that we will not have a SALT agreement in 1978, or at least one will not get before the Senate. That is the word from Senator Alan Cranston, who is now a very good vote counter in the Senate.

Is that your thinking as well, that we are not going to have a SALT agreement with the Russians during this next year?

THE PRESIDENT: I would be disappointed if we don't have a SALT agreement this year. We have made good progress on SALT. We started out with SALT I, the Soviets having a very heavy advantage, about a three to two ratio in their favor. President Ford and Secretary Kissinger made great progress, I think, at Vladivostok, and in their subsequent negotiations, to provide the first indication of equality. And we will maintain that posture of mutual advantage between ourselves and the Soviets.

We have added a new dimension, to have tight constraints on future deployment of weapons, both quantitatively and also the quality of the weapons, and to reduce actually the number of destructive weapons permitted.

We still have some negotiating to do. But we have made good progress on SALT. We have also been pleased with the results of negotiations with the Soviet Union on the comprehensive test ban to prohibit any testing of nuclear weapons at all.

And we have made progress, also, in trying to stop a military build-up in the Indian Ocean. My guess is that President Brezhnev would be likely to want to come here to visit after those three negotiations have made some substantial progress and where there is a prospect of immediate resolution of the remaining differences.

I would never approve a SALT agreement nor present one to the Congress that didn't have an adequate degree of verification of compliance, and which didn't protect the right of our own country to defend itself and to carry out our domestic and foreign policy. Whatever I put forward to the Congress will be good for our Nation.

We have had a maximum degree of involvement by the Congress. We have even had Senators in Europe at the negotiating table. And we have kept them informed as the progress is made.

So my guess is that 1978 will see us successful, and my guess is that when we present it to the Congress, the SALT agreement will be approved.

QUESTION: There are so many questions that I think we all have on foreign policy, but we are aware of the time so perhaps we might slide into the domestic issues.

Shortly before we went on the air you made news yourself about Arthur Burns and his replacement. Mr. Burns still has two years to go before he would retire from being on the Board itself of the Federal Reserve. Are you, or have you specifically asked him to stay? Obviously, some words from you might make the difference. Or do you have any other plans for him in government?

THE PRESIDENT: When I met with Chairman Burns, I told him that I understood he wanted to stay on the Board and that that would please me very much. He said that he had not yet made a decision. I then responded that if he decided not to stay on the Board, after a new Chairman is sworn in, that I would like very much to have him serve in some capacity. He is so wise. He has so much experience. His record is so superb. His integrity is perfect, almost. But I think he would still have good service to offer to our country. He said that he would not want to make any decisions within the next period just ahead, but that he would like to hear from me in the future. And I think the first decision that he would make is whether or not he would stay on the Board. My hope is that he will.

QUESTION: But did you give him any possibilities so he would have some choices perhaps to make of what governmental positions to take?

THE PRESIDENT: Not yet. I think either in economic affairs or foreign affairs, the field of human rights, the enhanced involvement of American citizens in taking initiative outside of government in the private sector—these are four areas where he and I have had discussions during this preceding year. He has shown an intense interest in them. He has been very excited about our progress in human rights. He has never seen me a single time this year that he didn't initiate a discussion about human rights, how profound he thought it was and how it exemplified what our Nation stands for. But what he would choose to do would have to be up to him. I would cooperate in every way to encourage him to continue to serve in the same capacity.

QUESTION: You sound like a man describing someone you just reappointed. Why did you replace him?

THE PRESIDENT: Chairman Burns, I think he served longer than anyone ever has before. He served two full terms. I thought it was time for us to have new leadership there. I particularly want to bring someone in, Bob, from the business community.

I think there ought to be some change in emphasis from time to time. I also wanted to get someone that would have the confidence of business and financial leaders here and around the world. As a matter of fact, when I informed Chairman Burns of my choice, he said that is a wise and worthy choice. He has known Bill Miller for years, and he said that he had been making a list of those that he hoped I might consider and he made a list of some he hoped I didn't consider.

Fritz Mondale said, "Why don't we share the list sometimes?" He said, "I could tell you a few of those you might consider." The first two or three names he mentioned were leaders in the business community. So these are the reasons that I thought it was time for a change. It is certainly no reflection on him.

QUESTION: Certainly Dr. Burns was a very symbol of what business wanted in that job and if Mr. Miller's philosophy is not very different from Dr. Burns', it is difficult to see why it was necessary to replace Dr. Burns.

THE PRESIDENT: Well, it was not an easy decision to make.

QUESTION: It was for personal reasons?

THE PRESIDENT: No, not at all.

QUESTION: Personal antipathy?

THE PRESIDENT: Not at all. I think it is accurate to say—and Dr. Burns would confirm this—that he and I have a close personal friendship. We never had any sort of disagreements when we were together. I have never criticized Chairman Burns either publicly or privately. But I have already explained the reasons why I thought it was time to make a change. I think two full terms there is adequate. That is as long as a President can serve and I think bringing in some new leadership into the Federal Reserve System will be beneficial.

QUESTION: I want to sketch a scenario, if I can. If, as the reports have it, you are considering recommending a tax cut of about $25 billion to Congress when it reconvenes, there are many who say that that will just about offset the increased taxes that we will have as a result of higher taxes on energy and Social Security. So it won't stimulate the economy in the manner you might like it to, and then in 1979 or 1980 you will have to come back and ask for another tax cut, and if you do that you will surely have defeated your goal of balancing the budget by 1981.

Do you have trouble with that scenario?

THE PRESIDENT: I think the benefits to be derived from our tax cuts in 1978 and 1979 will exceed any tax burdens that have been added on to the American people's shoulders by the Congress.

We have had fairly good economic success this year. The unemployment rate has dropped about 8 percent a year ago to a little bit less than 7 percent now, still pockets of high unemployment concern me very much. We have added 8 million net new jobs this year, the most we have ever had since the second World War. We have about 92 million people employed now. In the last half of this year, the inflation rate has dropped to less than 5 percent, although the underlying inflation rate is still 6, 6 1/2 percent. It is obvious that we need some economic stimulus next year and also I don't want the Federal budget to continue to grow in its proportion to the gross national product of our Nation.

It has now gotten up to about 23 percent. We are cutting it down now to a little bit above 22 percent and by the time my term is over in 1980, I would like to get this down to about 21 percent through careful management and wise spending of our funds.

I have to judge, though, between how much money we retain in the Federal budget and the Federal Treasury in order to balance the budget quickly, compared to how much we give back to the taxpayers in the form of tax cuts, to let them have the money to spend and to let the private enterprise system produce more jobs and a better life for us.

So I think that we have done well so far and I think we will make a much wiser decision on the tax reform package and tax reduction package for next year having gotten a good firm realization of the Social Security Tax changes and a fairly good hope of what the energy package will be as well.

QUESTION: I guess the question still is do you think that a balanced budget by 1981, which was a campaign promise, was a realistic goal for a man who is now in office, given all of the claims on the Federal budget?

THE PRESIDENT: Obviously, I can't guarantee that. We have obviously known that to balance the budget would be difficult. It depends upon how fast business invests, how many people are at work, which cuts down obviously on expenditure for unemployment compensation, welfare payments and there has to be some trade-off.

If there was an absolutely rigid fixation on a balanced budget, then there would be no chance for tax cuts. But I think when you take into consideration that we have a $25 billion tax reduction for the people next year with about $6 billion tax reductions this year, that is $31 billion, that is a major benefit to the people. I just can't give a firm commitment on how we will balance tax cuts versus a balanced budget by 1981.

QUESTION: Aren't you going to have just super growth, faster growth rate than anyone really predicted to be able to balance a budget by 1981? Isn't that what it boils down to?

THE PRESIDENT: It would take about a 10 percent annual increase in real terms in business investment with the present protections of economic need. We want to cut the unemployment rate down considerably and, of course, we want to deal with the problems of the cities. We want to meet the legitimate needs of our people and at the same time not let inflation get out of hand.

So balancing all of these factors is something that you have to do almost daily in making decisions from the White House.

QUESTION: Mr. President, it is reported that Vice President Mondale with you, of course, is working on a list of your top priorities for next year with the feeling perhaps that you had too many top priorities this year to get to Congress.

Can you tell us what the top two or three priorities would be and can you tell us if it would include a national health insurance program which organized labor feels you promised to introduce this year?

THE PRESIDENT: Yes, I intend to introduce a national health program to the Congress this year, late in this session. They can't pass it this year, but it will be introduced.

Dealing with the economy, which was just discussed, would be a top priority. Completing work on the energy package would be the first specific thing that we will do. One of the most important is to resolve the Panama Canal Treaty question.

About 75 years ago in the middle of the night the American Secretary of State signed the Panama Canal Treaty that presently is in existence. No Panamanian has ever signed it; no Panamanian ever saw it before it was signed. It was signed by a Frenchman who benefited financially from the terms of the treaty on behalf of the Panamanians.

That treaty gave us a chance to do a tremendous job in building the Panama Canal, keeping it open for international shipping. It has helped our country a lot. It is something of which we can be proud.

Presidents Eisenhower and Kennedy recognized that the present treaty was inadequate. President Johnson started negotiations to change it. Presidents Nixon and Ford continued, and we concluded it this year.

It is one of the most difficult political questions that we will have to deal with. It is going to take a lot of time in the Congress to pass it.

What we wanted was one that treated us and Panama fairly, and we got it. We wanted a treaty that did not put a financial burden on the American taxpayer, and we got it. We wanted treaties that would guarantee proper operation of the Panama Canal itself, for us and for foreign shipping, and we got it. We wanted treaties that would also guarantee us permanently the right to take what action we think necessary to keep the Canal safe, to defend it, and to keep it open for us to use, and we got it.

We wanted a treaty—two treaties there are—that would give us the right for expeditious passage in time of need or emergency, for our ships to go to the head of the line and go through the Canal without delay, and we got it. We wanted treaties that would be acceptable in the eyes of the international community, particularly in Latin America, and we got them.

So this is what we have tried to do under four Presidents, and we have finally succeeded. And I would say that would be one of the most difficult challenges that we have politically this year. It is absolutely crucial that the Senate ratify these treaties, and I think the terms are very favorable to us and to Panama.

QUESTION: You got all that in the treaty, Mr. President. Do you have the votes in the Senate?

THE PRESIDENT: I think we will get the votes in the Senate.

QUESTION: Do you not now have them?

THE PRESIDENT: I can't say for sure we do because many Senators still have not expressed their commitment to me or their opinion. But I was talking to President Ford this past week who is strongly supportive of the treaties, along with Secretary Kissinger and others, and he said that in his speeches to college groups and others around the Nation, that he is getting an increasingly favorable response from the audience. I think the public opinion is building up for the treaties.

QUESTION: Can we interpret this as a beginning of a new campaign on your part to get out and sell the treaty? You have been criticized for having left the ground to the opposition somewhat. Are you going to make a major effort personally to try to sell it?

THE PRESIDENT: Yes. I consider it one of my most important responsibilities.

QUESTION: Can you meet the deadline? President Torrijos has set April, which he says is urgent, and Panama's patience can be exhausted.

THE PRESIDENT: I don't feel any constraint to operate on the deadline, but both Senator Byrd and I and the leaders of the Senate all hope we can resolve that issue early in the year, certainly I think by April.

QUESTION: On that—since, by the way, to get back to my original questions—it seems your priorities next year are similar to your priorities this year, energy and the economy. But in October, you and President Torrijos issued a joint statement to remove the doubts about the rights of the United States to defend the neutrality of the Canal and also the right of ships to pass promptly through it. A number of Senators felt they might be more comfortable with this if it were actually written into the treaty.

Would you be willing to see the treaty amended so that it would reflect this understanding, this statement between you and General Torrijos?

THE PRESIDENT: No. I think it would be good to have a signed agreement between me and President Torrijos and he has indicated he would be glad to sign that statement that was made and of course, I would, too. I think the Senate could express an understanding that the treaty was being approved by them with the understanding that this was a proper interpretation. But to actually amend the treaty would require Panama to have another referendum on the subject and they have already had one.

Many people in Panama think that the treaties are too favorable to the United States. And I don't think it would be fair to them after they negotiated in good faith to cause them to have a completely new referendum. I would certainly hate to have two ratification votes in the Senate, separated by several months. So I think that the Senate can very well express its understanding of what the treaties mean.

We can exchange documents with the Panamanian leader. To amend the treaties, though, I think would be inadvisable.

QUESTION: Since we are talking about the Congress, what are you going to do about the energy bill now? It has been going on for six months now. There seems to be a deadlock in the Conference Committee. I saw a poll taken by your own pollster that said 44 percent of the people in this country still are undecided about whether it is a good bill or not. What do you do now? Do you start it over? Do you stay with the Conference Committee? What happens?

THE PRESIDENT: There is not a problem with the Congress, There is not a problem with the House. The problem is with the Senate Conference Committee that is dealing with the crucial issue of natural gas. There are eighteen Members on the Senate Conference Committee. They have been divided nine and nine ever since the conference began. And I would hope that a compromise could be worked out that could be acceptable to me, to the House Members, and to the Senate conferees and to the Senate quite early in the next session.

QUESTION: How can you tell that?

THE PRESIDENT: There are private signs.

QUESTION: Would you be willing to sign legislation that permitted natural gas prices to go above the figure $1.75 per thousand cubic feet if that would mean it would pass?

THE PRESIDENT: I haven't excluded any reasonable compromise solution from a bill that I would sign. My only requirements are that the bill in my judgment be fair to the consumers of this country, that the bill in my judgment give an adequate shift away from excessive consumption of oil and natural gas to other alternative supplies and also have conservation of energy on top of that and also that the bill not bankrupt the Nation, not be too great a burden on the budget itself.

If those requirements are met, then I will sign the bill. I still favor the proposal that I made to the Congress last April 20th, and very close to that is what the House passed back in August. I can see good indications of compromise solutions that would meet my requirements that have already been divulged to me by conferees. When I come back from my overseas trip ten days from now, we will play an active role in trying to encourage the Senate leadership and the conferees to negotiate with a great deal of enthusiasm and I think there will be a growing realization in our country of the importance of this bill.

It hurts our domestic economy, it hurts our foreign economy, it weakens the price, the value of the dollar. We imported this year about $45 billion worth of oil in addition to what we consumed of our own oil.

It is a very heavy drain on our economy, on international oil supplies and the Nation needs it very badly. And I think as the conferees and the Members of Congress see this need in a more and more dramatic way expressed here in our country and by leaders overseas, then I think they will act. We also have had encouraging word from the OPEC nations this past week when they froze the price of oil for another year (or six months). I think they did that at least partially on the basis that the Congress would act to cut down on the excessive consumption of oil in this country.

I think there will be a great pressure internationally for increased prices of oil and therefore higher inflation if the Congress doesn't act. It is a very important issue. I think most of the Congress Members still now feel the importance of what they are about to do. I don't think there is any doubt they will pass this legislation early in the session.

QUESTION: Looking back a little retrospectively in domestic issues, is there any domestic issue which just baffles you?

THE PRESIDENT: There are a lot of them that I don't completely comprehend. I have been criticized for introducing too much legislation. I have been criticized for not introducing enough legislation. I have been criticized for dealing too much in specifics and trying to learn too much about the government and how it works, how the economy functions and what the Congress does, their attitudes, and organization of the Congress and the Federal Government agencies.

But this is my nature. I think having come into Washington for the first time serving the Federal Government, I had an obligation to learn. I enjoy it. I obviously realize that there are many things that I don't completely comprehend.

QUESTION: I had an example in mind of a particularly intractable thing about which in the plethora of proposals that have come out there is no very innovative solution yet—that is, the question of unemployment among black youth in this country, very very high percentages. Is that one of the issues that at the moment just looks baffling and intractable—how to deal with it given the other priorities?

THE PRESIDENT: The unemployment rate in general is intractable and difficult. The inflation rate seems to be frozen at about 6 1/2 percent, and the pockets of unemployment among black youth in particular have been a great challenge to me, that we have not yet successfully resolved, either me or my predecessors. We did add 425,000 new jobs, and most of them were specifically oriented toward people who have been chronically unemployed.

In addition, we had about a $4 billion public works program. Ten percent of that money had to be spent with minority contractors to help emphasize black youth unemployment.

We also contemplate in the 1979 fiscal year budget emphasizing anew our interest in solving the higher unemployment rate among black young people. But this is one of those problems that is difficult to solve.

When I went to London in May for the International Economic Summit, this was the issue that every foreign leader said was becoming their most difficult and crucial issue. In England and Germany and France and Japan, in Canada and Italy, there was unanimous agreement among us that this was one of the most intractable and difficult issues of all.

Just recently, in Rome, Secretary Marshall from our Department of Labor went on an international meeting concerning youth unemployment. We are making some progress in our country.

We had during the summer and fall as a result of a $21 billion economic stimulus package more people put to work every week than even during the New Deal days with the WPA and the CCC. But it is a hard thing to solve.

We have added 4 million new jobs this year, and still have a big unemployment rate. But I think we are making progress. The basic thing is that government can't provide all those jobs. They have to be initiated through business investment brought about by proper tax decisions and proper economic decisions made by Congress and by business themselves.

But I think the progress that we are making in '78 will be even greater than this year.

QUESTION: Mr. President, I wonder about unemployment generally, whether we don't have to as a society, as a system of government, re-define what is an acceptable level of unemployment.

It has now been running about 7 percent, and people talk about an unemployment rate of 4, 4 1/2 percent, as being acceptable. That is a long drop, to get to 4 1/2 percent.

Do you think we have to redefine what is an acceptable level of unemployment, realistically?

THE PRESIDENT: No, I would hate to do that.

QUESTION: Or politically? But economically and practically it is very hard to see how it can be dropped that far that fast.

THE PRESIDENT: I believe we can get it below that. We have, as you know, a different system economically than most even democratic democracies. We provide welfare assistance and unemployment compensation for people who are out of work. And habitually in our Nation when demand drops for a product, the companies lay off even temporarily some of their workers. In a nation like Japan, they keep those workers on the job. They pay them a lower salary, and the production is held down by partial unemployment.

But I have seen good progress made. I think it was either October or November we added 900,000 new jobs, but there were just about that many new people who came into the labor market that month. Nobody anticipated that.

One reason for that is that as people see their neighbors getting jobs, who had been unemployed for a long time, then housewives or students who are still in high school and others apply for jobs and they become part of the labor market, which makes the unemployment rate stay high even though employment goes up to the highest level in the history of our Nation.

QUESTION: Mr. President, at the end of your first year in office, and it is almost New Year's Eve—and that is the time for people to take stock, and when they take stock they are a little more critical than maybe they should be. I would like to give you a list of those who currently say they are unhappy with it.

Labor is unhappy because they say you are dragging your feet on the medical insurance bill; and on full employment business is unhappy. They just don't have confidence in you. The blacks are unhappy again because of full employment and lack of it, and what Robin just brought out, and I talked with Vernon Jordan who had expressed his unhappiness with you last July and still feels the same way, he says. Women are unhappy because of your stand on Federal aid to abortion, and there aren't enough women appointed to administration positions. Striking farmers are holding up their tractors in Plains.

Who is your constituency or, to put it another way, who is happy?

THE PRESIDENT: Barbara, I think this is inherent and almost inevitable in a free Nation like ours. The news media legitimately reports the disharmony and the arguments and the debates because they are more exciting than the achievements .

It is good for us to remember at the end of this year that we live in the strongest Nation on earth—militarily the strongest, economically the strongest, politically the strongest—a Nation that is a leader worldwide, that is trusted, that is making progress, dealing with the developing nations, the Western European nations, Latin America, making progress toward controlling atomic weapons.

Domestically God has blessed us with tremendous natural resources, a free enterprise system that lets people benefit from their own contributions, their own initiative.

We have so much in common. We are a Nation of highly diverse people, different people, but we are one people and we have come from almost nothing 200 years ago to this position of sustained leadership and prosperity. The standard of living in our country for even the poorest person far exceeds the average living standard in many nations of the world. We are unselfish, and I think the threat to our country is that we might in grasping for advantage or in emphasizing differences lose that sense of common commitment and common purpose and a common future that binds us together and makes us great.

I don't have any fear about the future. I think that when I make mistakes or when the Congress makes mistakes or when we delay in solving apparently insoluble questions, our country is so strong and so vital and the people are bound together so closely that we can prevail in any case.

And I think the expressions of dissatisfaction, although they are legitimate in many instances, are overemphasized. I think our country is much greater than that.

QUESTION: Again, looking back on this first year of the Presidency, Senator Hart wrote—Senator Gary Hart—wrote a piece recently in which he said that you had demythologized the imperial Presidency, but he wondered whether you also had not sacrificed some of the psychological weight and power that the Presidency had accumulated since Roosevelt's time to your detriment.

I was wondering. For instance, you spoke out very strongly against the oil companies, accusing them of trying to rip off the American people, very, very strong words, and yet the oil companies seem relatively unperturbed. Are you at all concerned that in making yours as a Presidency of the common man and ridding yours of some of the imperial trappings you may have thrown away some of the clout?

THE PRESIDENT: Many people think so. The pomp and ceremony of office does not appeal to me, and I don't believe it is a necessary part of the Presidency in a democratic Nation like our own. I am no better than anyone else. And the people that I admire most who have lived in this house have taken the same attitude. Jefferson, Jackson, Lincoln, Truman have minimized the pomp and ceremony and the pride, personal pride that accrues sometimes to Presidents.

I don't think we need to put on the trappings of a monarchy in a Nation like our own. I feel uncomfortable with it. But I doubt if I feel quite as uncomfortable as the average citizen.

QUESTION: Mr. President, speaking of Abraham Lincoln, Abraham Lincoln said just toward the end of his Presidency, he said, "I must confess that events have controlled me rather than the other way around."

I wonder, looking back over your first year, how do you feel about this first year?

THE PRESIDENT: I feel good about it. It has been exciting and stimulating and challenging and sometimes a frustrating experience for me.

QUESTION: Were you controlled by events?

THE PRESIDENT: Yes, I think so. I have tried to represent what the American people want me to be and what they are. I noticed one of the news commentators the other night say that when I said during the campaign that I wanted the Government as good as the American people that it was demagoguery.

I don't think that is accurate. The American people are good and decent and idealistic. And I think they want their Government to be good and decent and idealistic.

One of the most popular things that I have tried to do is to express to the world our own people's commitment to basic human rights, to freedom, independence, and autonomy, the worth of a human being, whether they live here or in Russia or in South America or in Uganda, or China. And I doubt that there is a national leader in the world now who doesn't think about human rights every day and how his or her actions are measured against a standard that the world is beginning to demand.

So I think what I have tried to do is to see what is good in our Nation, in our people, in our past, and try to preserve it and to deal with changing events to the best of my ability. I have got a good Cabinet. I have had good cooperation and support from the Congress who recognized my newness in Washington. And overall, although I see great problems ahead of us, I feel confident.

I had my staff—the National Security Council—ready to give me an analysis of the world situation as it was a year ago, and the comparison doesn't look bad. I think we are trusted now where we weren't before, say in Africa, primarily because of the influence of Andrew Young.

I believe that our intentions are recognized as being good. So in all I think it has been a good year for us.

QUESTION: Mr. President, do you ever come back from the Oval Office, which is not that many feet away, and come back to the Residence and sit down and reflect on the day's events and what is going on in the world, and think, my God, this is a bigger job than I expected it to be; I am not sure I am up to this?

Do you ever have those moments of self-doubt?

THE PRESIDENT: Well, I have sober moments when I am not sure that I can deal with problems satisfactorily. But I have a lot of confidence in myself. Sometimes I go in the back room and pray a while. And a few times I have walked through this mansion where every President has lived except George Washington, since 1801, and I have thought about the difficulties and the tragedy that existed in the lives of many of them and feel myself to be fortunate. But I don't feel inadequate because I feel that even political opponents want me to succeed, and I couldn't have asked for better cooperation and support than I have gotten from those who have helped me in this job.

QUESTION: Can you tell us what you think has been your greatest single achievement this past year and also even though we hear that you don't have sleepless nights, everyone makes mistakes, what do you think your biggest mistake has been?

THE PRESIDENT: I think my biggest mistake has been in inadvertently building up expectations too high. I underestimated the difficulty and the time required for Congress to take action on controversial measures. It is much easier for me to study and evolve and present legislation to the Congress than it is for them to pass it in its final form. And I have dashed some hopes and disappointed people that thought we might act quicker.

I think that the achievements are not measured in how many bills were passed and how many bills I have signed or even my harmony with the Congress. If I have achieved anything, it has been to restore a tone to our Nation's life and attitude that most accurately exemplifies what we stand for. I use the human rights issue as one example. It gratifies me to know that the Nations in Africa now look to us with friendship and with trust, whereas, just a short time ago, they wouldn't permit our Secretary of State to come in their country.

It gratifies me to see a burgeoning friendship with Latin American Nations and to see our NATO allies now recommitting themselves to strong military commitments and it gratifies me to see some progress being made in relieving tensions between ourselves and the Soviet Union. We are making slow, steady progress. We are attempting many things simultaneously. Sometimes they get confusing because they are so voluminous and there are so many of them.

But I think having our Nation and its government represent more accurately the hopes and dreams of the American people is a general accomplishment of which I am most proud.

QUESTION: Mr. President, when you were still running for office, you told me in an interview—when I asked you what your weakness was, you said perhaps a difficulty to compromise and it was a difficulty with the Georgia Legislature and it might be a difficulty with the Congress. Has this year in Washington been an education in compromise?

THE PRESIDENT: Well, yes. I am not sure if I had an adequate education yet because I still find it difficult to compromise. But I am learning. One way that I have learned since I have been here to avoid having to compromise so much is by involving the congressional leaders in the decision, in the initial stages. When we evolved the Reorganization bill and when we put together the Energy Department, when we evolved the Social Security bill and other measures that were controversial, we consulted very closely with congressional leaders ahead of time. So I am trying to avoid having to yield to my weakness, which is a difficulty in compromising. I am learning every day, I think.

QUESTION: Mr. President, maybe we can all come back next year at this same time.

THE PRESIDENT: Well, I hope so.

QUESTION: On behalf of all my colleagues, I want to thank you very much for having us here this evening, however.

THE PRESIDENT: Thank you, Tom. I have enjoyed it very much.

QUESTION: Thank you, Mr. President.

10

INTERVIEW WITH THE PRESIDENT, NOV. 13, 1978

Public Papers of the Presidents, Bill Moyers

Bill Moyers and Jimmy Carter have much in common and always seem to bring off a good interview. This interview took place in the oval office, Nov. 13, 1978, and was taped for later broadcast on PBS.—*Editor*

MR. MOYERS: Mr. President, a philosopher you have read and quoted, Søren Kierkegaard, once wrote an essay called "For Self-Examination." Confession and examination have a long history in your church, although not usually on television. With your permission, I'd like to ask a few questions for self-examination.

If there is a single dominant criticism by your supporters of the Carter administration, it is that for the first 18 months there was no single theme, no vision of what it is you want to do. Are you going to try to, in the next 2 years, mold a Carter vision of the country?

THE PRESIDENT: Well, I think it was also Kierkegaard who said that every man is an exception. And the multiplicity of responsibilities that a President has, the same issues that our Nation has to face, I think, causes some lack of a central focus quite often.

We're dealing with the question of a strong national defense, some concern about the good intentions of potential adversaries like the Soviet Union on the one hand. At the same time we are struggling valiantly to find common ground on which we can assure peace between us and better friendship and a minimization of the distrust.

We, at the same time—we're dealing with SALT, are trying to bring peace to the Mideast, to Cyprus, to Namibia, to Rhodesia, to Nicaragua, exerting a leadership role in our country that the rest

---

From *Public Papers of the Presidents,* Jimmy Carter.

of the world sometimes expects. And then, of course, on domestic issues, they are so broad—trying to have a strong farm economy, increase exports, stabilize prices with an anti-inflation program, meet the necessary demands of many interest groups in our Nation who are quite benevolent. So, to bring some tightly drawn, simplistic cohesion into this broadly diverse responsibility is almost impossible.

I think in some cases previous Presidents have had their thrust identified with a simple slogan only in retrospect. I know that Roosevelt's New Deal was identified well into his term, and when he used the expression in a speech, he had no idea that it would categorize what he'd brought to the country. So, I think that only when an administration is looked at in maybe at least a recently historical perspective can you get a central theme.

We are trying to restore trust in government. We're trying to have enhancement of world peace, focusing on human rights, and at the same time exemplify what I tried to express in the campaign, and since I've been in office, as well, that my party and what I stand for is a proper blending of both compassion and competence.

In the past we've not been able to bridge that gap adequately. I think we've made a step in the right direction, but how to bring one or two phrases or a slick, little slogan to identify an administration in its formative stage or even in its productive stage is almost impossible.

MR. MOYERS: If I could put it another way, T. S. Eliot once said that every large, new figure in literature changes our perception of literature. I think the same is probably true of the Presidency. It represents something of what the country is all about. You're the most recent representative of that tradition, and I'm wondering if, 2 years into your administration, you know what it is you'd like to leave.

THE PRESIDENT: I don't think my goals have changed much since I began thinking about running for President, even 4 years before I was elected, and in the last 2 years.

There's no doubt that our Nation had been damaged very severely by the Vietnam war and by the Watergate scandals and by the CIA revelations. And I think our people were also beginning to suspect that many key public officials were dishonest, not exactly forthcoming in telling the truth, and that there was no respect for our own country among the vast majority of nations in the rest of the world. There was some doubt about our own allies and friends that we espoused who were personifications of human rights violations.

And I think in all those respects—how people look upon our government, either from the point of view of an American citizen and also foreign leaders and citizens—that we've made good progress toward reaching the goal of restoring that accurate image of a good nation with integrity and purpose, openness, and also with a President who speaks accurately for the people themselves.

One problem has been that in the openness that I've tried to create, there comes with debate on complicated issues an absence of clarity. The simplest decisions that I have to make, as I told the FFA convention in Kansas City last week, are the ones about which I know least, that the more you know about the subject, all the complexities on both sides, the detailed, intricate arguments, the more difficult it is to make a decision. If you don't know much about a subject, you can make a very quick and easy decision.

But I think that we have made good progress in correcting some of the defects that existed in our Government, and I feel that history will look with favor now.

MR. MOYERS: As you talk, it occurs to me that not since 1960 has a President finished two terms in the White House. Kennedy was elected and assassinated, Johnson was elected and discredited, Nixon was elected and disgraced, Ford was appointed and defeated. Would you like to be the first President to finish two terms since 1960?

THE PRESIDENT: Well, I haven't decided that yet. I would like to be worthy of that honor, and if I decided to run for reelection in 1980, I intend to win. But I can see why it's difficult for a President to serve two terms. You are the personification of problems, and when you address a problem, even successfully, you become identified with it. And that's what the responsibility of the Presidency is.

MR. MOYERS: Is that why, Mr. President, this disorder has been growing around the Presidency? For almost 15 years now, there is a sense of almost as if the American people or a substantial representative of the American people have silently withdrawn their support from the Presidency, no longer look to it as the symbol of the Nation as a whole.

THE PRESIDENT: I think that's true. But there were some special circumstances that relate to those Presidents you mentioned. Kennedy was assassinated. I don't think that was any reflection on the Presidency itself. It was just a tragic occurrence that I hope will never be repeated.

Johnson was, I think, looked upon by the country as primarily the one responsible for the continuation of the Vietnam war, and the war was around his neck like an anvil, pulling him down. I think he did the best he could to terminate the war, and I know he suffered personally because of the loss of American lives in Vietnam.

Nixon, of course, his successor, had the special problem with Watergate, and Ford was identified with the pardon of Nixon and didn't have long enough to get himself established, I think, to stay in office.

So, there have been special circumstances, but I don't believe that it is inherent in the office that you would be forced out of office because of some adverse occurrence.

MR. MOYERS: You don't agree with one of your predecessors that it's a splendid misery?

THE PRESIDENT: No. I think that was President Nixon who said it was a splendid misery.

MR. MOYERS: Quoting before him some earlier—it was Adams, I think—

THE PRESIDENT: Before Watergate, yes.

No, I've not been miserable in the job. I might point out that it's voluntary. Nobody in my memory has been forced to serve as President. And as a matter of fact, in spite of the challenges and problems and, sometimes, disappointments and criticisms, I really enjoy it.

MR. MOYERS: What's the hardest part?

THE PRESIDENT: I think the hardest part is the attempt to correlate sharply conflicting ideas from worthy people. The easy problems don't arrive on this desk. You know, the easy problems are solved in the life of an individual person or within a family or perhaps in a city hall or a county courthouse or, at the worst, in a State capitol. The ones that can't be solved after all those intense efforts arrive here in the White House to be solved, and they're quite difficult ones. And I think the attempt to correlate those conflicting ideas probably bring about the most serious challenge to a President.

MR. MOYERS: You said not long ago, "I feel like my life now is one massive multiple-choice examination, where things are put in front of me and I have to make the difficult choice." Can you give me an example of that?

THE PRESIDENT: Yes. I haven't found anything easy about this job. But I didn't expect it to be easy when I came here. Well, I mentioned one earlier, the fact that we have to be very protective of our Nation's security and cover every eventuality if we don't make progress toward peace with the Soviet Union.

At the same time, we have to explore every possibility to have a peaceful relationship with the Soviet Union, to alleviate tensions and to find common grounds on which we can actually build friendships in the future. And these two are not only extremely complicated, each side of that possibility, but apparently are in conflict.

MR. MOYERS: What do you think the Soviets are up to, Mr. President? I mean, do you see them as primarily a defensive power, seeking to solidify their own position in the world, or do you see them as an aggressive power, seeking to enlarge their position in the world?

THE PRESIDENT: Well, to be perhaps excessively generous, but not too far off the mark, I think, first of all, they want peace and security for their own people, and they undoubtedly exaggerate any apparent threat to themselves and have to, to be sure that they are able to protect themselves. At the same time, as is the case with us, they would like to expand their influence among other people in the world, believing that their system of government, their philosophy is the best. This means that we have to plan in the future, in the presence of peace between us, to be competitive with them and able to compete both aggressively and successfully.

But I would say that those are their two basic motives, as is the case with us—security for themselves and to have their own influence felt in the rest of the world as much as possible.

MR. MOYERS: There is a school of thought which says that their aim is to achieve superiority over us in both conventional and strategic weapons and that we must therefore not settle to be equal with them, but to have superiority over them. These are the hard choices you're talking about. Where do you come out in that debate?

THE PRESIDENT: They will never be superior to us in national strength nor overall military strength. We are by far the stronger nation economically. Our productivity capacity is superior, and I think always will be.

We've got a vibrant, dynamic social and political system based on freedom, individuality, and a common purpose that's engendered from the desire of our own people, not imposed from above by an autocratic government. I think our absence of desire to control other people around the world gives us a competitive advantage once a new government is established or as they search about for friends. We are better trusted than the Soviet Union. They spend more than twice as much of their gross national product on military matters, but we are still much stronger, and we will always be stronger than they are, at least in our lifetimes.

We are surrounded by friends and allies—Canada in the north, Mexico in the south—two open and accessible oceans on the east and west. The Soviets, when looked at from the perspective of the Kremlin, are faced with almost a billion Chinese, who have a strong animosity and distrust toward the Soviets. Toward the west, in Eastern Europe, their allies and friends can't be depended on nearly so strongly as our own. They have a difficult chance to have access to the oceans in an unrestricted fashion; their climate is not as good as ours; their lands are not as productive.

And so, I think that in any sort of present or future challenge from the Soviet Union, our Nation stacks up very well, and I thank God for it.

MR. MOYERS: But do you think the number one mentality which you hear many people espouse is a healthy mentality? Is the whole question of being number one one that can ever result in anything but an increasing escalation of tensions and increasing arms expenditures?

THE PRESIDENT: In nuclear weapons, which is, you know, where our competition with the Soviets is most direct, we've both accepted the concept of rough equivalency; that is, we are just about equal. They have heavier warheads; we have more of them. We have three different systems for delivery of warheads—if we ever need to, and I don't think we ever will have to—that are mutually supportive. We have a much higher developed electronics technology; our surveillance systems are probably as good or better than theirs. Our submarines are quieter than theirs.

We've got an advantage in having a tremendous reservoir of a free enterprise business system that can be innovative and aggressive. We have a much closer correlation between the production of civilian or peaceful goods on the one hand and military on the other.

So, I think that in the case of nuclear weapons, we have an equivalency with them, and they recognize it, and vice versa. Both of us realize that no one can attack the other with impunity. We can absorb, even if we had to, an attack by the Soviets and still destroy their country, and they know it, and vice versa.

So, I think that the horrible threat of surety of mutual destruction will prevent an attack being launched. We don't intend to evolve and neither do the Soviets intend to evolve a capability to destroy the other nation without ourselves being destroyed by nuclear forces.

In the case of land weapons, as I said before, the Soviets have vulnerable borders. They have neighbors whom they can't trust as well as we. And they face even in the nuclear field three other nuclear powers who are potential adversaries in case of a crisis—the Chinese, the British, and the French—in addition to ourselves. We don't have any of those as potential adversaries for us.

But I think for any nation to have a macho attitude, that we're going to be so powerful that we can dominate or destroy the other nation, would be counterproductive. And I don't think that even if we wanted to do that, either we or the Soviets could have that capability.

MR. MOYERS: Let me apply the multiple-choice, difficult options equation to a couple of other contemporary and very live issues. One is Iran. What are the options facing you there?

THE PRESIDENT: Well, we look on the Shah, as you know, as a friend, a loyal ally, and the good relationship that Iran has had and has now with ourselves and with the other democracies in the world, the Western powers as being very constructive and valuable. Also, having a strong and independent Iran in that area is a very stabilizing factor, and we would hate to see it disrupted by violence and the government fall with an unpredictable result.

The Shah has been primarily criticized within Iran because he has tried to democratize the country and because he's instituted social reforms in a very rapid fashion. Some of his domestic adversaries either disagree with the way he's done it, or think he hasn't moved fast enough or too fast, and deplore his breaking of ancient religious and social customs as Iran has become modern.

MR. MOYERS: But he was also criticized, Mr. President, for running a police state—political prisoners—

THE PRESIDENT: That's exactly right. I think the Shah has had that criticism, sometimes perhaps justified—I don't know the details of it. But I think there's no doubt that Iran has made great social progress and has moved toward a freer expression of people. Even in recent months, for instance, the Shah has authorized or directed, I guess, the parliament to have all of its deliberations open and televised, something that we don't even do in our country here.

MR. MOYERS: You think this is all too late?

THE PRESIDENT: Well, I hope not. I don't know what will come eventually. I would hope that a coalition government could be formed rapidly. At the present time there's a quasi-military government. The Shah has reconfirmed his commitment to have open and democratic elections, maybe within 6 months or 8 months. I hope that would be possible.

Our inclination is for the Iranian people to have a clear expression of their own views and to have a government intact in Iran that accurately expresses a majority view in Iran.

MR. MOYERS: But can we do anything to encourage that, or are our hands tied?

THE PRESIDENT: No, we don't try to interfere in the internal affairs of Iran.

MR. MOYERS: We did put the Shah in, but you're saying we can't keep him in.

THE PRESIDENT: I think that's a decision to be made by the people of that country.

MR. MOYERS: Does it hurt you sometimes to have to sit back and do nothing when you know there are large stakes in a part of the world beyond your influence?

THE PRESIDENT: Well, we don't have any inclination to be involved in the internal affairs of another country unless our own security should be directly threatened. And that's a philosophy that I have espoused ever since I've been in the national political realm.

I just think we've learned our lessons the hard way, in Vietnam and in other instances, and we've tried to be loyal to our allies and loyal to our friends, to encourage one person–one vote, majority rule, the democratic processes, the protection of human rights. Obviously, we have not always succeeded in encouraging other people to measure up to our own standards, but I think we've been consistent in our effort.

MR. MOYERS: But this is again where some criticism arises in some circles in this country, who say the Soviets have a stake in what happens in Iran and they are free to move clandestinely or any other way that they wish. But if we take the position that you're espousing, we'll sit back and do nothing when we should be in there covertly or clandestinely or overtly, taking a tough stand, saying that we may not like the Shah but we need him in power. You're saying that day is over, that we cannot do that.

THE PRESIDENT: No, we have made it clear through my own public statements and those of Secretary Vance that we support the Shah and support the present government, recognizing that we don't have any control over the decisions ultimately made by the Iranian people and the stability of that region. The absence of the success of terrorism, of violence, the anarchy that might come with the complete disruption of their government is a threat to peace.

We don't have any evidence that the Soviets, for instance, are trying to disrupt the existing government structure in Iran nor that they are a source of violence in Iran. I think they recognize—they have a very long mutual border with Iran, and a stable government there, no matter who its leaders might be, is valuable to them.

This might change. If it becomes obvious that the Shah is very vulnerable and that other forces might come into power, the Soviets might change their obvious posture. But that's the observation that we have now.

MR. MOYERS: What about the Middle East, Mr. President?

THE PRESIDENT: I have put hundreds of hours in both preparation and direct negotiation with the leaders in the Middle East, particularly Egypt and Israel. And Secretary Vance, even to the extent of abandoning some of his other responsibilities in foreign affairs, has tried to bring about a successful conclusion of the peace treaty negotiations. There, again, we don't have any authority over anyone else. We can't use pressure to make the Israelis and Egyptians come to a peaceful settlement of the disputes that have divided them.

The Camp David framework, which was almost miraculous in its conclusion—it seems more miraculous in retrospect than it did at the time—is a sound basis for peace between Egypt and Israel. There's no doubt that both nations would be highly benefited by peace.

MR. MOYERS: But yet the talks seem to be at an impasse as of tonight.

THE PRESIDENT: The present disagreements, compared to the benefits to be derived, are relatively insignificant. The benefits are so overwhelming, in comparison with the differences, that I hope that the Egyptians and Israelis will move toward peace.

MR. MOYERS: What's holding it up tonight?

THE PRESIDENT: At Camp David it was a framework, it was an outline that had a lot of substance to it, but it required negotiation of details and specifics. And there is no way that you could have a peace treaty with all of the ends tied down and all of the detailed agreements reached, the maps drawn, the lines delineated, time schedules agreed, without going far beyond what the Camp David outline required.

And so, both sides have demanded from the others additional assurances far above and beyond what Camp David said specifically. This is inherent in the process. And I think in some cases, in many cases, the two governments have reached agreement fairly well.

Now I don't know what's going to happen. We hope that they will continue to work in reaching agreement, to understand one another, to balance the consequences of failure against the benefits to be derived from the success, and be flexible on both sides.

These are ancient arguments, historical distrust not easy to overcome. And the frustrating part about it is that we are involved in the negotiations, but we can't make Israel accept the Egyptians' demands, nor vice versa. We have to try to tone down those demands and use our influence. I don't know what will happen about it. We just pray that agreements will be reached.

MR. MOYERS: Are you asking both sides to make further concessions?

THE PRESIDENT: Oh, yes—every day and night. We ask both sides to please be constructive, to please not freeze your position, to please to continue to negotiate, to please yield on this proposal, to adopt this compromise. These have been and are our efforts on a constant basis.

It would be horrible, I think, if we failed to reach a peaceful agreement between Israel and Egypt—

MR. MOYERS: What would happen?

THE PRESIDENT: —and then see our children, our grandchildren, future generations look back and say these little tiny technicalities, phrases, phrasing of ideas, legalisms, which at that time seemed to be paramount in the eyes of the Egyptian and the Israeli agreements, have absolutely no historical significance. And that's basically what the problems are.

MR. MOYERS: Are you saying that the impasse as of today is because of technicalities and not major principles?

THE PRESIDENT: Yes, compared to the principles that have already been resolved and the overall scope of things, the disagreements now, relatively, are insignificant.

MR. MOYERS: Egypt wants to tie the present negotiations, I understand, to some future resolution of the Gaza Strip and the West Bank. Israel is resisting that. Who's being more stubborn?

THE PRESIDENT: Well, I wouldn't want to start saying who's being more stubborn. I think there's adequate stubbornness to be allotted to both sides.

MR. MOYERS: You mentioned grandchildren, and I heard you say after Camp David that at one critical moment that was resolved because of somebody thinking about grandchildren. Would you tell me about that?

THE PRESIDENT: It might be a mistake to attach too much importance to it, but during the last few hours of negotiations at Camp David, when it looked like everything was going to break down then, Prime Minister Begin sent me over some photographs of me and him and President Sadat and wanted me to autograph them. And the issue at that time was Jerusalem, which was an almost insurmountable obstacle that we later resolved by not including it at all in the framework. And instead of just putting my signature on it, which President Sadat had done, I sent my secretary, Susan Clough, over and got the names from one of his aides of all his grandchildren.

So, I personally autographed it to his granddaughters and grand-sons and signed my name, and I carried it over to him in one of the most tense moments and I handed it to him. And he started to talk to me about the breakdown of the negotiations and he looked down and saw that I had written all of his grandchildren's names on the in-dividual pictures and signed them, and he started telling me about his favorite grandchild and the characteristics of different ones. And he and I had quite an emotional discussion about the benefits to my two grandchildren and to his if we could reach peace. And I think it broke the tension that existed there, that could have been an obsta-cle to any sort of resolution at that time.

MR. MOYERS: What does that say to you about the nature of these problems and their resolution?

THE PRESIDENT: Well, you know, when you put the problems in the focus of how they affect people, little children, families, the loss of life, the agreements and the need for agreement becomes para-mount. When you put the focus in the hands of international lawyers and get it down to technicalities—is a certain event going to take place in 9 months or 8 1/2 months or 10 months; is this going to happen before that; is this demarcation line going to go around this hill or through the hill, on the other side of the hill; can the obser-vation towers be 150 feet high, 200 feet high, 125 feet high—the human dimension of it becomes obviously paramount. But when the negotiators sit around a table and start talking, the human dimen-sion tends to fade away, and you get bogged down in the legalisms and the language and the exact time schedule, when from a historic perspective they have no significance.

Another problem has been—and this has been one of the most serious problems—at Camp David we didn't have daily press brief-ings, and this was the agreement when we started here in Washing-ton, that neither side would make a direct statement to the press. As you know, this has not been honored at all, and it's created enor-mous additional and unnecessary problems for us.

MR. MOYERS: You mean leaks from both governments are—

THE PRESIDENT: Not just leaks. I mean, almost every day I see inter-views in the national television of at least one of the sides in the dis-pute.

And also at Camp David I was working directly with the heads of state. Here we work with the negotiators, and the negotiators then refer their decision back to the head of state or the cabinet. The cab-inet reverses themselves, reverses the negotiators on a language change or one word, and in effect you get the most radical members of the governments who have a major input into the negotiating process, rather than having the heads of state there 100 yards away so that they can resolve those issues once and for all.

So, I think the followup to Camp David has been much more time-consuming and much more frustrating than it was when the three of us were primarily leading the discussions.

MR. MOYERS: I read that the Camp David log showed that you spent 27 1/2 hours with Sadat and 29 hours with Begin, and 9 hours alone with Sadat and 6 hours alone with Begin, with no one else in the room, the way FDR used to do with Churchill.

Do you think that you could resolve most of these large issues we face if you could just get people in a room like this and talk to them? It used to be said Lyndon Johnson could have done much better had he been able to persuade people one on one instead of having to use television and public speeches. Do you think that other problems you face could be resolved if you could meet nose to nose, in a sense, with the adversaries?

THE PRESIDENT: I couldn't guarantee success, but I think, obviously, the likelihood of success would be better.

MR. MOYERS: This goes back to something you said earlier, too, where what you try to do is never seen in the singular way in which you're trying to do it, that you become many things to many people. How do you resolve those contradictions?

THE PRESIDENT: Well, that's inevitable. The most pressing problem on my hands, on my shoulders, is not to present to the people of the world a simplistic and simple character as a President or as a person.

The agenda for an average day for me is incredibly complex, you know, and I shift from one subject to another—from domestic affairs to foreign affairs, from one country to another, from one issue to another. And there's no way for me to say what I did in this one single day in a few words, so that the complexities are inevitable. The only thing I know to do about it is to try to address each item on its own merits and make a decision that I think at that time is the best for my country and my people.

The advantage of having good advisers is very great, and I do have good advisers. I've been criticized because I studied details of issues too much, but that's my nature. And I think on occasion it pays rich dividends, in that I am able to understand the complexities of an issue when a final decision has to be made and not depend entirely on advisers who don't have the knowledge that I, as President, can have uniquely.

But this is a fond hope, I guess, of every politician, to be universally admired, to have all of your themes clearly defined, to have everything packaged beautifully so it can be examined from all sides without doubt, to have one's character be recognized clearly, and to have universal approbation of the people that you try to represent. All those things are hopeless dreams.

MR. MOYERS: Pat Caddell made a speech recently in which he said— Pat Caddell is one of your associates—in which he said that a President can succeed by doing poorly because the people out there don't think he can do well. Do you think that's true?

THE PRESIDENT: [*Laughing*] I hope I don't have to prove that.

MR. MOYERS: You were criticized, I know, talking about details, for keeping the log yourself of who could use the White House tennis courts. Are you still doing that?

THE PRESIDENT: No—and never have, by the way.

MR. MOYERS: Was that a false report?

THE PRESIDENT: Yes, it was.

MR. MOYERS: But seriously, is the job too big? Is the United States Government, which is a $500 billion enterprise, now too big to be managed by a single chief executive?

THE PRESIDENT: No. I wouldn't want to—I say that, recognizing that no one person can do it all. But the structure of the American Government is still the best that I can imagine. There's a tremendous sharing of responsibility between the different branches of the Federal Government, an adequate sharing of responsibility between myself and Governors of States and mayors and county officials at the local level of government, between government and private citizens. These balances have been evolved historically, and I think they've grown to their present state because in each instance when a change occurred, tests were made and the best arrangement triumphed.

But it would be a serious mistake to try to run a government like this with, say, committee. And I'm thankful that my Cabinet can be either hired or fired by me. I consult with my Cabinet or listen to them, but I make a decision. I don't have to have a vote and go by the majority vote in my own Cabinet. And if you had, say, a three-person President, one perhaps involved with foreign affairs, one with domestic affairs, one managing the bureaucracy itself, I think it would be much worse than what we have now.

I like the constitutional arrangement, where you have an executive with constitutionally limited powers and a voice with which to express the aspirations and hopes of our country accurately, I hope, to the people.

MR. MOYERS: Was Camp David the high of your administration so far?

THE PRESIDENT: Well, I'd say the first 12 1/2 days were probably the lower of my administration; the last half day at Camp David was one of the highest. It's hard to say.

MR. MOYERS: What's been the lowest moment for you? Were you aware, for example, this summer of the growing doubts about your competency to be President?

THE PRESIDENT: Well, there was a rash of news reports, cover stories in the weekly magazines, and editorial comments around the Nation expressing concerns about my ability to run the Government.

I'm not sure they were any more condemnatory nor critical than they were about previous Presidents, all the way back to Abraham Lincoln; even before. Each President has been criticized and castigated as incompetent and dastardly, even.

MR. MOYERS: Your polls had fallen very sharply this summer as well.

THE PRESIDENT: Well, they had—not as low as the polls fell for, say, Harry Truman during his own administration, but lower than I liked. But I never had any particular concern about that, because I could see in the evolutionary stage, for instance, in my dealings with Congress, progress being made toward eventual decisions by Congress that showed that the 95th Congress had a very good record of achievement. And I think in the confrontations I had with the Congress, when we disagreed on two or three items, I prevailed because I think I was right and established principles that will be good for the future.

But I've never had any doubt about my own resolution. I recognize my own limitations and faults. I'm not omniscient. I'm certainly not omnipotent. I have limited powers, limited authority, and I try to overcome those inherent defects in the office itself as best I can.

MR. MOYERS: What people were saying in circles where I was listening was that Jimmy Carter accepted an energy bill that was not what he wanted; Jimmy Carter settled for a tax bill that was at odds with his conviction; Jimmy Carter had set aside an aggressive fight for welfare reform; he lost his hospital containment costs; he didn't push on education. In a sense, people were saying that Jimmy Carter, who said he was going to bring competency and efficiency to government, was being routed on every front and settling, compromising for what he had said before he didn't want. And from that came a perception, I think, of a weak President, of a President who is being defeated in one front after another.

THE PRESIDENT: The final legislative agenda as it was passed, I think, is a great credit to the Congress and shows a good compatibility between them and me and has been a matter of pride for all of us.

The fact that we had very few Members of the Congress defeated in the last election, compared to previous off-year elections, is good. We still have more than 60 percent Democrats in the House, about 60 percent in the Senate, I think about 60 percent in the Governorships, is an endorsement of what the Democratic Party has done.

But I think I need to be fair in saying that there have been times when I've had to compromise, below what I had asked the Congress to do or had demanded of the Congress. We got about 65 percent of the energy bill that we originally proposed to Congress in ultimate savings in imported oil, about 2.5 million barrels a day savings compared to 4.5, for instance.

I would like to have gotten the entire thing. I'm not out of office yet and will come back to try to get some more in the future.

MR. MOYERS: But take the tax bill, Mr. President. During the campaign, you said repeatedly our tax system is a disgrace to the human race. The tax bill you signed was a bill that gave the biggest breaks to the wealthiest taxpayers and the smallest breaks to the smaller taxpayers. Did you sign that bill in conscience?

THE PRESIDENT: That's not exactly fair, because although the bill fell far short of the reforms that I advocated, the bill does bring substantial tax reductions to all taxpayers. And it's a fairly balanced bill, as far as that goes.

It was necessary that a bill be passed, and compared to the version that the House passed or compared to the version that the Senate passed, the compromise that was brought about was superior to either one of those.

Had I vetoed that bill after the Congress sent it to me, we would have had an enormous increase in taxes on the American people as of the first of the year; not only the loss of roughly $20 billion in tax reductions that we've added, but also we would have lost, say, roughly $13 billion in tax reductions that had been passed the previous year.

So, there was a case that was a difficult decision to make. When I met a few days before the Congress adjourned with the leaders of the House and Senate—Al Ullman in the House, Russell Long in the Senate—and said, "This is what I will and will not accept," they complied with my request substantially. And although it was short of what I would have preferred, my vetoing of that bill would have been a very serious mistake.

MR. MOYERS: This explanation, this rationalization, which is necessary in this town on a lot of compromises, raises the question about where you think the Democratic Party is going. As you know, Democrats have a tradition of using the Government's powers to correct the imbalances and the injustices of the capitalist economy, to innovate, to equalize, to take risks. Republicans are elected generally to manage, to stabilize, to pull in the horns a little bit.

Howard Baker is going around town saying—the minority leader of the Senate—saying that "The Democrats are singing our song, and it's a Republican song." And what a lot of people are saying has been reborn in Washington is a conservative administration with a Democratic President with Republican intuitions. Do you think that's fair? Isn't the Democratic Party coopting the Republican philosophy?

THE PRESIDENT: No, I don't think so. The Democrats have always been a party of compassion and concern about the people of our country. We've always been eager to extend a helping hand to somebody who hasn't had an adequate chance in life to stand on one's own feet, to make one's own decisions, to control one's own destiny, to have an education if they didn't have one, to have a house to live in, to have better health care, better food, security in one's old age, better highway systems. These are the kinds of things that the Democratic Party has always espoused and has always pursued.

I saw quite early in my administration as Governor of Georgia that we had an undeserved reputation as Democrats of not being fiscally responsible and not being competent in management. One of the major thrusts of my own Governorship was to reorganize the government, to get control of the bureaucracy, to cut taxes, to budget carefully, and I ran my campaign for President on that platform. And we've had remarkable success since I've been here.

We will have cut the budget deficit more than half compared to what the Republican administration had when they went out of office.

We will have passed civil service reform to get the bureaucracy under control, for a change. We've had $28 to $30 billion in tax reductions. At the same time we've had the largest allocation of increased funds for better education the country's ever seen. We've had help to cities and other local governments that's almost unprecedented. We've sustained a home building rate of over 2 million a year.

So, we've been able to combine, through tough, competent fiscal management, both the delivery of good services to our people and also tight budgeting, cutting down deficits, cutting taxes. And the combination of those two, in my opinion, is not incompatible. You can't educate a child with inefficiency and waste and corruption. You can't feed a hungry person with inefficiency or waste or corruption. And I think that this is a reputation that the Democrats have now assumed, legitimately so, of competent management, that we did not enjoy in the past.

And I can understand why the Republicans are complaining, because they can no longer allege successfully that the Democrats can't be both compassionate, concerned, and competent.

MR. MOYERS: If you were a teenage black youth in the ghetto, if you were one of those millions of people who are surplus in our economy, who have no positive role in our economy or our society, would you have taken much encouragement from the results last week of that election?

THE PRESIDENT: Well, that's hard to say, when you analyze the results. The Republicans picked up a few extra seats in the House—I think about a dozen—and a few extra seats in the Senate. That obviously should not bring encouragement to anyone that the Republicans have more seats.

MR. MOYERS: I mean the rhetoric that many Democrats use, the rhetoric almost everyone used, in talking about cutting back, retrenching, cutting taxes, all of which would add up to a different kind of approach to government than the traditional Democratic posture.

THE PRESIDENT: I see what you mean. That's hard to say, because for a single person who's out of a job, the most important thing is to get a job. In the last 20 months or so, we've added almost 7 million net new jobs to the American economy. We've cut the unemployment rate about 25 percent.

In the case of agriculture, we've increased farm income, net farm income about 25 percent, and as I say, sustained additional commitments to better education, better housing, and so forth.

Now, however, there's a general feeling among those who are in the very low levels of income and those retired people who have a fixed income, that the most serious threat to our Nation is inflation. And I think the Congress candidates and those running for Governor as well recognize that controlling inflation had to be given a very high priority.

With that comes a need to have tight budgeting decisions made, a reduction in deficits, and a demonstration to the Government and also to the private parts of our economy that we are going to be fiscally responsible.

I think in the long run the alleviation of inflation in a person's life is almost as important as an increase in wages or an increase in prices that one can get for products sold.

So, there is a new emphasis, I think, on the control of inflation, but it doesn't mean that we've abandoned searching for new jobs, nor the better life for the people who live in our country.

MR. MOYERS: But it is likely, isn't it, that if you succeed in your inflation fight, some people will be put out of work?

THE PRESIDENT: I don't believe that's the case. We don't project that to happen. I think there will be an increase in the number of jobs available every year that I'm in office. The rate of increase might slack off and level off some, but I don't think there will be a net loss in the number of jobs in our country.

MR. MOYERS: A lot of private economists are forecasting a turndown by 1980. How can you avoid that if you really keep the pressure on interest rates and housing construction and the pressures to stop the growth of inflation? Do you have some new trick in the hat?

THE PRESIDENT: No. There is no trick, and there again it's a difficult decision that you just have to balance. But whether we can continue to build up enormous deficits by spending money we don't have, and benefit the American people, is a serious question. I don't think we can.

I think we've got to have careful budgeting, a more accurate focusing of Government services to meet the needs of those who need it most; combined with a restoration of confidence in our Government's ability to handle both fiscal, monetary, and administrative affairs. And there are times when those are in conflict. But we now have 10 years of inflation that's averaged about 6 1/2 percent, and I think that almost every economist, even those who think we might have a recession next year, agrees that we have got to cut down on the inflation rate.

MR. MOYERS: Some of your people this morning were telling me that they sense a new attitude on your part, a new spirit of confidence. And they attribute it to the fact that in your mind you've made some very tough decisions on the inflation front and are going to stick with them. Is that true? Are their perceptions accurate?

THE PRESIDENT: I don't feel that I'm more confident or more aggressive or more sure of myself than I was before. We've made some difficult decisions ever since I've been in office. It seems to me, almost daily, difficult decisions have had to be made. But, obviously, the longer I'm in office, the more I'm aware of the needs. I understand the Government structure better. I know more of the leaders both within Washington and outside Washington who help to shape our Nation's policies and shape its future.

We've now finished the 95th Congress work. I think they passed about 6 or 700 bills which help to clarify my own programs. We're trying to take advantage of what the Congress has decided, and I think I'm certainly more aware of and more sure of the opportunities and limitations of the Presidency itself.

MR. MOYERS: What have you learned about this town?

THE PRESIDENT: I like Washington very much. We came here as newcomers.

MR. MOYERS: To say the least.

THE PRESIDENT: To say the least. I didn't know the congressional leaders. I didn't know the news media representatives, except those who followed me in the campaign. Neither did they know me. I had a lot to learn about the bureaucratic structure of the Government. I was not privy of course to secrets involving national defense or international relations, and I really spent 18 months or so not only as a President but also as a student trying to learn what I didn't know before.

There have been no serious disappointments on my part. I told some news people the other night at a supper at the Mansion that there were two things that had been unpleasant surprises. One was the inertia of Congress, the length of time it takes to get a complicated piece of legislation through the Congress, and the other was the irresponsibility of the press.

MR. MOYERS: Irresponsibility of the press?

THE PRESIDENT: Yes.

MR. MOYERS: What do you mean?

THE PRESIDENT: Well, quite often news reports have been inaccurate when I think a simple checking of the facts with a telephone call or a personal inquiry could have prevented a serious distortion of the news. And also there's a sense of doubt or even cynicism about the Government and about programs or proposals, brought about I'm sure by the Vietnam experience, of the fact that the public was misled during Watergate and perhaps even the CIA, as I mentioned earlier.

But I think that a lot of that was caused by my relative inaccessibility and by the lack of knowledge on my part of the press and vice versa. And in the last few months we've taken steps to make sure that we understand each other better, so that I have an ability and my Cabinet Members have an ability to present the facts clearer to the American people through the press, and vice versa.

MR. MOYERS: Is this the work of your media czar, Mr. Rafshoon? What did he tell you about how to get the message out?

THE PRESIDENT: Well, it was a common belief that all of us had that we needed to have a clearer access to the public through the press in an undistorted way, a truthful way, not to try to cover up any mistakes we made, and also to have it understood among those who report the news that they can have access to me or to Jody Powell or to Hamilton Jordan or members of the Cabinet or others if there is a question that arises approaching a deadline, that they can make a telephone call and say, "Is this or is this not accurate?"

We all recognize the devastating consequences of ever making a misleading statement or telling a falsehood, because our credibility would be damaged. And we've bent over backwards (not) to do that. But I think that we've made some progress in this respect.

And I understand the Congress a lot better now. I know the speed with which legislation can be expected to move through the Congress. I understand the complexities of the committee system, the interrelationships between the House and the Senate.

And also I think we're doing a much better job in letting the press have access to the facts.

MR. MOYERS: The hour is past. Should we stop?

THE PRESIDENT: I think perhaps we'd better, if the hour's over.

MR. MOYERS: Well, on behalf of Public Broadcasting, I thank you for your time.

THE PRESIDENT: Thank you, Bill.

NOTE: The interview began at 1:30 p.m. in the Oval Office at the White House. It was taped for later broadcast on the Public Broadcasting Service.

11

ENERGY, JUNE 1, 1979

Public Papers of the Presidents, John Dancy

The topic of this interview is one of the most frequently discussed but frustrating issues dealt with by Carter. A unified national energy policy was a major initiative of his administration. He assumed an energy bill would pass early but it did not. He made so many energy speeches that the American public grew tired of hearing them. Finally, a watered down energy bill passed in October of 1978.—*Editor*

MR. DANCY: Mr. President, you've been meeting with oilmen this past week to get firsthand information from them on the shortages. I'd like to hear from you what we can expect in terms of supplies in June, July, and August.

THE PRESIDENT: I'm meeting with both the oil people and also consumers and other groups.

We have a permanent problem with oil supplies. We lost 200 million barrels of oil because of the problems in Iran. The last 2 weeks, oil imports have increased somewhat.

We believe that in the summer, we'll be better off than we were in May, which was perhaps our worst month, but even at best, in the summer, we're going to have no more oil or gasoline than we had a year ago. And demand for gasoline, because of more automobiles and a lack of conservation ethic or commitment, is going to cause some continued shortages.

We have relieved the spot shortages, I think, to some degree in California, primarily because of the small increase in supply and also because of strong conservation efforts made by the people of California.

From *Public Papers of the Presidents,* Jimmy Carter, June 1, 1979.

MR. DANCY: Let's talk about that demand problem for just a moment. The latest NBC News–AP poll shows that 65 percent of the people in the country simply don't believe that there is a gasoline shortage. Is there a shortage in this country?

THE PRESIDENT: Yes. In April of 1977, more than 2 years ago, I proposed to the Congress a comprehensive energy policy for the first time in the history of our Nation. After 18 months of tough debate and argument, the Congress passed not one bit of legislation concerning oil. It's that difficult.

The Congress hears from the special interest groups, particularly the oil lobby. They very seldom hear from the American people. We have now come back to the Congress with a package that will work—slow, steady, carefully monitored decontrol of oil to get the Government out of it and to let the free enterprise system work, which will improve conservation, increase domestic exploration and production, and also open up an opportunity to decrease imports and dependence on foreign supplies. There will be some increase in the price of oil and gas inevitably, no matter what we do.

So, we're going to tax the oil companies very heavily—they can keep 29 cents out of every dollar—with a windfall profits tax. The windfall profits tax will go into an energy security fund. That fund will grow year by year because of increase in OPEC prices and because of increase in prices on domestic oil because of its shortage.

That energy reserve fund, or security fund, will be used to alleviate the heavy burden on the poor families of our country, to improve mass transit, which we need, and to provide a reservoir of money for research and development to develop other sources of energy—solar power, geothermal, gasification, liquefaction of coal.

The essence of it is this: If the American people will work together and accept the fact that we do have too much demand for limited supplies of energy, our country is strong enough to resolve the problem. We have the capability to resolve the problem. But we've got to face it frankly, and we've got to work together.

MR. DANCY: But people are skeptical about this. And one reason seems to be that the crisis appears and disappears mysteriously. One week there's a gasoline shortage in California. The Governor of California comes here and talks to you, and you say that, "Well, the situation is going to get better." And the next day Jody Powell says, "Well, it's not going to get all that much better." How can people know what to believe?

THE PRESIDENT: Sometimes people don't want to face an unpleasant fact. That's a characteristic of my own, and it's a characteristic of the American people as well.

May was a very bad month. In the latter part of last month, May, we did have an increase in imports of oil. The California people helped a great deal, because they recognized the problem. Perhaps at first they overreacted to it, but eventually they began to use more rapid transit, they began to share automobiles, they began to observe the 55-mile-per-hour speed limit. The odd-even days imposed by Governor Brown helped to some degree, and the problem was partially alleviated.

The problem is not going away. Even at the best of circumstances in June or July, we are still going to have less gasoline available in California than they had a year ago. So, it won't be good. It will be better than it was in May.

MR. DANCY: Mr. President, the poll also shows that 55 percent of the people don't believe that you or the Congress are doing a good job of managing this gasoline shortage. How do you restore, you and the Congress, restore some faith in your leadership?

THE PRESIDENT: That's a hard question to answer. I don't claim that the Government has done a good job with the energy problem; it hasn't. I would say last year, the Congress passed about 65 percent of the legislation that I had put forward 2 years ago on energy. We have not yet had the political courage or ability to deal with oil. We're not only the world's greatest consumer and waster of oil, we're also one of the world's largest producers of oil, and the oil lobby is extremely powerful in Washington. And it's been difficult to deal with this subject.

If the people ever get aroused enough to demand action, there's no doubt in my mind that the Congress will act. I think we have an excellent chance now to get the windfall profits tax passed, which will discourage waste, encourage production in America, and set up a reserve fund to explore other sources of energy. If this is done, it'll be a major step forward. And I think under those circumstances, the people will begin to see that the Government is doing its best.

We don't have a good record at all so far. But part of their need is for people to realize that we do indeed have a problem, that we can solve it if we work together, and that they will encourage the Congress to act.

MR. DANCY: Do you believe that the debate over energy has become so political, so highly emotional that when people vote against, say, the standby rationing plan, for example, they are, in effect, voting against you and against your leadership?

THE PRESIDENT: I don't interpret it as a personal attack on me or a rejection of leadership. It's an inability or unwillingness to deal with an unpleasant subject.

The problem is with us on a permanent basis. We're going to have to quit wasting oil; we're going to have to increase American production; we're going to have to decrease imports from foreign countries; we're going to have to shift toward more use of rapid transit; we're going to have to shift toward more research and development of other sources of energy to replace oil. Those are facts. You can't get away from them. And I think we've made a tremendous amount of progress in the last 2 years, because there's a growing awareness that we do indeed have a problem.

Now we're in a phase of trying to find an easy way out or trying to find a scapegoat to blame for the problem. But if we all work together, as I say, our country is strong enough and able enough to deal with this problem and not let it become a crisis.

MR. DANCY: You've been trying to build up supplies of home heating oil, I know.

THE PRESIDENT: Yes.

MR. DANCY: And one way that you have done that is the Government has offered the oil companies a $5-a-barrel subsidy in order to encourage them to go into the world market and buy that oil and import it so that we'll have enough heating oil in the wintertime. But our European Common Market allies now say that this is bad, because it is shifting the problem to them and it's raising the world price of heating oil.

How do you answer this criticism?

THE PRESIDENT: We've had two shortages identified recently, in addition to the one that you've described. One was tractor fuel to get our crops planted. I think we successfully weathered that potential crisis period. We were planting as much as 5 million acres of crops per day, and we didn't have any serious spot shortages, because the Governors—Republicans and Democrats—the Agriculture Department, the Energy Department, and the White House worked together on it.

We have another potential shortage next winter, and that is with home heating oil. I have committed myself to build up reserve supplies of home heating oil so that our people, in the Northeast, particularly, won't go cold this winter.

We were having a problem because some refineries that make home heating oil, say, in the Caribbean, because of high prices in Europe, were shifting that oil to Europe when we should have had access to buy it for American homeowners.

So, we did try to impose and did impose a difference in the price to make us competitive in that market. The Europeans didn't like part of what we did, but I think it'll help us to alleviate that potential crisis.

MR. DANCY: Gasoline prices were the leading cause last month of the big jump in the cost of living in the country. Isn't there a great danger in all of that for your anti-inflation program?

THE PRESIDENT: Yes. I might point out that this increase in price that we've experienced has been under so-called Government controls, and the slow, carefully monitored, phased out Government controls, I think, will help to alleviate the problem over the long run. We'll still have a problem; it'll help with it.

Obviously, the price of energy is something that I cannot control. We can do our best to alleviate the problem.

We have been asked by the OPEC nations, who have been the cause of the great increase in prices, to cut back on waste and consumption. Our European allies look at Americans using twice as much oil per person as they do, with the same standard of living, and say, "Please cut back on waste and on the consumption of oil."

I'll be meeting with the leaders of six major nations, democratic nations, in Tokyo, the last of this month, and that will be one of the high, important points on the agenda. How can the consuming nations reduce our demand for imported oil in return for which the OPEC nations would agree to stabilize supply and also to stabilize prices? This has to be a multinational approach. It's one of the greatest responsibilities on my shoulders, as a leader of a great nation, and also on the shoulders of others who represent the major consuming nations.

We've not yet successfully addressed it. We have to be courageous and tenacious, we have to tell the people the truth, the people have to believe the truth, and we have to work together. There is no magic answer to a very difficult question.

MR. DANCY: Finally, the poll does show that there is a rising awareness of the energy problem. When people were asked about it, they now place it number two behind inflation as one of their concerns. I would assume that you find that encouraging.

THE PRESIDENT: Yes, I do find it encouraging, but also I think it illustrates vividly that the two are tied together. As long as we have excessive demand for a given level of supply of energy, it creates enormous increase in prices, and those prices for oil and for other sources of energy wind up increasing prices for almost every product that we use. So, successfully addressing the energy question will take us a great step down the road to successfully solving the chronic inflation problem.

MR. DANCY: Mr. President, thank you very much.

THE PRESIDENT: Thank you, John.

NOTE: The interview began at 11:35 a.m. in the Oval Office at the White House. It was taped for broadcast on the NBC television network on June 3.

The transcript of the interview was released on June 2.

12

INTERVIEW WITH THE PRESIDENT, JAN. 7, 1980

Public Papers of the Presidents, John Chancellor

The following excerpts from the Chancellor interview deal with foreign policy matters. Parts of this interview were broadcast on NBC later that week.—*Editor*

MR. CHANCELLOR: Well, specifically, sir, I was wondering about aid, military aid, to Pakistan.

THE PRESIDENT: Yes. This is a commitment that I am ready to make. We have already assured President Zia, who's the leader of Pakistan, directly with a telephone communication from me the day, very shortly after the invasion, and since then through emissaries, that we're willing to join other nations in giving necessary protection to Pakistan and meet their legitimate defensive military needs. This is not a threat to India, an adjacent country, but it's an ability for Pakistan to repel invasion if it should occur and particularly to let Pakistan be known as a strong nation able to protect themselves, so that a possible invasion will be prevented.

MR. CHANCELLOR: Have there been any specific communications within the last 48 hours on this between yourself and General Zia or the two governments involved?

THE PRESIDENT: Through diplomatic emissaries, yes; not directly between me and Zia.

MR. CHANCELLOR: Are you able to expand on that, Mr. President, about the amount of aid or how it would be delivered or what it would be?

From *Public Papers of the Presidents,* Jimmy Carter, Jan. 7, 1980.

THE PRESIDENT: No. There are three factors that have to be considered. One is the degree to which other nations will join in with us in providing economic and military aid; secondly, the amount of aid and the specific form of it that the Pakistanis would like to have; and thirdly, of course, I'll have to go to the Congress to get authorization to provide the American portion of the aid that's decided to be given to Pakistan.

MR. CHANCELLOR: Can you tell us what other countries might also be supplying aid to Pakistan?

THE PRESIDENT: I think it would be better to let them speak for themselves.

MR. CHANCELLOR: Would they be Western, industrialized countries?

THE PRESIDENT: Yes, mostly, and also some of the Mideast countries perhaps, who have the wealth and the ability to help to finance part of the aid.

MR. CHANCELLOR: So you're really putting together a package of aid for Pakistan.

THE PRESIDENT: Yes. Some people call it a consortium. I don't want to predict at this point what other nations might do, because the evolution of this so-called consortium is still in the embryonic stage, but we want to accommodate Pakistan's needs. And obviously, with our complete absence, some of the regional countries are obviously consulting with one another and will help themselves individually.

MR. CHANCELLOR: Somalia, Oman, and Kenya have offered us the use of naval and air facilities. Will the United States accept any of those offers?

THE PRESIDENT: Yes, we're considering the use of some of those facilities. We don't have any definite agreement yet, but that's the kind of thing that I think is important to our Nation to prepare for the long-range meeting of any threat to the peace in the Mideast–Persian Gulf–northern Indian Ocean area.

MR. CHANCELLOR: Mr. President, as a journalist it sometimes seems to me as though the Soviet Union, which will become a net importer of petroleum during the 1980's, is really going for the Persian Gulf. They're trying to control that part of the world. Is that your view?

THE PRESIDENT: I think that's one of the factors that we believe is extant. No one can know what the Soviets' plans might be, but I think we've got to be prepared for that eventuality, and the best way to prepare for it is to prevent its occurrence. The arousing of world opinion to recognize the threat that the Soviets project to that area of the world is an important first step, particularly the marshaling of common condemnation of the Soviets for what they've already done. The strengthening of countries in the area that might be threatened, so that they can repel any potential invasion, is another very important element. And I think the third thing is to make sure that our own country realizes that we've got a long-range commitment to be made and that the responsibility and the sacrifice economically to prepare for it must be shared by all of us.

One of the important elements involved in the question you asked is the Soviets' need to produce more of their oil and gas. High technology is an element of that. And the punitive aspects of a partial trade embargo against the Soviet Union for those very valuable items is a cautionary message to the Soviet Union that I think they are perfectly able to read and must read.

MR. CHANCELLOR: Could I ask you about Iran, sir, and where we stand now in terms of the hostages?

THE PRESIDENT: We've always had a few basic principles to guide me since I've been involved in meeting this absolutely illegal and abhorrent act. One is to protect the long-range interests of our country; secondly, to protect the lives and the well-being of the hostages; third, to seek their release; fourth, to avoid bloodshed if possible, but still to protect our interests if necessary; and lastly, to make sure that a strong majority of the nations of the world understand that Iran is a criminal actor in this process and that we are the aggrieved party, and to keep world support for our position.

We've had four votes in the United Nations Security Council. We've not had a negative vote yet; we've only had four abstentions. When we took our case to the International Court of Justice, the vote was 15 to nothing in favor of our position.

And I think that Iran must realize—there are some responsible people in Iran—and the world must realize that Iran is at this moment involved in a criminal act, a terrorist act. And it's not a matter of negotiating on a diplomatic basis between two nations. This is a matter of condemning Iran for international terrorism and for kidnaping. And I think those purposes that I've described are and will be our basic principles until those hostages are home safe.

MR. CHANCELLOR: If some Americans are put on trial in "show trials," what would your reaction be to that?

THE PRESIDENT: I would rather not give specifics, but we are prepared to take action that would be quite serious in its consequences for Iran.

MR. CHANCELLOR: And I can't draw any further details on that out of you today, sir?

THE PRESIDENT: No, I don't think it would be good to go into details.

NOTE: The interview began at 4:10 p.m. in the Oval Office at the White House. NBC News broadcast portions of the interview during the week. ·

13

MEET THE PRESS, JAN. 20, 1980

Public Papers of the Presidents,
Bill Monroe, Carl Rowan, David Broder
& Judy Woodruff

This interview took place at the beginning of the campaign for the 1980 presidential election one day before the Iowa caucuses. Carter had refused to campaign in Iowa and was accused of participating in this interview for political gain in a forum in which he could not be challenged by his opponents. The questions are hard-hitting and cover many aspects of foreign and domestic developments. This interview was broadcast live from NBC studios in Washington, D.C., on both NBC Radio and Television.—*Editor*

MR. MONROE: Our guest today on "Meet the Press" is the President of the United States, Jimmy Carter.

Mr. President, assuming the Soviets do not pull out of Afghanistan any time soon, do you favor the U.S. participating in the Moscow Olympics and, if not, what are the alternatives?

THE PRESIDENT: No. Neither I nor the American people would support the sending of an American team to Moscow with Soviet invasion troops in Afghanistan. I've sent a message today to the United States Olympic Committee spelling out my own position: that unless the Soviets withdraw their troops within a month from Afghanistan, that the Olympic games be moved from Moscow to an alternate site or multiple sites or postponed or canceled. If the Soviets do not withdraw their troops immediately from Afghanistan within a month, I would not support the sending of an American team to the Olympics. It's very important for the world to realize how serious a threat the Soviets' invasion of Afghanistan is.

From *Public Papers of the Presidents,* Jimmy Carter, Jan. 20, 1980.

I do not want to inject politics into the Olympics, and I would personally favor the establishment of a permanent Olympic site for both the summer and the winter games. In my opinion, the most appropriate permanent site for the summer games would be Greece. This will be my own position, and I have asked the U.S. Olympic Committee to take this position to the International Olympic Committee, and I would hope that as many nations as possible would support this basic position. One hundred and four nations voted against the Soviet invasion and called for their immediate withdrawal from Afghanistan in the United Nations, and I would hope as many of those as possible would support the position I've just outlined to you.

MR. MONROE: Mr. President, if a substantial number of nations does not support the U.S. position, would not that just put the U.S. in an isolated position, without doing much damage to the Soviet Union?

THE PRESIDENT: Regardless of what other nations might do, I would not favor the sending of an American Olympic team to Moscow while the Soviet invasion troops are in Afghanistan.

MR. MONROE: Thank you, Mr. President. Our reporters on "Meet the Press" today are Carl T. Rowan of the *Chicago Sun-Times,* David S. Broder of the *Washington Post,* and Judy Woodruff of NBC News. We'll be back with our questions in a minute.

[*At this point, the program was interrupted for a commercial announcement. Mr. Monroe then resumed speaking as follows:*]

We'll continue the questions for President Carter with Mr. Rowan.

MR. ROWAN: Mr. President, you spoke earlier of a serious threat to peace. Just how serious is this situation? Are we potentially on the verge of conflict with the Soviet Union?

THE PRESIDENT: As I said earlier, Mr. Rowan, this in my opinion is the most serious threat to world peace since the Second World War. It's an unprecedented act on the part of the Soviet Union. It's the first time they have attacked, themselves, a nation that was not already under their domination, that is, a part of the Warsaw Pact neighborhood. They have used surrogate forces, the Cubans, to participate in other countries like Angola or Ethiopia.

This is a threat to a vital area of the world. It's a threat to an area of the world where the interests of our country and those interests of our allies are deeply imbedded. More than two-thirds of the total exportable oil that supplies the rest of the world comes from the Persian Gulf region in Southwest Asia.

My own assessment is that there have been times in the years gone by that we have had intense competition with the Soviet Union and also an effort for accommodation with the Soviet Union and for consulting with them and working with them toward peace. This is an action initiated by the Soviets—and I am still committed to peace, but peace through strength and through letting the Soviets know in a clear and certain way, by action of our own country and other nations, that they cannot invade an innocent country with impunity; they must suffer the consequences.

MR. ROWAN: In that connection, Mr. President, your critics say that the Soviets are moving because they've seen weakness on your part. They don't believe you or the American people will fight. If they move into Pakistan or into Iran, will you use military force?

THE PRESIDENT: We've not been weak. We've been firm and resolved and consistent and clear in our policy since I've been in the White House. We've had a steady increase in our commitment to the strength of our national defense, as measured by budget levels and also measured by the tone and actions that I have taken and the Congress has taken. We've strengthened our alliances with NATO, both in the buildup of fighting capability and also, lately, in the theater nuclear force response to the Soviet threat with atomic weapons. We've also let it be clear that we favor the resolution of intense differences that have destabilized the Middle East and the Persian Gulf region.

The most notable advance has been the peace treaty signed between Israel and Egypt, and we have reconfirmed our commitment to Pakistan of 1959. We are committed to consult with Pakistan and to take whatever action is necessary, under the constitutional guidelines that I have to follow as President of our country, to protect the security of Pakistan involving military force, if necessary.

In addition to that, we're increasing and will maintain an increased level of naval forces in the northern Indian Ocean and the Persian Gulf region. And we are now exploring with some intensity the establishment of facilities for the servicing of our air and naval forces in the northern Indian Ocean, Persian Gulf region. These actions have been initiated ever since I've been in office. They are consistent and clear, and we are concentrating on them now with an increased level of commitment because of the Soviet invasion of Afghanistan.

MR. MONROE: Mr. Broder?

MR. BRODER: Mr. President, the timing of this appearance the day before the Iowa caucuses suggests a political motive. Why did you accept this appearance when you have refused to appear any place where your challengers could confront you directly?

THE PRESIDENT: Mr. Broder, in a time of crisis for our country I believe it's very important for the President not to assume, in a public way, the role of a partisan campaigner in a political contest. Our country is in a state of crisis, and this has been a consistent policy that I have maintained since the Iranians captured and held hostage Americans in Tehran. I do not consider this to be a campaign forum, "Meet the Press," and I'm not here as a partisan candidate.

As you well know, we have been presenting my views very clearly to the American people in multiple ways—my own appearances before the press, my briefing of groups in the White House, the sending of surrogates for me to Iowa. I think my positions and the actions that I've taken have been very clear, and my appearance on this show is an opportunity to give you, for instance, a chance to ask me questions about issues that are important to the American people.

MR. BRODER: A colleague of mine printed this question 3 weeks ago, at the time that you canceled out of the Iowa debate, as an example of what you might have been asked, and I'd like to ask it.

THE PRESIDENT: Fine.

MR. BRODER: With all due respect, we still have 5.8 percent unemployment. Inflation has risen from 4.8 percent to 13 percent. We still don't have a viable energy policy. Russian troops are in Cuba and Afghanistan. The dollar is falling. Gold is rising. And the hostages, after 78 days, are still in Tehran. Just what have you done, sir, to deserve renomination?

THE PRESIDENT: Well, since I've been in the White House, I've done everything possible to strengthen our own Nation, not only militarily but economically and politically and, I think, morally and ethically as well. We've strengthened our alliances with our allies, which has been pointed out already on this program. We've dealt not only with peace for our country but peace for others, working with the British in Rhodesia, working with the Egyptians and Israelis in the Middle East.

We have tried to expand American friendships among other nations on Earth, notably being successful in retaining our friendship with the people of Taiwan, opening up a new and friendly relationship with the recognition of a fourth of the world's total population in China. We've had, I think, a great improvement in our own Nation's relationships with countries, as expressed by recent United Nations votes.

Domestically, I've dealt with the Nation's crises and problems as best I could, working with a Congress that sometimes acts too slowly. Since the first day I've been in office, we've been addressing the most serious threat to our Nation domestically, and that is inflation, tied very closely with energy.

Energy is the single most important factor in the increase in the inflation rate since I've been in office. Just in the last 12 months, OPEC has increased energy prices by 80 percent. As a matter of fact, all of the increase, for practical purposes, of the inflation rate since I've been in office has been directly attributable to increase in OPEC oil prices.

When I was elected, the prime threat to our country was extremely high unemployment. We've added a net increase of 9 million jobs, and we've cut the unemployment rate down by 25 percent. This has been a very good move toward the strengthening of our Nation's economy. We've cut down our balance of trade deficit. We have seen a very clear increase in net income for Americans above inflation, above taxes paid, of about 7 1/2 percent. Corporate profits have gone up about 50 percent. And I think our Nation is much more unified. And I believe, in addition to that, there's a greater respect for the integrity and the truthfulness of the Government of our country. So, we've made some progress.

I might say that I don't claim to know all the answers. They are not easy questions to address. They are not easy problems to solve. But our country is united. We are struggling with these very difficult and complicated questions, and I think that they need to be pursued further, hopefully in a second term for myself.

MR. MONROE: Ms. Woodruff?

MS. WOODRUFF: Mr. President, you said in an interview recently that the invasion of Afghanistan had changed your opinions of the Russians more drastically than anything else since you had been in office. Why did it take almost 3 years for you to discover the true intentions of the Soviet leadership?

THE PRESIDENT: I've never doubted the long-range policy or the long-range ambitions of the Soviet Union. The fact that we have consistently strengthened our own Nation's defense, after 15 years of a decrease in commitment to our Nation's defense vis-à-vis the Soviets, is one indication of that. All of the actions that I described earlier—the strengthening of NATO, the movement into the northern Indian Ocean, the search for peace in the Mideast, and so forth—were directly because of the ultimate threat by the Soviet Union to world peace.

But it is obvious that the Soviets' actual invasion of a previously nonaligned country, an independent, freedom-loving country, a deeply religious country, with their own massive troops is a radical departure from the policy or actions that the Soviets have pursued since the Second World War. It is a direct threat because Pakistan [Afghanistan],* formerly a buffer state between the Soviet Union and Iran and the world's oil supplies and the Hormuz Straits and the Persian Gulf, has now become kind of an arrow aiming at those crucial strategic regions of the world. So, this is a major departure by the Soviet Union from their previous actions.

Their long-range policies have been well understood by me then and still are.

MS. WOODRUFF: And yet your administration didn't take any steps to offset the huge increases in the number of Cuban troops in Africa in recent years. Soviet combat troops are still in Cuba today, despite your statement last fall that their presence was not acceptable. In light of this failure to counter Soviet aggression earlier, do you accept any responsibility at all for the Soviet calculation that they could move into Afghanistan with impunity?

THE PRESIDENT: Well, the Soviets have seriously misjudged our own Nation's strength and resolve and unity and determination and the condemnation that has accrued to them by the world community because of their invasion of Afghanistan. As you know, Cuban troops went into Angola long before I became President. And the Soviet brigade, about 2,000 to 2,500 troops, have been in Cuba since the early 1960's. There has obviously been a buildup in the Soviet adventurism in the Horn of Africa, in Ethiopia. These moves were of great concern to us.

But the point that I would like to make clear is that we have always had a very complicated relationship with the Soviet Union— based on cooperation when we could together move toward a peaceful resolution of the world's problems, like the negotiation of the SALT treaty, and competition with the Soviet Union when our interests were at cross purposes in any region of the world. I think our strength has been clearly demonstrated. The resolve of our Nation has been clearly demonstrated. The support of our allies has been clearly demonstrated, and indeed, the support of the world in the condemnation of the Soviets' recent invasion has also been clearly demonstrated.

---

*White House correction.

Times change and circumstances change. Our country has been one that does commit itself to the preservation of peace, but peace through strength, not weakness. That has been our policy. That will still be our policy.

MR. MONROE: Mr. President, is there any specific new hope for ending the hostage crisis with Iran?

THE PRESIDENT: I can't predict the early end of that situation. The concern that I feel about the hostages today is just as great as it was a month ago or 2 months ago. Our policy on the Iranian capturing of our hostages has been clear and consistent. It's an abhorrent violation of every moral and ethical standard and international law. It's a criminal act: a group of terrorists, kidnapers, seizing innocent victims and holding them for attempted blackmail in an unprecedented way, supported and encouraged by government officials themselves. Our response has been clear: to protect, first of all, the short-term and long-range interests of our country; secondly, to protect the safety and the lives of the hostages themselves; third, to pursue every possible avenue of the early and safe release of our hostages; fourth, to avoid bloodshed if possible, because I have felt from the very beginning that the initiation of a military action or the causing of bloodshed would undoubtedly result in the death of the hostages; and fifth, and perhaps most difficult of all, is to arouse and to sustain the strong support by the vast majority of nations on Earth for our position as an aggrieved nation and the condemnation of the world for Iran for this direct violation of international law. It's an abhorrent act.

I don't know when the hostages will be released, but we will maintain our intense interest in it. We will maintain our commitment to every possible avenue to carry out the policies I've just described to you, and we will maintain, as best we can, the full support of the rest of the world. And that concerted pressure from many sources, including the recent sanctions that we have initiated against Iran, I believe and I hope and I pray will result in the safe release of our hostages. I can't predict exactly when.

MR. MONROE: How do you answer criticism, Mr. President, that your administration bungled the admission of the Shah to this country, chiefly by not providing guaranteed protection to the American Embassy in Iran after American diplomats had warned that there might be this kind of trouble and there had been, in fact, a seizure of the Embassy a few months previously?

THE PRESIDENT: I don't have any apology at all for letting the Shah come here as an extremely sick person—

MR. MONROE: What about protection of the Embassy, Mr. President?

THE PRESIDENT: —for treatment. The Embassy had been attacked in the past. Embassies around the world are often subjected to attacks. In every instance the Iranian officials had joined with our own people to protect the Embassy of the United States. Following the seizure of the Embassy earlier in the year, we had carried out a substantial program for the strengthening of the Embassy's defenses. After the Shah came here to the United States for treatment, and we notified the Iranian officials of that fact, we were again assured by the Iranian Prime Minister and the Iranian Foreign Minister that the Embassy would be protected. It was, indeed, protected for about 10 days, following which the Ayatollah Khomeini made a very aggressive and abusive speech. And when it was attacked by militant terrorists, the Iranians, the Iranian Government withdrew their protection for the Embassy. It was an unpredictable kind of thing. This has never been done, so far as I know, in modern history, to have a government support a terrorist act of this kind, the kidnaping of hostages, and the holding of them for attempted blackmail.

But there was no stone unturned in our attempt to maintain relations with Iran, which is in our interest, and at the same time to protect our people.

MR. MONROE: Mr. Rowan?

MR. ROWAN: Mr. President, some of our allies are now saying that Iran already is in chaos and that if the U.S. puts the economic screws on, that country could fall apart and make it easy for the Soviet Union to pick up the pieces. Are you listening to this or are you still going to put the screws on Iran?

THE PRESIDENT: That's been a constant concern of mine, Mr. Rowan.

What we want is a unified Iran, not fragmented. We want a stable and independent Iran, and we want a secure Iran. But we cannot accept the abhorrent act, supported by the Iranian officials, of the terrorists holding Americans hostage. We have decided to take action against Iran, with the presence of our naval forces to prevent injury to our hostages; and secondly, to impose, with an increasing degree of severity, sanctions against Iran that would encourage them to release the hostages.

There has been, obviously, a new element introduced into the Iranian hostage crisis in recent weeks with the Soviet invasion of Afghanistan. My belief is that many of the responsible officials in Iran now see that this major threat to Iran's security and the peace of Iran is becoming paramount, and that there will be an additional effort on their part to secure the release of the hostages and remove the isolation of Iran from the rest of the civilized world.

But I think our actions have been well considered. We have taken every element of caution about the possibility which you describe. And in my judgment, the best thing for Iran to do now is to release the hostages, to seek redress of their alleged grievances in the international fora and the courts of the individual nations, and to begin to strengthen themselves against the possible threat by the Soviets now addressed toward them in Afghanistan.

MR. MONROE: We have less than a minute and a half. Mr. Broder?

MR. BRODER: In view of what you just said, Mr. President, are you prepared to accept a delay or postponement of the imposition of the economic sanctions against Iran?

THE PRESIDENT: No. Those sanctions will be pursued by ourselves, unilaterally, and joined in by as many of our allies as will agree. We have had very acceptable support by our allies in this imposition of sanctions against Iran, and we've had overwhelming support in the International Court of Justice and in the United Nations from many nations who've observed this situation. So, I will not postpone the imposition of sanctions.

MR. MONROE: Ms. Woodruff?

MS. WOODRUFF: Mr. President, in 1976 you castigated the Republicans for what you described as a "misery index" of some 13 percent. That "misery index" is now up to 19 percent. What do you think about it now?

THE PRESIDENT: Well, obviously, when a nation is in a state of crisis—a deep obsession and concern with the holding of innocent Americans and an acknowledged threat to world peace by a Soviet invasion of Afghanistan, with high inflation brought about by, in my opinion, unwarranted increases in the price of oil—this preys on the mind of Americans. We are taking action, as I've described on this program and previously, to alleviate these concerns, and I believe that the unity of America has been paramount. I believe the future will hold a better prospect for the alleviation of those tensions.

MR. MONROE: Thank you, Mr. President, for being with us today on "Meet the Press."

NOTE: The interview began at 12 p.m. in the NBC studios in Washington, D.C. It was broadcast live on radio and television. Mr. Monroe of NBC News was the moderator for the program. Following the interview, the President returned to Camp David, Md.

14

MR. PRESIDENT, AUG. 10, 1980

60 Minutes, Dan Rather

In this conversation, Rather probes some of the more sensitive areas of the first three and a half years of the Carter administration. Specific issues raised by Rather include: the economy (inflation was running at 14.8 percent); energy; the Billy Carter/Libya affair; the Iranian hostage situation; Afghanistan (an area in which Rather had personal experience); and the Olympic boycott. Finally, Rather persuades Carter to grade himself on foreign policy, domestic policy, energy, the economy, and leadership.—*Editor*

RATHER: To the world, Jimmy Carter is a President in some serious trouble with some very large problems: the hostages, Afghanistan, the economy, his brother Billy, his low standing in the polls, the lack of enthusiasm for him by leaders of his own party. And yet, you walk into the Oval Office of the White House, as I did last Friday, and you find a man seemingly unperturbed. Nothing to worry about. Every incumbent President is under some kind of siege. It goes with the territory, he'll tell you. There is no mistaking what the President is saying. Anybody who raises the possibility that Jimmy Carter can't beat Ronald Reagan is talking through his hat. More than that, so is anyone who raises the possibility that Jimmy Carter may not be his party's nominee.

Mister President, the convention is about to begin. Is there any doubt in your mind that you'll be the nominee?

PRESIDENT CARTER: No, there's no doubt in my mind that I will be the nominee.

RATHER: If I may, I'd like to follow up on that, because we may find ourselves at some disagreement. I brought along the latest CBS tally of delegates.

PRESIDENT CARTER: Yes.

RATHER: We try to stay in touch with the delegates, have over the period of this campaign, and I'm told that just today our compilation is that 429 Carter delegates told CBS News they disapprove of the way you're handling the economy, 241 Carter delegates said they disapprove of how you're handling foreign policy, and 113 Carter delegates disapprove of how you're handling your job in general.

PRESIDENT CARTER: When you quote those figures, they sound very impressive, but you have to remember that you're talking about a total of more than 3,000 delegates, a substantial majority of whom—about 60 percent—support me. And although someone might disapprove of something that I do with foreign policy or the economy or the rate of inflation and so forth, the fact that they prefer me above other candidates in the Democratic Party—and certainly against any Republican—is a significant thing. We don't claim to be perfect. We've made some mistakes in the minds of many people. But I think that my prediction that I'll be the nominee will be carried out next Thursday.

RATHER: Because Mr. Carter is so confident that he is the choice of the majority of the delegates, last week there were Kennedy people clinging to the hope that he might somehow release all the delegates to vote as they please. No way will that happen, say his campaign manager and his chief of staff. But the issue is so crucial to the nomination, we decided to put it right to the President. Is there a possibility, despite the denials, that he would release his delegates?

PRESIDENT CARTER: No.

RATHER: Any chance of that happening at all?

PRESIDENT CARTER: None at all.

RATHER: None whatever?

PRESIDENT CARTER: No. We have had some of my very strong supporters point out to me, Dan, that if I should release the delegates, after their rule for loyalty and against the brokered convention is confirmed, that it would be a demonstration of strength. There is no doubt in my mind that if I release those delegates, they would still vote for me, 98 percent of them. They have signed a pledge to vote for me, and they would not violate their word of honor.

RATHER: Mister President, with all respect, let me make the opposite argument, which I know you've heard—but there are any number of people who make the following points, and included among these people are many who like you, support you, and still think you can win—make the argument: things change. The primaries covered many months. Many events have happened since then; people have changed their minds since then. Your own job rating in the polls is at an all-time low (indistinct) since the poll started. Leaders of your own party are concerned. So why not, whatever the—the moral principle may be as you see it, why not have an up-or-down vote of confidence at this convention?

PRESIDENT CARTER: We went through a long series of reforms to say that once the voters go to the polls and choose a nominee, later the delegate is chosen to represent that expression of support for a certain candidate—myself or Senator Kennedy or whoever—and then that delegate is supposed to go and accurately represent the voters. They are not my delegates. They are the people's delegates who are sending them.

RATHER: Mister President, surely you are aware that not only the leadership of the Democratic Party, but those Democrats who are running for offices from county judge up through state legislature, U.S. Representative, are as of this moment, many of them, absolutely petrified, that with you at the head of the ticket that it's going to be a wipe-out for the Democratic Party in November.

PRESIDENT CARTER: (laughs) Dan, that's a gross exaggeration.

RATHER: Is it?

PRESIDENT CARTER: Sure it's an exaggeration. It—I—you know, Democrats don't get petrified when poll results go up and down.

RATHER: I agree with you they do go up and down. They come and they go.

PRESIDENT CARTER: Sure they do.

RATHER: I think, number one, you would agree that, over the past year and a half's period, that while there have been ups and downs, that the trend for you has been down. Would you agree with that?

PRESIDENT CARTER: No.

RATHER: You would not?

PRESIDENT CARTER: Well, Dan, right now they're down, the polls are down. This time four years ago we were—we had an enormous lead over President Ford. And as you know, the final results in November were very close. Last October, September, November, when Senator Kennedy was deciding whether or not to run for President, the polls showed that if he should run, that I would be defeated by a margin of three or four to one. And many people who advised him very closely predicted to him that, if he ever should announce as a candidate, that I would probably withdraw and not even go into the contest since my prospects were so hopeless. So, at that time I was at an abysmal low.

The—the polls that count in a democratic society like ours are the polls that are conducted among the people on Election Day. There is no doubt in my mind that in November I will be elected President, because in my entire lifetime there has never been a sharper difference between two parties and two men than there will be in 1980. The only possible time that would even approach the significance of this election was when Barry Goldwater ran against Lyndon Johnson. That was a sharp difference. The same degree of difference, even an—a greater difference, exists in 1980.

RATHER: Mister President, I know that you'll agree that one of the major differences between this year's election and 1964 is that you have a record that you have to—to run on.

PRESIDENT CARTER: That's right.

RATHER: The—President Johnson was an incumbent of sorts in '64, but he did not have a long record at that time. Now, in your record— you promised that you'd have inflation down to 4 percent by the end of your first term. Fact is inflation is running—my last look was 14.8 annual inflation rate. You promised you'd have balanced budgets by the end of your first term. You haven't had a balanced budget any year; there's no balanced budget in sight. You promised that you would reform the tax system. You said that our tax system was—and I quote directly—that it's a "disgrace to the human race." Unquote. Tax system remains pretty much the same. You promised that you would reduce the number of federal agencies from 1,900 down to 200. There's still 1,500 federal agencies.

Now, it strikes me that any reasonable person looking at that record would say that's a record of ineffective leadership.

PRESIDENT CARTER: I think you'll find in the election months ahead that your prediction will not come true.

RATHER: I've been wrong before, as you know. (President Carter laughs)

PRESIDENT CARTER: Some of those things we attempted and could not accomplish. We've had a substantial increase in government—

government services. We've had a substantial reduction in the number of federal employees who deliver services to the American people. We've had a sharp reduction in the deficit that's been achieved between my own Administration and that of—of President Ford's. We've had consistent economic goals that we have achieved.

RATHER: When we pointed out a string of economic failures, the President referred us to his successes: in increasing jobs, cutting back on regulatory agencies, and paving the way for a revitalization of industry.

He said he thought he had done a good job in holding down inflation and interest rates, considering the way oil prices had skyrocketed since he took office. He then gave us a few sketchy details of his new economic plan, the one he mentioned briefly in his address last week to the convention of the National Urban League. It would, he said, take advantage of taxes on so-called windfall profits.

PRESIDENT CARTER: This is a $227 billion fund that's taken from the excess profits of the oil companies that will be invested in the conservation of energy, revitalization of our transportation system and the production of synthetic fuels and the production of energy from the solar power and from coal, and will create literally hundreds of thousands of jobs the first year, and millions of jobs over the next decade.

RATHER: Is it a coincidence, just a coincidence, that that's being proposed just before the convention?

PRESIDENT CARTER: No. This—this possibility for us to put into effect the benefits of the windfall profits tax—which, by the way, Governor Reagan wants to repeal and so-called "unleash," to quote him, the oil companies—has been the result of three years of hard work. And only this year, early this year, has it finally got to be a part of the American law and the American tax system.

RATHER: Let's get back to the convention and politics. Any chance that you would consider replacing Mr. Mondale as your vice presidential running mate?

PRESIDENT CARTER: No, none at all. I think Fritz Mondale is not only the best partner that a President ever had in this—in this office, but also the—the best Vice President.

RATHER: Under the provision of the Democratic charter to be adopted this week, under the charter, there's a provision that discrimination or prejudice based on sexual orientation is prohibited in all party affairs. Now, realistically, do you think all Democratic candidates in all portions of the country can run on that?

PRESIDENT CARTER: No. The Democratic Party and the candidates and the voters are so completely fragmented and disparate and—and—and are such strong individuals that each one would have a different approach to almost any part of the Democratic platform. And that's obviously one of those controversial issues, as is abortion, gun control, the Equal Rights Amendment, and so forth. So I don't think you could have unanimity on—among Democrats on any issue.

RATHER: Mister President, I do not wish to spend much time on the Billy Carter affair. I'm sorry. I know that you would like to spend a great deal of time on that at this particular time. (President Carter laughs) But in listening to you on Monday evening, it appeared to me that you were attempting to frame the issue incorrectly—perhaps not purposely so, but incorrectly—that you argued that Billy never influenced American policy on Libya.

PRESIDENT CARTER: Yes.

RATHER: Now, it seems to me that that's not really in dispute, but the issue is that you may have showed a lack of judgment in permitting Billy to lead the Libyans on when you should have and could have stopped him right away.

PRESIDENT CARTER: There are several issues. I think the most important issue was whether or not anyone in the White House or in my Administration had done anything illegal or improper, and the answer is that no one did. And the other question was whether Billy had any influence on me or whether he had any influence on anyone in the government, and the answer is he did not. And the third question is did he try to influence me relating to Libya, or anyone in the government, and the answer is that he did not.

RATHER: What did you do to let the Libyans know that Billy wouldn't have any influence on you whatsoever?

PRESIDENT CARTER: The Libyans, I think, were able to observe whether or not our policy changed with respect to the delivery of airplanes and so forth, and of course they saw that our policies did not change.

RATHER: In retrospect, might it have been a mistake not to have sent a message clearly, publicly, to the Libyans that if you have any idea that Billy has any influence with me, I want to make certain you understand that he does not. Looking back on it, would that not have been something that you should and could have done?

PRESIDENT CARTER: Dan, since your question is hypothetical in nature, let me give you a hypothetical answer. If I had known in March that Billy had received any sort of loan or payment or money in any fashion from the Libyans, then I should have done what you just described. Had—had I known that he had any sort of financial relationship with Libya, I would have made it clear to Billy and to Libya that this was a non-productive effort that might have been mounted by Libya.

RATHER: Mister President, have—have you suggested to Billy that he return that money forthwith to the Libyans?

PRESIDENT CARTER: I have not talked to Billy about Libya under any circumstances since the first day of July.

RATHER: Do you think it would be a good idea if he returned the money to Libya?

PRESIDENT CARTER: I think it would be, yes. The—the last thing I said in my press conference statement was that I was deeply concerned about Billy's receiving any money or favors from Libya and his possible obligation to Libya, but that under no circumstances in the past or the future would he have any influence on me in our relationship with Libya, and under no circumstances in the past or future would I derive any direct or indirect benefit from Billy's relationship with Libya, either while I'm in this office or after I leave this office.

RATHER: But you would like to see him return that money as soon as possible?

PRESIDENT CARTER: Yes, that would be my preference.

RATHER: Have you talked to your mother about this problem, Mister President?

PRESIDENT CARTER: Yes.

RATHER: What did she say, sir?

PRESIDENT CARTER: I think I won't relate the private conversation with my mother.

RATHER: I'll respect that, sir.

PRESIDENT CARTER: Thank you.

RATHER: Mister President, there's been some obfuscation—I'm not, again, certain whether it was purposefully done or not—about will you or won't you debate, on the same platform, Governor Reagan and Representative Anderson. Will you give me a yes or no answer about that?

PRESIDENT CARTER: The answer's yes, but I would like to pursue that answer just one step further. The most important thing is—is for me and Reagan, just the two of us, to have a complete ability and opportunity to debate every issue, domestic and foreign, that's important to the American people. I hope we'll have several debates. That's one part, and that's the most important part. The other part that I have said is that I would participate in a debate along with Governor Reagan and any other candidate who has qualified in enough states where he had a theoretical chance to be elected President if he carried all those states, and that would certainly include John Anderson, the former congressman.

Rather: So you are prepared to debate on the same platform during the campaign both Governor Reagan and Representative Anderson?

President Carter: That's correct.

Rather: I—I believe you've said—correct me if I'm wrong—if you haven't said, may I assume that you think Representative Anderson, if he stays in the race, would take more votes from you than he would from Governor Reagan?

President Carter: Well, let me put it this way, Dan. I'll be running against two Republicans; one Democrat, two Republicans. I think it would be too early for me to get into the role of characterizing how Reagan differs from Anderson and so forth, but I'm willing to do it. I don't have any choice in the matter. My preference would be to run against one person.

Rather: Do you have any indication, do you have any suspicion, that Governor Reagan and/or some of his supporters are putting money into Anderson's campaign in hope of hurting you?

President Carter: No, I don't.

Rather: If I may carry this forward just one additional step.

President Carter: Yes.

Rather: I thought perhaps it might be informative, and we might have a good time with it, for that matter. Could you give me, if you will, what you consider to be the single biggest asset and the single biggest weakness of Representative Anderson?

President Carter: Well, the single biggest asset, I guess, would be an absolute capability to take different positions on different issues to accommodate the circumstances. And he—

Rather: And his biggest weakness?

President Carter: —he's not bound by any sort of party commitment or platform or convention support. He's just a—a—a freewheeling agent that can change his position as he sees—as he sees fit. The biggest weakness would be that he doesn't have the structure of—of a party organization behind him, and he's—he's never won a primary. He entered numerous numbers of primaries and caucuses, and he never won one. And he's characterized, I think, at least by many people, as someone who—who lost and who abandoned his own party ostensibly to continue a personal campaign. I—I—I say that not in derogation of him. I—I'm trying to answer the question. That's a—the freedom is a—is an asset, and the lack of a—of a structured campaign and—and having a series of victories behind you I would say would be a detrimental factor. But I've never thought this through ahead of time. I didn't anticipate the question. (Laughs)

RATHER: I'm glad to hear that. I'd hoped that we'd be able to ask at least one.

PRESIDENT CARTER: That's one.

RATHER: Senator Kennedy. His greatest weakness, greatest asset.

PRESIDENT CARTER: I think his greatest asset is the heritage that he bears with the Kennedy name. And in many of the finest elements of his two brothers, he has carried forward those fine elements. I—I don't want to try to assess his—the—the negative factors that he—that he has to bear. I think the main thing is that he didn't wind up with enough delegates to get the nomination.

RATHER: Biggest strength, biggest weakness, Governor Reagan.

PRESIDENT CARTER: Well, I think Governor Reagan's biggest strength is the fact that he's been so successful in capturing the Republican nomination after formidable opposition from some very attractive opponents. The biggest weakness is his stand on the issues.

RATHER: In brief, Mister President—because I'm sure you could speak the rest of the afternoon on this next one—principal strength, principal weakness, Jimmy Carter.

PRESIDENT CARTER: I think our record in dealing with difficult issues without flinching—war, peace, for ourselves in the Middle East; an adherence to human rights; dealing with energy and economic matters; never evading a difficult question—will be appreciated by the American people. So, I would say that is a great strength, along with three and a half years of experience, which the American people can assuage and/or judge, rather—can—can judge. And the biggest problem is the fact that we still face uncertain and difficult times.

RATHER: In talking about our foreign policy, the President called the Carter years the most difficult and most complicated of times, with dozens of countries struggling for independence and a voice in the world. What the voters will have to judge, he said, was how well he has balanced these new facts of international life with the national interests of the United States.

What would be wrong with setting a deadline, a date for the Iranians to release our hostages? Say, "By October first, our hostages have to be out, or I, the President of the United States, will consider this an act of war by the Iranians."

President Carter: If we were dealing with a rational government, what you propose would be feasible. We are dealing with a group of fanatics who have violated every principle of human decency and human rights in holding 52 absolutely innocent Americans hostage, away from their families, away from freedom, away from communication with the outside world, away from medical attention, for the last months. So, we are not dealing with rational people. Secondly, there is no government there with whom we can deal. The elected president has no power at all. He's given authority under the constitution to choose a prime minister. He can't even choose his own prime minister. He and the secretary of state, or the foreign minister, both want to have the hostages released. They have lost power because of it. So, we're not dealing with rational people, and a threat or a deadline I'm afraid and I believe might very well result in the death or the injury to our hostages.

Rather: Do you believe that it would be more likely that the hostages would be freed if Governor Reagan was elected? After all, there'd be a good reason then: that the Iranians might want to make a gesture to a new administration; you would have been removed as the man, as they see it, responsible for protecting the Shah. It might be a way to get it off dead center, it strikes me. Does it strike you that way?

President Carter: No. We have had intelligence reports from quite early this year that the Ayatollah Khomeini may be considering holding the hostages until after our election in order to try to influence Americans in how they voted. I don't know if that's an accurate report or not, but—but it may be that after a certain event occurs—after Ramadan this next few weeks, after the speaker and the prime minister are chosen by the new Majlis, some change in tone of world events, maybe our election—there will be triggered in the Iranians' minds a commitment to release the hostages. I can't predict when it will be. But I don't think the election of a certain person in our country as President will be the determining factor at all.

Rather: Mister President, on the day that you announced the plan to boycott the Olympics, you said the Soviet military presence in Afghanistan—and I quote—"is the most serious threat to world peace since the Second World War."

PRESIDENT CARTER: Yes.

RATHER: Do you really mean that?

PRESIDENT CARTER: Certainly since the Soviet invasion and domination of the Eastern European countries that now comprise the Warsaw Bloc, yes. Afghanistan was formerly a buffer nation between the Soviet Union and Pakistan and Iran. That buffer has now been changed into a wedge between Pakistan and Iran.

If the Soviets thrust southward and try to take, say, Iran, with its oil resources and—and have a dominant presence around the Persian Gulf, it would have an enormous strategic importance and a threat not only to ourselves but to every nation on earth dependent upon oil from that troubled region. It's crucial that we stand firm against the Soviet Union, and it's equally crucial, maybe even more so, that we get as many nations as possible to join in with us. We joined a hundred and three other nations in this—in the United Nations to condemn the Soviet invasion and to call for their withdrawal. Subsequent—

RATHER: Mister President, (indistinct) effective—sorry to interrupt.

PRESIDENT CARTER: I'm sorry.

RATHER: I mean, that—that was totally ineffective, was it not?

PRESIDENT CARTER: I don't think it's ineffective at all. The Soviets have—have now stood condemned in an unprecedented way not only by ourselves in the Western world, but also by the Moslem countries, some of whom were formerly intimate friends of the Soviet Union, and the non-aligned movement. We restrained the shipment of feed grains to the Soviet Union, and got 50 other nations to join with us in boycotting the Olympics. We also decided to register our young men for the draft.

I might say this is a sum total of a very effective political and economic move. I might add, coincidentally but importantly, Governor Reagan opposed registration for the draft, Governor Reagan opposed the restraint on the sale of American feed grains to the Soviet Union. Governor Reagan opposed the boycott of the Moscow Olympics. And when he was asked what would you do to meet the threat of the Soviet Union in Southwest Asia in the invasion of Afghanistan, he replied, "I would put a naval blockade around Cuba in the Caribbean Ocean."

RATHER: You told the world through your National Security Adviser that the Soviet brigade in Cuba was unacceptable; then you accepted it. Now, what kind of signal does that send out to friend and foe alike?

PRESIDENT CARTER: Dan, that brigade has been in Cuba since 1962. It has no capability of attacking the United States. When the Soviets were in Berlin and built the Berlin Wall, President Kennedy said that Berlin Wall is—is unacceptable. The Berlin Wall is not acceptable to the American people, and it—to the same degree the presence of a Soviet brigade in Cuba is unacceptable to us. It doesn't mean that we're going to invade Cuba to root it out or invade East Berlin to tear down that wall or invade Afghanistan to root out the Soviet troops. It means that the world will never accept the reason for the presence of those troops in Cuba or the troops in Afghanistan or the Berlin Wall.

RATHER: Mister President, do you recognize how pervasive the feeling is in the country that you have not managed well Afghanistan, what—what's happened in Afghanistan, the Iranian situation, the Cuban situation, and foreign policy in general? Now, you travel around a good deal. You must have heard it yourself. I—I hear it at truck stops, coffee shops, cafeterias. What I hear, Mister President, is, "Jimmy Carter's a good and decent man," and a lot of people say, "I like him." But a lot of people will say, right behind that, "I think the job's too big for him." Seems to me that the—the essential point here is one of leadership and management of the country's foreign policy and domestic policy. Do you hear that? Do your people tell you that?

PRESIDENT CARTER: I—every time I watch the evening news, I hear it, and see the results in the polls; and obviously hear it from reporters and from private citizens. I am proud of what we have done and what our nation is. In nuclear strategic capability, we are making great progress. In the strengthening of NATO and our other alliances around the world, we have made great progress. In keeping our nation at peace, mine is one of the few Administrations in history where our nation has been at peace for three and a half years. And I pray it'll be at peace until I leave this office. We have spread the benefits of peace to other countries like Israel and Egypt. We have stood firm for our basic principles of human rights, and we've seen democracy come to nations like Zimbabwe and Nigeria and to several countries in this hemisphere.

RATHER: What do you consider to be your major mistake this year, Mister President?

PRESIDENT CARTER: In retrospect, you can pick out some things that might have been done if you had known ahead of time that events that are unpredictable would have occurred. Had we known ahead of time that the Iranians would have seized our hostages, we may—could have taken some different step. It's hard to know what could have been done. Had we known ahead of time that the Soviets would have invaded Afghanistan, we may have taken some additional measures. But not being able to know those things ahead of time, you can't say what could have been done.

The President has a unique responsibility. You can't share it with others. Quite often your advisers are divided fifty-fifty on a very important issue. Sometimes your advisers are wrong. The President is—has the ultimate responsibility. And in order to deal with those potential crises in such a way that they—they don't become actual crises, there is a—a lonely, important decision-making process that goes on within the mind of one person, the President. And if he makes a mistake in judgment that's a serious—of serious dimensions, it could affect the future of the entire world.

RATHER: Mister President, you recently directed your staff to make report cards on their employees. Now, in specific areas I'm going to ask you to grade yourself A through F. (President Carter laughs) Foreign policy.

PRESIDENT CARTER: Dan, this is a little bit embarrassing, because I'm highly prejudiced and—

RATHER: I recognize that, but you also have prided yourself on your candor and straight talk.

PRESIDENT CARTER: (laughs) You put me on the spot. I would say maybe a B or a C-plus on foreign policy. But I'd like to equivocate some, if you'll permit me as a politician, by saying that the maintenance of our nation at peace and strong is such a dominant factor that I—that it may be that a—that a more disinterested observer would give me a little bit higher grade. (Laughs)

RATHER: You give yourself a C-plus, but you think a B-minus might be justified?

PRESIDENT CARTER: I think a B-minus. Let's say a B-minus.

RATHER: Overall domestic policy.

PRESIDENT CARTER: Under the circumstances, I think about a B. The—the actual results, maybe a C.

RATHER: On energy, specifically.

PRESIDENT CARTER: Very good. I think we've done better on energy than we had anticipated, and that's one of the great achievements of our Administration, is putting into place under the most difficult possible circumstances an energy policy that'll—that will pay rich dividends in the future. I'd say an A in that.

RATHER: A in that?

PRESIDENT CARTER: I think so.

RATHER: On the economy? You can't give yourself an A on the economy, can you?

PRESIDENT CARTER: Well, that's what I was really referring to about actual results, because the inflation rate and unemployment are too high, and that was the C that I gave myself before.

RATHER: And on leadership?

PRESIDENT CARTER: Well, in international affairs our country is still a leader. On human rights, there's no doubt that we are a leader. In military strength, we are a leader. There is a—a growing realization in this country and in my own mind, however, that we are no longer dominant, in that we cannot enforce our will on others. That's an inevitable consequence of changing times. So, I would say that on leadership, reasonably good; maybe a B. I don't want to be held on account of those scores. I'll see what the American people say in November. (Laughs).

15

CARTER INTERVIEW EXCERPTS, AUG. 22, 1980

The Boston Globe, Curtis Wilkie

This interview was conducted by Curtis Wilkie, one of the *Globe* editors, and deals mostly with Soviet relations, the Strategic Arms Limitation Treaty, and the presidential campaign.—*Editor*

QUESTION: Mr. President . . . you mentioned in your speech presidential Directive 59 (a change in nuclear strategy from destroying Soviet population centers to hitting military targets and leadership shelters), and there's been some controversy. Does your embrace of that suggest that you believe a limited nuclear war is a possibility, that it's possible to fight, to have a limited nuclear war that won't expand?

CARTER: I think if nuclear war should erupt, that there would be a high likelihood of it escalating into a much broader nuclear conflict. That's a presumption under which I do my own thinking and planning. If I could just look philosophically for a minute, when anybody decides in this country to run for President, you're not involved in the campaign very long before you realize that you have got to be prepared, if necessary, to use nuclear force in order to protect the existence of our nation and as a real deterrent to prevent other nations from making a pre-emptive strike. It's not an easy decision to make . . .

In the privacy of discussions among myself and (West German Chancellor) Helmut Schmidt and (French President Valery) Giscard d'Estaing and (British Prime Minister) Margaret Thatcher and others, we discussed this issue as human beings who will have to make

---

the ultimate decision to launch a nuclear strike in order to defend our countries. When I first became President, I launched into a thorough analysis of the options that a President has to respond to an attack delivered against our country. I felt then and (former Secretary of State) Cy Vance and (Secretary of Defense) Harold Brown, (national security adviser) Dr. (Zbigniew) Brzezinski and other very close advisers, including the Vice President, agree that we needed to have a more flexible capability for a response. Not just all-out attacks on all population centers plus military bases and command posts in the Soviet Union, but at least as an interim step, hopefully, limiting the scope of nuclear weapon use, an ability to concentrate, at least in the early stage, pending circumstances, all command and military outposts to the exclusion of the industrial centers and the great population centers.

We have the capability to do that now. It's a constantly evolving procedure. . . . It's been well understood by all of us. I don't recall exactly if we started those first consultations between State and Defense and the White House late in 1977 or in 1978. It was after I had a chance to assimilate, to study and to learn about our nuclear capability and the flexibility that was there. I think, as I said to the Legionnaires, that having that additional flexibility enhances the security of our country and helps to prevent war.

QUESTION: Don't you fear, as some do, that it makes nuclear war more thinkable from the Russian perspective if they can engage in a limited nuclear . . .?

CARTER: In my private talks with (Soviet) President (Leonid) Brezhnev, along with the private talks that I had with the European allies, there is an absolute realization of the horrible prospect of nuclear warfare. I have never seen anyone, Soviet or American or Western, who didn't recognize that fact, too. Nobody thinks that you can have a little, small nuclear war as a frivolous part of a conventional confrontation. It is a major recognized escalation that might lead to warlike catastrophe, and that's generally understood. But I think it's good for our allies, for Americans and for potential adversaries to know that we do have the technological capability and the command capability to be flexible in our response.

We have the ability, through almost instant observation, to know the degree and the origin of an attack against our country, but only a limited period of time within which I can decide on the response. And it's a step forward. I think the problem was that it wasn't adequately explained to the American people, maybe to the degree that I just explained it to you in this brief period of time. And also there was a directive by me to Harold Brown to thoroughly brief Ed Muskie on the elements that involve State, and that was going to be done and he tried to make an appointment two or three times and it wasn't done, then a leak came out in the paper before we anticipated it.

QUESTION: You didn't authorize the leak, did you, Mr. President?

CARTER: No sir. We were taken aback by the leak . . .

QUESTION: But you probably have a pretty good idea of where it came from?

CARTER: You probably have a better idea than I do.

QUESTION: Mr. President, on that same point . . . do you have any concern about, it seems to me the primary focus of the campaign to date has been who can arm the country fastest and greater. Does it bother you, this concentration on blackening the skies, so to speak? That's what the debate seems to have been lately.

CARTER: Our policy on defense capability and priorities has been to spell (them) out over a four-year period. We've had a very careful, measured, methodical improvement in defense capability approved by the American people, I think, and by Congress. And we've also projected a five-year plan in the future that spells out how much we expect to spend and for what general purposes, so that the people understand where they're going now, after this year.

I tried in the statement to the American Legion not only to emphasize defense capability, but also the importance of correlating defense with diplomatic efforts to preserve peace, to enhance human rights. I emphasized, probably almost excessively, the need for nuclear arms control and negotiations, and also have spelled out the importance of Third World nations, and called on the Legionnaires to support our foreign aid program. I didn't expect to have a rousing response to that, but I think it's important to lay down a marker that the threat of strategic considerations is awesome and that you can't concentrate on just one factor of military strength. I hope that, with some move toward resolution of the Afghanistan invasion problem, that we can rejuvenate quickly and enthusiastically the consultations and negotiations with the Soviets to go beyond what SALT II prescribes to much more drastic reductions in nuclear weapons on a balanced basis.

QUESTION: Can I ask you something, Mr. President, about your overall kind of tonal notions of leadership. I was reading the Time magazine interview with Vice President (Walter) Mondale in which he said that you loved details. He said the President loves details.

CARTER: I loved details more the first couple of years than I do now.

QUESTION: One fellow who was running against you last year, I asked him to describe to me the essence of President Carter. And he said, "The best thing I can say is also the worst thing: He's a good staff man." And with (former California) Gov. (Ronald) Reagan appearing to run for chairman of the board and boasting about his ability to delegate authority and your known reluctance to, do you think you're going to change your style of leadership?

CARTER: Well, I don't agree with your presumption about me. I'll accept the presumption about Reagan. A better source, maybe one to believe more quickly, would be the Cabinet members who work with me. I think if you interrogated (Interior Secretary) Cecil Andrus or Harold Brown or the rest of them, you would find that they run their departments as they choose. They make weekly reports to me and, of course, at the Cabinet meetings they report and when we have a difficult decision to make as far as our policies, I make the proper judgment.

The first two years I was in office, I literally worked day and night. I got up every morning at 5 o'clock and I was working until 5 o'clock in the afternoon. . . . I felt it was necessary because I needed to know the interrelationship among the agencies and departments in the complex structure of government, the relative priority of budget decisions that I had to recommend to Congress. I had to know the identity and character of the nations and their leaders with whom I had to deal. I had to know some of the history of things right up to the present time, how it was modified or affected by Truman or Eisenhower or Nixon or Ford or Kennedy and Johnson. There was a breadth of knowledge that I felt that I had to have.

As I said in my acceptance speech, there are not any easy answers in the Oval Office. The ones that come to me for resolution are the ones where HUD (Housing and Urban Development) and Labor can't resolve it between them. Or where governors or mayors or county officials cannot solve their problems in a state or a local place. These are difficult decisions, and you'd be surprised, perhaps, at how many recommendations I get where my counselors are sharply divided . . . I'm the one that has to make a decision. At that point I don't have time to go and study all the interrelationships between or among these different agencies and who has which responsibility and what . . . is involved . . . I have to make a judgment that day. I might have a thousand or maybe dozens of things to decide that day. And someone has got to make an ultimate decision, and it's the President.

On a matter of international importance that might lead to the destruction of this country, or if it's a choice between peace and war, that decision probably has to be made in a hurry. I don't have time to call a national security council meeting when I get a flash message saying that the Soviets are doing this or (Egyptian President Anwar) Sadat has said that or (UN Secretary General Kurt) Waldheim is planning to do this. I've got to understand a little bit ahead of time. So it suits my nature as an engineer and an embryonic scientist, and also as someone who's been involved in government to know enough about my job, to make a decision as best I can when I have to in a hurry. . . . But I have no apology to make for the homework that I do.

This is the most important job in the world, and it's one of the most difficult jobs in the world. And just as you in your job devote enough time and effort so you don't have to depend on subordinates to make your ultimate decisions, that's what I feel as President. There's nobody that can make those decisions for you. And when I'm out on the side of a creek tying flies or catching trout and the military walks out and hands me a message, I don't have time to call a conference of the national security council. I've got to make a judgment based on my knowledge and experience. So I don't think there's anything wrong with that. I don't lose sight, I believe, of the direct responsibility and overall strategic consequences of my decisions. I hope I've answered your question.

QUESTION: Mr. President, another question on style. It seems (California) Gov. (Edmund G.) Brown and Sen. Kennedy and yesterday Ronald Reagan all have criticized you for blaming the nation's problems on the American people; they refer back to the malaise speech and that's been a constant line used. Do you regret that speech or think it was misinterpreted, or do you, in fact, blame the American people for some percentage of the problems and their inability to face up to the situation?

CARTER: I think, (with) the possible exception of an extemporaneous Law Day speech I made in Georgia when I was governor, that's the best speech I ever made. I reread some of my speeches in the last few weeks—that is a darn good speech. I have seen my political opponents extract one little, tiny phrase out of it, where Americans had lost their confidence and believe our nation could not face the difficult issues successfully and had given up in trying to meet the energy challenge, but I would urge you to take 15 minutes—I know it's valuable time—and just reread this speech. . . . I don't have any apologies to make for that speech.

QUESTION: Have you seen a change in the country?

CARTER: Yes.

QUESTION: How?

CARTER: I think the response to the energy question has been notable, until . . . I don't attribute all of it, I don't want to exaggerate the importance of the speech, but there has certainly been a profound change in the attitude of the American people and the press in the last 12 months concerning whether or not the energy crisis was the moral equivalent of war or was a profound challenge to our country or could be resolved. I think there's a firm realization now that did not exist 12 months ago, that this is a crucial issue and that Americans can resolve it and that we can have a better life in the process and not make a personal, deleterious sacrifice.

QUESTION: Speaking of the mood of the people, it seems you may be in some trouble with minorities, and to some extent that means cities. What are your thoughts on that?

CARTER: Again, I don't agree with your premise. Even against an extremely attractive candidate like Kennedy, among the black voters, for instance, I did very well, I think, on a nationwide basis had a heavy majority. It's very difficult against him because of his stand on issues, which is always perfect with them, and the history of his family and so forth. There is a fear on the part of many minorities and leaders, at least until now, about the consequences of a Reagan victory. I think the natural rapport that I have with and the realization of the differences between what the Republicans did by Reagan's stand, compared to what I and the Democrats stand for, will give us good (support).

QUESTION: Will you discuss the role you perceive at this point Ted Kennedy playing in the campaign and this other distinguished gentleman from Massachusetts?

CARTER: Tip (House Speaker Thomas P. O'Neill Jr.) tells me what to do on all matters of great interest. Whenever I disagree with Tip, I ask Millie (O'Neill's wife) for a judgment.

QUESTION: Mr. President, there've been contradictory statements attributed to American commanders and state department officials about the level of our support for Gen. Chun (Doo Hwan) in Korea. Could you address that, and also the question of whether we're withdrawing more troops?

CARTER: We have a long-range schedule for withdrawal of troops incrementally as we assess South Korea's ability to defend herself against any possible North Korean intrusion. After I got in office, we did a complete analysis based on aerial surveillance and other means of the North Korea defense capability. It was much greater than we had presupposed. . . .

We have been deeply concerned about Chun and some of the policies he's put forward. I understand now he might step down as general to become president. We also are concerned about the upcoming trial of Kim Dae Jung (the trial began last Thursday) and are letting our concern be expressed very clearly to the Koreans. We have some limited influence, although it's not great, on their internal political situation under (former) President Park (Chung Hee), and under the new leaders our influence is limited, and we've got the option of expressing our extreme displeasure by withdrawing our forces, which might destabilize that whole region of Asia and have deleterious effects for us on the one hand or accepting some political development of which we disapprove. We would like to have a complete democracy, with full and open debate, free press and elected leaders. The Koreans are not ready for that, according to their own judgment, and I don't know how to explain it any better.

QUESTION: Mr. President, are the Polish strikes part of a bigger chain in Eastern Europe?

QUESTION: Can I add to that? If the Soviets were to move troops into Poland what would be your response?

CARTER: I can't answer that because I don't want to. We have decided, as a matter of national policy, to make minimal comments about Poland during this time of instability there. It's obvious that, in some of the other countries, such as Romania, to some degree Hungary, certain Yugoslavian communities in Eastern Europe behind the Soviet bloc, there's been a growing sense of independence. They express their views more clearly on occasion than they did before. The Warsaw Pact demanded and put forth by the Soviets is quite often debated and the debates are reported in public, which has not been done that much in the past. In the United Nations, there's not as clear a delineation of discipline among all the Eastern European countries, as imposed by the Soviet Union, as there was some years ago. We hope, and I might say we expect, that there will be no further Soviet involvement in Polish affairs because of this series of strikes and demands for more political and economic improvements. But I can't predict that for sure. But we were being very reticent as a government in not expressing our views because, I think, it would be destabilizing and might work counter to our purposes.

QUESTION: Just to follow that up, during this period, do you have any communications with the Soviet Union about what they might do?

CARTER: We have fairly very frequent communications with the Soviets. We communicated with them yesterday, for instance, to express our displeasure at the jamming of Western radio broadcasts. They jammed the Germans, BBC (British Broadcasting Corporation) and Voice of America, which is a contravention of the Helsinki agreement. We expressed our displeasure there. My presumption is that they were trying to conceal from the Soviet citizens the Voice of America reports on the Polish strikes.

Carter (facing camera) on the *U.S.S. Pomfret,* circa 1950
(Courtesy Jimmy Carter Library)

Judge Robert Jordan administers the oath of office to Carter, swearing him in as Georgia's 76th governor (Courtesy Jimmy Carter Library)

Anwar Sadat, Carter, and Menachem Begin meet at Camp David,
September 5, 1978 (Courtesy Jimmy Carter Library)

Sadat, Carter, and Begin at the signing of the Framework for Peace,
September 17, 1978 (Courtesy Jimmy Carter Library)

Carter examines the voter registration list
at a polling site during the 1989 Panamanian elections
(Courtesy the Carter Center from *Talking Peace*/Dutton Children's Books)

Rosalynn Carter, former chairman of the Joint Chiefs of Staff Colin Powell,
Carter, and Senator Sam Nunn visit Haiti in February 1995 to assess
progress on preparations for elections (Courtesy the Carter Center)

Carter joins more than seven thousand volunteers in a drive sponsored by the Atlanta Project to identify children who need immunizations, April 1993 (Photo © 1993 Michael A. Schwarz)

PART 3

POST-PRESIDENTIAL
CONVERSATIONS

16

INTERVIEW WITH JIMMY CARTER, NOV. 29, 1982

Miller Center Interviews, Carter Presidency Project, Steven H. Hochman, et al.

This interview with former President Jimmy Carter took place November 29, 1982, and is part of a research document from the White Burkett Miller Center of Public Affairs at the University of Virginia.

The document is housed in The Jimmy Carter Library in Atlanta and was previously unpublished. Those participating in the interview with Jimmy Carter were Steven H. Hochman, Assistant to President Carter; Richard F. Fenno, Jr., University of Rochester; Erwin C. Hargrove, Vanderbilt University; Charles O. Jones, University of Virginia; H. Clifton Mc-Cleskey, University of Virginia; Richard E. Neustadt, Harvard University; Kenneth W. Thompson, University of Virginia; David B. Truman, President Emeritus, Mt. Holyoke College; and James S. Young, University of Virginia.

The interview in its original form is 76 pages long. It has been shortened for this book.—*Editor*

CARTER: I'm eager to participate and cooperate fully. I don't have any hesitancy about putting myself in your hands and I presume the best way to go about it, Jim, will be just for you all to ask questions because you know the gaps and what you want. I do hope that we can work out some way of having the record available in the presidential library that we will build. I think that should be a very beneficial addition to the library. Many of the people who have served in the administration have agreed to put their own personal papers in the library, even all the hostage families are putting their personal letters and so forth in the Carter Presidential Library, just so they'll be preserved and made available later on for historians and students.

YOUNG: I'm sure we want very much to do this and to see that done.

CARTER: If there are problems about accessibility, or constraints that your other interviewees have prescribed, then we'll certainly work out a way that is responsible for honoring those. The best thing, I think, would be to have questions, Jim, and I'll try to answer them.

YOUNG: I'll start off with a large one. People who study presidencies and who study campaigns note that there's quite a disparity between the world as it seems on the campaign trail and the world that one finds in Washington. There are a whole set of questions I think we would like to ask you about how you organized your administration, particularly your staff, or that transition as it may have evolved over time. Also we would like to know about some of the things that you felt you had particularly to address in establishing your presidency in the Washington environment. My first question is a very general one. Can you give us your thoughts on what you anticipated, not so much in terms of what problems were yet on your agenda, but what you anticipated when you came to Washington? Did you foresee what you would have to do and what demands would be made on you in your relations with that governmental establishment? Then, we can pick up some particular questions on that.

CARTER: I'll probably ramble in my answer because the question rambles. I began considering a nationwide race in 1971 when I had only been in the governor's office a few months, not distinguishing at that time between the vice presidency, and the possibility of being on someone else's ticket, and being president. It was really only after that time, during 1972, that I decided to run for the presidency itself. But throughout my governor's term, at least, I was preoccupied with how the presidency and the federal government should react to problems and issues that I had to face as a governor. I was very active in the southeastern region dealing with all the agencies of the federal government as they dealt with education, transportation, public welfare systems, those kinds of things.

In the reorganization of the Georgia state government, we also sought advice from other governors and administrations around the country. Although I was primarily concerned with my duties as governor, it was always a constant factor in my mind, how would this relate to the presidency itself? Shortly after the Democratic convention in '72, when I endorsed and in fact made the major nominating speech for Scoop Jackson, we began to make plans for my candidacy for the presidency itself. That accentuated my interest, and I began to make an agenda of what I thought the presidency should encompass. With personal experience on domestic issues and some defense issues, and with just a modicum of opportunities in the foreign field, I joined the Trilateral Commission and took a lot of trips to other nations to learn as much as I could about international affairs. But I can't say that I accomplished very much with the trips, except that they were primarily trade trips for Georgla. One of the things that I did was to study the relationships between our country and the Japanese and Chinese, and another one was to go to the Mid East and spend about a week traveling around the important places in Israel, the Golan Heights, and along the Jordan River and so forth. So from the early stages of my gubernatorial experience, I was in effect preparing and assessing issues and questions that I thought might be addressed from the White House, and after the first year, from the presidency itself.

I thought I would be running against Kennedy and Wallace and I didn't think many Democrats would have the temerity to do the same thing on a serious basis. Although Wallace stayed in the race, Kennedy withdrew and when Kennedy withdrew, there were ten or so very well-known and formidable Democratic opponents who came forth to challenge me which was disconcerting.

When we began the direct campaign, just driving around first of all with Jody and me all by ourselves, I had a chance to learn even more about domestic issues from a broader perspective in Iowa and California, Texas, New Hampshire and so forth. Small groups, sometimes not any larger than this, were either curious about me as one of the potential candidates, or quite often younger people who were newcomers to politics actively wanted to support me. I listened to their problems and their concerns, their suggestions about agricultural policy and defense matters, what they were concerned about in SALT and non-proliferation. So I began to expand my mind a little bit further than I had, during that campaign itself. Later, as I got to be well known, and had some success in the early Florida straw ballot and the Iowa caucus and so forth, then I became one of the focal points for the press and had to prepare myself much better to answer questions that were much more probing and that were engendered within the national press in Washington where they were much more knowledgeable about past history or current events than was I. I turned to people in whom I had confidence to help me. These included people in foreign/defense fields that I had known, primarily in the Trilateral Commission and many of whom later became members of my administration, such as Harold Brown, Dr. Brzezinski, Jerry Smith, Cy Vance and others. It was an educational program on a crash basis. By the time I won the nomination (as you know I didn't have any remaining opposition by the first of June so it was obvious that I had the nomination won), I didn't have to horse trade or negotiate with other leading candidates either for the vice presidency or any positions on the cabinet. I was quite free to make these decisions over a period of time as I chose. The one I had to make before the convention, obviously was the choice of the Vice President. And after that we had a strong lead in the public opinion polls. It was distorted greatly by the conflict between Reagan and Ford where neither one of their supporters would agree in interviews to support the other. It gave us a highly distorted position as a favorite before both conventions. But that went away fairly rapidly and as you know the Ford/Carter race was decided on a very narrow basis.

But in spite of that, between the conventions and the initiation of a general election campaign, I had a chance to have extended and definitive meetings down here in Plains at the Pond House where my mother now lives. We would carefully prepare the agendas and spend all day, or sometimes two days, with distinguished Americans who were the most knowledgeable, Democratically-oriented political leaders that we could identify on every conceivable domestic, foreign, and defense issue. At the conclusion of those long sessions that were organized by people like Stu Eizenstat or Dr. Brzezinski or sometimes Charlie Schultze or Juanita Kreps, we put together a growing understanding of what issues I would have to face when I was elected. After the election, of course, my primary responsibility was to put together a cabinet and further to define a specific agenda for the initial weeks of the administration. I also had to try to get acquainted with the members of the Congress with whom I would be working. I turned over to Jack Watson and to my son Chip and a few others the responsibility for the transition period and the actual arrangement for the taking over of the government, and they did a good job of that. But I wasn't very deeply involved in that respect.

In that process, a number of potential workers in the administration, I would say mostly at the sub-cabinet level, were identified because of the good work that they did in the transition months. I've covered in the book in some degree, and Hamilton would probably be better qualified than I to discuss this, the process that we used to screen candidates—and I think this is where Charlie Kirbo could be very helpful to you. Charlie went to Washington on several occasions and he would, in his own inimitable way, talk to distinguished lawyers in Washington, the heads of some of the lobbying groups, that would be a minimal factor, and also to the people in the Congress that we knew, such as Ed Muskie and others. He would then say, who do you think would be the best person to be the Secretary of State, or Secretary of Defense, or head of HEW, and so forth. We narrowed those down. In those processes, we began to learn more about the agenda that ought to be mine when I became President. As I interviewed these people, on an average I interviewed from three to six candidates for a cabinet post personally, I would ask for their ideas. When I talked to Harold Brown or Charlie Duncan, for instance, I would ask them what they thought ought to be done in the Department of Defense to make it more efficient, to eliminate waste and to have a more orderly and methodical procedure for establishing defense priorities and so forth. It was the same thing with HEW, same thing with transportation, so as I interviewed people who might be cabinet officers, I extracted from them their ideas on the top priorities in their mind in their own departments.

At the same time, I was meeting with congressional leaders, who were fairly deferential to my ideas during the transition phase. They came down to Plains; we met at Herman Talmadge's farm; I went to Washington. I met with every chairman of every major committee in the House or Senate. I had an all-day session at the Smithsonian with both Democratic and Republican leaders and all my cabinet officers who were involved in important defense matters, just to talk about the agenda for defense and foreign policy. It was there I decided to move aggressively on Camp David, which was the Mid East and to move aggressively on normalization relations with China, on the Panama Canal treaty, on SALT II and so forth. Those kind of decisions were made during that time. Fritz Mondale worked very closely with me in trying to decide which ones of those items we could pursue the first year, which ones should be left until later, which ones were potentially incompatible, which ones would overbook the agenda.

As I said in my book, I still have mixed emotions about this. There's a general consensus, which I presume you all have encountered, that we tried to do too much too fast, and I think as far as creating an image of consistency, achievement, or authority is concerned, this is right. But whether we could have actually accomplished more by having a more limited agenda, I have my doubts. As Bob Strauss said, and I put this in the book: if we had got 85 percent of what we wanted, it seemed that the public impression was that we had lost 15 percent, which is probably inevitable. But we did accumulate over a period of time an image of not getting what we wanted. I think in general we had a fairly good success rate.

I was experienced as a governor. I think I did a good job as governor. I did a lot of innovative things all of which have stood the test of time. So I took that experience to Washington, but there were at least two remarkable differences. One was just that the Washington environment was much more of a major factor than was the Atlanta environment on a comparative basis. I could ignore the people in Atlanta who were the social, business, and media leaders, if I so chose, with relative impunity and deal primarily with the members of the legislature. There was a much more isolated relationship between the legislative and executive branch on the one hand, and the general public and the news media on the other, than was the case in Washington where the lobbyists and the law firms and the news media leaders, in particular the columnists and others, were such an important element of government in Washington. And I underestimated that. I don't think there's any doubt about it.

It didn't take us long to realize that the underestimation existed but by that time, we were not able to repair that mistake. I'm not trying to rationalize too much, but in retrospect as I wrote the book and thought about it a lot and got probed on every side from Steve and from my editors and Jody and Hamilton and Zbig and others who read it over before it was published, I'm just not sure that there was not an inherent incompability there. Whether I could have overcome it by having a series of private luncheons or suppers at the White House for the news media in the first few weeks, I have my doubts. But I'm willing to grant that that's a possibility. Later we did, as you know. I invited to the White House every executive officer or news commentator or notable columnist or reporter who I thought shaped events in the nation, probably a hundred, all of the ones that we thought were the most important. Jody and Jerry Rafshoon and a few of the friends that we had in the press helped us make out the list and I would spend several hours with them at night answering their questions, talking to them about major issues, but I'm not sure how much good it did.

I had a different way of governing, I think, than had been the case with my predecessors, and the public and the press were still in somewhat of a quandary about how we managed the affairs of the White House. I was a southerner, a born-again Christian, a Baptist, a newcomer. I didn't have any obligations to the people in Washington for my election. Very few of the members of Congress, or members of the major lobbying groups, or the distinguished, former Democratic leaders had played much of a role in my election. There wasn't that tie of campaign interrelationship that ordinarily would have occurred had I not been able to win the nomination by myself. I just didn't have that sort of potential tie to them, and I think they felt that they were kind of on the outside.

YOUNG: Could I just interrupt a moment? During the transition you noticed that the congressional leaders were very deferential to you, at that time, and so you were in for a rude shock later on. After the transition (Bert Lance has talked a little bit to us about this but not much), did it come as a shock to you to see this developing declaration of war on you by Washington? I wonder if during all of this intensive work that was being done preparing for the standard transitional matters and agendas and programs and recruitment to the departments and screening, you were being fully informed about what kinds of problems you might expect down that road with what we call "Washington" or the Congress in particular? The Congress wasn't telling you; congressmen you were seeing were not telling you, "you're going to have a big problem with Congress," I presume, at that point. Was this a source of concern in your transition teams, or did it more or less catch you by surprise?

CARTER: I don't think it was a source of concern that I recall. Obviously, we had seen the problems that Nixon and Ford had had with Congress, but it was a Democratic Congress. I expected when I went into the White House to have a much more harmonious relationship with the Democratic Congress than did occur. There's no question about that. The basic agenda that we presented to the Congress at that time was carried out. It was supported and evolved between me, Bob Byrd, Tip O'Neill and the other Democratic leaders. There was a similar economic circumstance then to what we have now: high unemployment, a long period of stable oil prices, the inflation rate being fairly low, extraordinary deficits for those times—sixty-six billion dollars, I think, was Ford's last deficit that I inherited, and the main program that we had was to stimulate the economy and to create jobs. There was no incompatibility between me and the Democratic leaders on those basic issues. That was a major thrust, along with the energy package which passed the House as you know by August and then took us three more years to pass the Senate. I think the first example of congressional incompatibility was what I described in the book with the reorganization bill and with Jack Brooks' opposition. I found very quickly then that there was no Democratic discipline and there was no inherent loyalty to me. I had to get the votes individually from Democrats or Republicans wherever I could get them. It didn't take me long to learn that my original transition expectations were not going to be realized. That misapprehension didn't extend for months and months after I was inaugurated. I was disabused of those dreams within the first few days.

THOMPSON: Mr. President, I wondered whether if you had it to do over again in identifying this other sector of your administration, namely the people who did have reputations in Washington, you would have checked a little more carefully or your staff would have to be more specific about the antagonist-adversary-advocate reputation of some of those people? You mentioned Blumenthal. I have a good deal of experience in the difference betweeen making presentations at the

Rockefeller Foundation to Bob Lovett, to Douglas Dillon, to, although he was President, Dean Rusk and all the others, and the kind of antagonist relationship you had with Mike Blumenthal and some others who came into the administration. I wondered if in this trust relationship thing the relationships with cabinet members and with outsiders would have been any different if you had had this other type, or if you somehow could have identified the 1970 Robert Lovett's or the people who were accommodators and adjustors rather than antagonists in their powers?

NEUSTADT: George Shultz–types of human being.

CARTER: Well, I had some of the George Shultz–types. I don't think you could say that Harold Brown was antagonistic. Cy Vance and others weren't that way. I have nothing but good feelings toward Mike Blumenthal. I think Mike did an excellent job. Mike is naturally feisty and he protects his turf, maybe to excess. But I thought he was superb and I still think he's a good guy. When I asked Cy Vance to serve as Secretary of State, the first man he wanted to be his deputy was Mike Blumenthal and that's how I first got to know Mike. In interviewing Mike and in talking to others about Mike for the Deputy Secretary of State job, I decided he would be best placed in the Secretary of the Treasury's job. Later we got Warren Christopher, really as a second choice, but he turned out to be exemplary. The only cabinet officer that I felt was excessively independent was Joe Califano. Joe was operating his own shop. He would make major decisions concerning controversial matters and announce them publicly and never inform me. Joe was an integral part of the *Washington Post* cocktail party circuit. But at the same time, as long as Joe served, he and I got along well. I would call him in and chastise him on occasion for making an announcement without letting me know ahead of time, but in general the announcement he made was compatible with my basic policy. So in all the changes that we'd made in the cabinet, the only one that still leaves a slightly bitter taste in my mouth is Joe Califano. The rest of them I think were fine and they served well. As you know, we didn't make a change at all for thirty months. It's probably an unprecedented thing. When they left, it was relatively pleasant. Jim Schlesinger wanted to leave earlier, as I mentioned in the book. As soon as the first energy package was passed, he sincerely wanted to leave after he got the Energy Department partially established. It wasn't completely established. Later, I think about six or eight months later, he came back and again wanted to leave and I urged him to stay. I don't have any feeling of disappointment or a sense that I didn't do a good job in choosing the cabinet, even including Califano, who I think did a good job while he was there.

NEUSTADT: I told these fellows . . . , I asked their permission to ask you this question.

CARTER: You can ask anything you wish.

NEUSTADT: Well, I read Joe Califano's book and I said to myself, "Why didn't President Carter fire him sooner?" I said this to Joe and he did not speak to me for quite some time after that. If one reads it as an outside observer, you see time after time where you are quite gently and politely suggesting something, or saying something, or inferring something, or there's noise coming from the White House, all of which is just disregarded by Califano. From this, I induce that to get his attention you have to hit him over the head. My impression is you didn't hit him on the head for quite a long while. Maybe Joe was used to having to live with Lyndon Johnson, who did hit him on the head quite often. Give me comment.

THOMPSON: Could I just have one sentence? We had a long interview with Steve's former boss, Dumas Malone, that's going to go out on television and the fellow kept pressing him about what was it that was unique about the whole Jefferson culture and he said "politeness." Is there anything in southern tradition that made it difficult to deal with Califano?

CARTER: That's a good point. I didn't read all of Joe Califano's book but I read parts of it. My impression is that in writing his book, Joe described a lot of things as being unilateral decisions or accomplishments on his part when I and everyone else played a significant role. There was great consultation. A lot of the ideas that Joe eventually implemented came from Stu Eizenstat or on occasion from me and others. Joe took credit for all of them as though he was a lot more independent than he was. He was more independent than my staff members including Stu and others wanted him to be. But he didn't particularly displease me. And it was really approximately the time I went to Camp David and had people come and advise that I think unanimously folks said, Mr. President, you've got someone in your cabinet that's not loyal to you and he's running his own shop and his comments in private and in public are not favorable to you, and they asked the same question that you said, "Why don't you fire this guy?" At first, I was not inclined to do it. Later, I became convinced that Joe ought to go. I called Joe and I said, "Joe, I've been pleased with what you've done. In general, the accomplishments of HEW have been gratifying to me, but there's such a severe incompatiblity between you and my White House staff and other cabinet officers that I think it would be best for you to step down. There was no argument about it. I said I'd like to make the transition as pleasant as possible. I even invited Joe and his family to use Camp David if he wanted to spend a few days to talk to his children and so forth and even for me and Rosalynn to be there that weekend. He finally decided he would go up to Maine or somewhere; they have a vacation spot. So there was not an unpleasant confrontation between me and Joe Califano. As I said, it wasn't up until he was actually fired that I felt at all inclined to fire him.

THOMPSON: Could I follow up?

CARTER: Please do because I don't think I've answered your question adequately.

THOMPSON: This seems to stand in such dramatic contrast to your proper moral indignation about Ambassador Sullivan and your words about firing him immediately.

CARTER: I should have fired him. Should have fired him and I should have fired Haig. Those are the only two that I think back on that I should have discharged. I expressed my desire to discharge both men, but I listened to the advice of Vance and Brown in both cases, both men were very strongly opposed to my discharging Haig and later Sullivan, so I didn't do it. But in retrospect, I should have fired them. In fact I instructed Cy Vance to bring Sullivan out of Iran. And Cy delayed it and he came back again and again as was his manner and tried to convince me that we should send a deputy secretary of state in there to run things, assistant secretary of state, I think, and to ease Sullivan out after the crisis had passed. And I finally deferred to that. Brown and Cy both were convinced that if I brought Haig out of Europe at that time, it would disrupt matters in Europe with the nuclear weapons question and others. I don't remember exactly what issues were involved. So I deferred on both of those decisions. But in retrospect, I wish I had gone ahead and done it.

NEUSTADT: Both of these are cases of clear insubordination and not following instructions in policy.

CARTER: Yes. Sullivan was specifically insubordinate, and Haig was obviously running for President. Every time somebody would go to Europe to talk to Haig about our relationship with the NATO allies and so forth, Haig would use that forum, whether it was Ed Muskie or visiting Republican senators or a congressional delegation or even sometimes members of my own cabinet, and would denigrate what I was doing and what the Democrats in general were doing and promote himself as a potential candidate. One of the problems I had with Haig was his repeated concern expressed to others that I had moved Heiser out of Europe into Iran. But I don't have any hard feelings toward either man. I haven't really talked to them much since I went out of office, but those are the only ones that I remember that I should have fired earlier than I did.

YOUNG: So it was really for reasons of State and loss of effectiveness that you feel were the main objectives of the Califano removal?

CARTER: Yes. The other cabinet officers and the staff members almost unanimously said that Joe was just promoting himself, not cooperating with them and was basically disloyal. I never did detect that disloyalty to me, but I think knowing Joe's temperament, he's aggressive, he felt that he had been there with Johnson, he knew the social programs better than anyone else including the White House, and when something was done in a collegial way, as far as Joe was concerned, it was his program. But that's just his character and his nature and I should have understood it and did understand it.

HARGROVE: I have the impression in the first instance that you had the notion that, let's say Stu Eizenstat and DPS, for example, were not authorized to develop policy so much as to oversee and advise you. The lead would be given to a cabinet officer, such as Califano on welfare reform or Mrs. Harris on the urban package. In time, there was a discovery that cabinet departments had difficulty coordinating each other and you gave increasing authority to Stuart to play that coordinating role. Was there a gradual development and awareness that you needed your own staffs to screen, sort out, coordinate, make options more coherent?

CARTER: I don't believe so, although if there's an inconsistency between what I'm going to say and what Stu Eizenstat told you, I would trust Stu Eizenstat better than I would me because he was involved in the heart of it. When we evolved a new welfare program or an urban policy, I let Stu and Jack Watson, sometimes Frank Moore (if particular Congress members were interested at the early stages), evolve their concept of what the new urban policy would be. Jack Watson would have hearings around the country with mayors and governors and so forth. Then he and Stu would come and present to me a voluminous, sometimes fifty or sixty pages of options about what we might agree would be part of the ultimate urban package. I would require them to put on each item, sometimes thirty items, how much it would cost the federal government, how much it would cost or save the state and local governments, and if I agreed with it, I would just put a check mark on a memorandum which they had prepared. If there were options, then I would indicate my choice among the options. If I had further questions, then I would call Stu and/or Jack in and say, I don't understand this, will you explain it to me, and I believe it's going to cost more than this, why do you think it would cost so little? Once I signed off on that option paper, (I'm taking one of the most voluminous ones I can recall), then Stu would be responsible for the drafting of the proposed legislation. Stu would be responsible also for talking to the subcommittee chairmen who were involved. Frank Moore's staff would get involved at a later stage. So that's basically how we did it from the very beginning.

On occasion, the initiative would come from a department. For instance, on labor matters it would ordinarily be at least two departments, certainly HEW and Labor, or sometimes it would spill over into another one like Commerce or Agriculture. I didn't ever get involved at that stage. Either Jack Watson, or Stu, or most of the time both, would work out a composite proposal. It may be that the Secretary of HEW would strongly disagree with the Secretary of Labor or Housing and Urban Development. If so, and they couldn't resolve the differences with Jack Watson mediating, then I would let both of them come in and talk to me in the Oval Office or the Cabinet Room and present their opposing views. I would either make a decision at that point, still in the Cabinet Room, or the following day I would let them know what my decision was. It was a complicated sytem, but I don't know of any alternative, at least in my way of governing.

HARGROVE: I didn't mean to suggest that you delegated authority to Stuart to resolve things, but I do have the impression that you gave him gradually more authority to coordinate and try to make the options coherent, particularly in welfare reform and certainly in the urban factors.

CARTER: Yes, I certainly agree with that. Yes. As I became more familiar with the overall operation of government, and as we built up a base of generic policy that could be used as a guide for more specific policy evolution, then I trusted Stu and his staff to do much more than we did at first. Stu was one of those who didn't work for me in the state government. He evolved policy ideas even when I was a candidate for governor in '70 and then he was the one who did the issue analysis and worked up domestic policy proposals when I was running for President, so I knew him and I trusted him. But he didn't really have those four years of experience and training within the state government to know exactly how I did things. That didn't take long. I couldn't put a number of months on it, but I would say after the first rash of major proposals that went to the Congress, from then on we had our basic policies understood among each other and Stu had much more authority from then on than originally in making proposals on his own.

HARGROVE: Was there an analogue to Eizenstat in economic policy?

CARTER: It would be hard to separate Stu from the economic policy.

HARGROVE: OK. That's right. Because you really gave him the charter at least in one of micro-areas didn't you?

CARTER: Yes. Not just micro, macro also. For instance, when we devised a second-phase energy legislation, I would say that Stu played as large a role as Jim Schlesinger did. Stu had a large and very competent staff, as you probably know. Jack Watson had a tiny staff, always needed more, but I never did give them to him. He had a very small staff. I think Stu had more knowledge, intelligence, and resources on the domestic policy staff to play that larger role. This is not taking anything away from Jack's native intelligence and ability, but Stu had the resources to do all these complicated things. Much more so than say Frank Moore or Jack Watson.

HARGROVE: Did you really feel well served by the EPG mechanism or was there something that frustrated you about it?

CARTER: I never did feel well served by it.

HARGROVE: Could you spin that out, because I sensed that and I'd like to hear you talk about that?

CARTER: Well, the only reason I hesitate to answer is because I don't want to cast any further aspersions on Mike Blumenthal. But that was the crux of it. There was a constant friction there and I don't like— I think like all other Presidents—to deal with friction. You like to have things come to you in a harmonious fashion. You haven't got time to be a referee. And so that was a very serious problem for me.

    Charlie Schultze, on the other hand, would attend the same meetings. Schultze would brief me once or twice a week, and Schultze has an ability, which you probably noticed, to explain complicated things in a clear and enjoyable fashion. He's as good at that as Brzezinski is at international affairs. I really enjoyed Mr. Brzezinski explaining to me because he made it interesting and so did the cabinet officers. Well Mike wasn't that way. I think it was Mike's lack of natural leadership capability over that independent and disparate group that made the EPG ineffective for me.

HARGROVE: Did it change when Miller came along?

CARTER: Yes.

HARGROVE: For the better?

CARTER: For the better. Yes. Miller was the boss of that group, but he didn't aggravate anybody. It changed a lot.

FENNO: Before you talked about Mike Blumenthal and Joe Califano. I want to read an old saw that comes, I think, from Charles Dawes, who was Calvin Coolidge's Vice President. He said that "cabinet members are the natural enemies of the President." I think you may have answered that.

CARTER: I never did feel that way, really. I felt at ease with my cabinet members and even when Mike was having the problems that I've just described to you, I had more of a feeling of sympathy for him because, you know, I understood Mike's character. I know about his past history as a child and how he fought his way to one of the top positions in the corporate world. I know his assets and his capabilities and his intelligence and his courage. I admire all those things about him. That one element, though, was a problem. Mike and I have the finest relationship now. When I was in Detroit recently, I went out there, he just donated a very fine Burroughs computer to the Carter library and recently, when I was in New York, I spent the night with Cy Vance. I have a good relationship with all those former cabinet members. So I didn't look upon them as challenges or natural enemies. I looked on them as adequately supportive and as friends.

FENNO: So you are saying that even though you didn't check for loyalty at the time you appointed them, you weren't terribly concerned with loyalty because they were, in fact, loyal to you?

CARTER: Yes. They were. And I think even Califano in his own way was loyal. That's just his character. I think he saw himself as being much more knowledgeable about domestic affairs than anyone in the White House or the rest of the cabinet, having helped Lyndon Johnson evolve many of the Great Society programs.

TRUMAN: You said in your book that the Friday morning foreign policy breakfast was your favorite meeting of the week. Do you want to tell us a little bit about why?

CARTER: For one thing, it was uninterrupted unless it was an extreme emergency, and it was an informal group restricted in attendance. We discussed issues that were of utmost importance in a very frank way. It was a compatible group with me, Cy, Zbig, Harold, and sometimes others. It was a meeting above all else where I could make a final decision and ordinarily, the decision would be implemented. We would go through a list of agenda items. We didn't have a prepared agenda ahead of time, but Vance, Brown, Brzezinski, and I would have the agenda items. I would ordinarily cover almost all of the issues myself and then I would ask them for additional ones. I would see them crossing off their lists the things that I had already brought up. At the conclusion of it, Brzezinski would read the decisions that we had made or things that were postponed. That was an hour-and-a-half. We had a nice breakfast. It was early in the morning. All those factors put together, and I think primarily the fact that we could actually make some decisions there, was what made it attractive.

TRUMAN: I had a feeling that was going to be your answer, but I'd rather hear it from you.

NEUSTADT: I've got a more than one part question. Let me get into it this way. I want to start with the Vance-Zbig thing. You have a comment in the book where you were talking about the neutron bomb at the point where Helmut Schmidt had gone to his parliament for a vote, and you said that you went to call in Zbig and Cy Vance and it was clear that they had disregarded your warnings the previous summer and gotten you committed awfully far. Well that suggests what it suggests, and there are several other times in the course of the book where comparable things seemed to have happened to you. But that's the one I notice most sharply.

CARTER: Either that's not exactly an accurate memory of yours or I confused it in the book.

NEUSTADT: I've got the page. I don't want to misread you here or certainly not misquote you. But let me get exactly what it was that caught my eye.

CARTER: Well, the primary commitment had been made on the neutron weapon through the military commanders. They were always much more eager to reach agreement among themselves. Any kind of new weapon was not difficult to sell to the military leaders who were the defense ministers of the countries and who spoke with great authority. But then came the time when the political leaders, Helmut Schmidt and I, and prime ministers of the other countries had to implement. There was not a vacuum between those military leaders' meetings in Brussels and the nations' capitals around the Atlantic alliance. But there was not necessarily a compatibility between the two. And I was down somewhere in Georgia and all of a sudden got either a daily report from Cy or a weekly report from Zbig and realized how far we had gone at the military level in committing ourselves to the neutron weapon without any commitment at all from a single, European country that they would deploy or accept it. And that's when I went back to Washington and raised the roof.

NEUSTADT: What it says here is you met with the Vice President, and Secretaries Vance, Brown, and Brzezinski to express my concern about the issue. Then you quote from your diary, "they, (I took the 'they' to be those people), had generated a lot of momentum including an immediate agreement for me to produce these neutron weapons. My cautionary words to them since last summer have pretty well been ignored and I was aggravated."

CARTER: Right.

NEUSTADT: Well, it's a terrible problem for a President. I mean, I've seen it happen before. What I got out of this was that you had said, don't get me ahead of the Europeans, or words to that effect. Cautionary words last summer, don't get us over-committed, and the bureaucracy had churned away and these fellows hadn't stopped the bureaucracy and now you were faced with this thing. That's what I get out of it.

CARTER: Your basic premise is substantially correct. I think the nuance that I didn't adequately describe is in the word "they." The primary commitment was made on a military level by Brown and to a much lesser degree Brzezinski. I think that Vance was playing a secondary role completely and probably Fritz was removed from it altogether. That would be my basic memory.

The cautionary comments that had been made both in marginal jottings on routine memoranda and so forth or the thrust of those cautionary comments was that we don't want to commit ourselves to develop another new weapon unless we're sure that somebody's going to deploy it. As the issue became known to the public in Europe, it wasn't a particularly important issue over here, there were enormous political opposition efforts made to abort the neutron weapon. Helmut had himself committed to deploy the weapon, but under pressure he backed off. First, he told me he would only deploy the weapon if another European nation agreed to do so. The British immediately informed me when interrogated they would deploy them. Then Helmut came back and said only another continental European nation would suffice his requirement and there never was another European nation who was willing to deploy the neutron weapon. But I think your question related more to the process than it did to the facts. Is that right, Dick?

NEUSTADT: Yes. What I wanted to get at was, if this is right, you felt that your flank had not been guarded?

CARTER: That's correct. There was a justification for it in that habitually, historically might be a better word, the NATO alliance had worked on a premise that the military leaders would decide on a new weapon or a new strategy. The United States would take the public onus for their proposal and would, in effect, go ahead with enough momentum so that some of the weaker European countries could do it ostensibly with reluctance, but under pressure from the United States. I thought that was ill-advised. I think that, to be perfectly honest to my associates there, I hadn't expressed my concern or my change in policy well enough or clear enough to them. I didn't want the United States to develop a weapon and then force it on the Europeans. I thought that time had passed. This happened to be the first test case when it did come up.

NEUSTADT: You talked in the book about part of what got Brzezinski and Vance publicly tangled with each other was Cy Vance's aversion to public speaking and the need to have it done.

CARTER: I'd say advocacy would be a better word than speaking.

NEUSTADT: Well, that's what I mean. A public advocate, other than yourself; there has to be such a person and Vance did not do it and did not like it and did not want to do it. Somebody had to do it. Brzezinski did it. Then what I infer you to be saying or implying is that the moment Zbig did it, the media picked it up as a contest.

CARTER: That's right.

NEUSTADT: Now, one or two other places you say Zbig was a bit too competitive.

CARTER: Yes.

NEUSTADT: Once it became a contest, he entered in. Several of us know Zbig and we understand that quality. Did you monitor this?

CARTER: Yes.

NEUSTADT: Bother you?

CARTER: No. I monitored it. It didn't bother me.

NEUSTADT: OK.

CARTER: I put a lot of time in on this part of the book, and although I abbreviated it in the final version, I think I got the essence of it. Zbig, like Mike Blumenthal, was feisty and provocative and he had one difference: he didn't have to protect his turf. I don't think Zbig ever felt in four years that he was on shaky ground. I don't think he ever felt that Vance or Brown were coming between me and Zbig. Zbig and I had a relationship not nearly as close as Jody and I, but we joked with each other, we argued about issues, we were together four or five times every day. I started off my days meeting with Zbig. I was a student in many ways of Zbig's as far as the inner makeup of the Soviet Union and different ethnic groups and the history of Eastern Europe. I was an eager student of Zbig's and I enjoyed being around him. I recognized long before I ever was elected President Zbig's strengths and some of his possible weaknesses. Zbig put together a constant barrage of new ideas and suggestions and plans, and 90 percent of them in that totality would have to be rejected. Sometimes maybe 50 percent of them, I'm just estimating, would have some essence or benefit that if modified were good and some of them had to be rejected outright.

Zbig was not responsible for carrying out the policies that he advocated. He didn't have a bureaucracy to carry it out. The State Department was that bureaucracy that had to implement foreign policy. Zbig and I had a very close, easy, friendly relationship. We played tennis against each other. I went out to his house every now and then to eat with him, and his daughter and Amy were the same age. We had a good relationship. Also Zbig had an early record of being my supporter. He was my primary foreign policy advisor all the time I was running for President. He met me in San Francisco when I debated Ford in the second debate on foreign policy and defense. Zbig and I had breakfast that morning and Zbig cross-examined me on foreign policy issues just before I went into the debate with Jerry Ford. We were that close together. So I think through all that period, there was no doubt in Zbig's mind that he had a permanent, solid relationship with me. If I didn't like it, I told him in no uncertain terms. If Zbig said, I'd like to go to Taiwan or China or Germany, which he did a couple of times a week, I'd say, hell no, you're not going, you're going to stay here. He was always wanting to go somewhere as an emissary and very seldom did I let him do it. But when he went, he did a good job.

Now, Cy was not a shrinking violet or anything, but when we had a controversial policy to be presented to the public, Cy didn't want to do it. There were times when I didn't want his press secretary, Hodding Carter, to do it. I thought it ought to come from me or him. And if I wanted Cy to sit down with four or five of the top columnists, Scotty Reston, Joseph Kraft, and others, he wouldn't do it. And sometimes I would urge him three or four times, Cy this statement on Cuba or this statement on the Soviet Union, this statement on SALT or something needs to be promulgated to the public and I don't think I ought to be calling press conferences two or three times a week. He would say, I'll take care of it, Mr. President. First thing I knew Hodding Carter would have mentioned that issue in a daily briefing. So this was a constant. I'm not saying this in criticism of Cy, it was just the way he was. Brzezinski on the other hand was always eager to be the spokesman and he liked to be on *Meet the Press,* or brief the White House press corps on a non-attributable basis. So there were many times when I told Zbig to go ahead and do it.

I never, with one or two exceptions, knew Zbig to promulgate an issue that was contrary to my basic policy. There was a time when his rhetoric went too far, for instance, once concerning the Soviet Union and China as related to Vietnam and the invasion of Afghanistan and so forth. But in general, almost invariably, Zbig put forward ideas that were completely compatible with my own because he and I had spent hours or days or sometimes weeks discussing that subject. He knew my position as well as Jody did. When Zbig would say something, though, because of his appearance, because of his attitude, his statement which Cy could have made in a non-provocative way became provocative. The press not only assumed that this was a contest between Cy and Zbig and that Zbig had won, but also that Zbig was speaking contrary to my desires and, in effect, betraying me. I recognized that then and I recognize it now.

Cy was extremely valuable in his own way. His orthodox, careful, evolutionary plodding attitude and demeanor was compatible with what the State Department was. Zbig's more provocative attitude was compatible with what I thought the National Security Advisor ought to do, giving me a whole range of new ideas and letting me sift through them to see if they were good or bad. But in spite of all I've said, in almost every instance, Cy and Zbig were compatible. And at these Friday morning breakfasts, every now and then they had a difference as would Vance and Brown or Fritz and I. But there was no incompatibility there.

JONES: And Vance seemed to appreciate the way in which you used Zbig?

CARTER: No. Whenever Zbig went anywhere or said anything, it created tremors in the State Department. Vance was extremely protective of the State Department. When some of his subordinates, I don't mean Deputy Secretary, I don't mean Assistant Secretary, I'm talking about the Deputy to the Assistant Secretary. When someone on that level would come to Vance and express to him their displeasure, Cy would immediately leave whatever he was doing and come to the White House and tell me about it. Cy was very, very sensitive about any reflection on the State Department or any usurpation of its authority or vestige of influence to a fault. I understood that, I recognized that, I accepted it as Vance's natural temperament. I used the State Department as kind of anchor or screen to hold us back from doing things that were ill-advised, to point out all the reasons why something wouldn't work, and to make sure that we didn't take any radical steps. It was kind of a stabilizing factor.

JONES: Well, if Vance was not going to assume the role of public spokesman, in a way, he was almost put in the position of having to accept the fact.

CARTER: That's right, but he didn't accept it willingly. That's right. I'm talking about it a lot more today than the subject warrants. But I think he was the origin of a lot of misapprehension. From my perspective, this was about 2 percent of the foreign policy procedure. But for the press, it was about 75 percent of it. Therefore, it was a problem.

HARGROVE: I think what you just said is really the underlying truth. Do you think the balance that you structured of different kinds of knowledge, was a good one?

CARTER: Yes, I do.

HARGROVE: And that you kept it under control?

CARTER: From my perspective, it was no problem. For speculative press and, therefore, the public, whatever problem there was was magnified a hundredfold.

HARGROVE: But they deal in personalities. They don't look at these institutional realities.

CARTER: That's true. Not only did we have our Friday morning breakfast when all of us were right together and when I made the decisions and Zbig recorded and read back to the group what the decisions were. But they also had a weekly meeting of just the three of them, Vance, Brzezinski, and Brown, to work out any possible differences among their agencies that didn't have to be addressed personally by me. This dealt with personal matters and how the assistant secretaries related to one another and so forth. It was a good relationship. But there was that personality conflict or difference that was exaggerated and it intrigued the press I think more than any other single element of government.

YOUNG: I have a related question and it follows up something that Chuck Jones was asking this morning. Why didn't your administration get a better reputation for the many things it did well and for the few dramatic successes it had? It's also related to what you were just saying about the press. Is there something we should know about what's defective about the media beyond things we commonly read? For one thing, there is the suspicion of presidents after Vietnam and Watergate. The other half of the question is should there have been more of an effort on the part of the White House to cultivate an image apart from making sure that there was good policy?

CARTER: I don't really think I can answer either one of your questions, although they're excellent questions. I wrote a chapter in my book about the press, none of which was published.

NEUSTADT: That's a shame, but I understand.

CARTER: But I enjoyed writing it. I got a lot of it out of my system and when I read it over, a lot of it was somewhat childish. Jody and Steve and others prevailed upon me not to put it in the book. I just had a whole series of things where I knew the facts and the press had reported them erroneously. But you know, it wasn't necessary to dredge up all that stuff. Jody is writing a book of his own using a few major examples of what went on in the White House and what the press reported. I don't know how it's going to come out. I hope he's not seduced by being a member of the press too much.

I don't know how to answer your question. I told Bill Moyers as I put in the book, the greatest disappointments of mine in Washington were lethargy, inertia of the Congress, and irresponsibility of the press. That is a very serious problem. How to address it, I do not know. There's an inherent problem in the brevity of the press reporting which is read by the general public or watched by the general public, with thirty-two seconds on the evening news being about the most you can expect to get on a major issue. With news columns, it is the headline quite often that sticks in your mind no matter what's in the column. Obviously, a few periodicals like the *New York Times* and the *L.A. Times* write more definitive analyses. But the number of people who read those are not very great. I don't know how to resolve that question. It's something for the press to address. I never knew of any time when there was an investigative reporter, and there are some excellent ones, who tried to get the truth about an issue where the truth would be nonscandalous or nonprovocative.

When Rosalynn and I were accused of illegally washing bank loan funds through my warehouse and spending them in the campaign, never did a reporter come to me and say, Mr. President, is this true? Did you cheat or use this money illegally? There was nobody on the *Washington Post* or the *New York Times* who tried to investigate the allegations and discern if they were true. Their presumption was that an investigative reporter was supposed to prove that we had violated the law or had done something improper. The same thing applied to Billy and the same thing applied to Hamilton and the same thing applied to others in the administration. That's a part of the press that possibly can be corrected. If Columbia and that great journalism school and so forth would do some things, that's a possibility. They need to have investigative reporters on both sides, because the thing that I tried to point out in the book without belaboring the point is that once an accusation is made against somebody in the public arena, you cannot answer it. You can't prove that you're innocent unless you have a forum. And there's no element in the press inclined to prove the facts. Are you guilty or not? The presumption and the thrust is to prove that you're guilty. Ultimately, the only place that you can go is to something like a Senate investigative committee. Eventually, Billy had to do that, Bert Lance had to do that, and I had to do it in writing concerning the Billy-Libya case. There was an investigation by Paul Curran in New York about the warehouse allegations. Eventually, after an enormous expenditure of time and actually private money, not public money, we were able to prove that we were basically innocent. But that adversarial relationship where the press presumes that you are guilty is another defect that I don't think is going to be resolved easily.

Finally, there's a conviction in the press, at least there was when I was in office, that since Nixon and Johnson had lied or misled the public concerning Vietnam and the bombing of Cambodia and Watergate and so forth, surely we must be doing the same thing. If they investigate it long enough, they would discover these skeletons in our closet. We recognized it, and we had to deal with it. If there is an article in the paper, and particularly a paper like the *Washington Post,* which is remarkably irresponsible at times, for a president to respond to, it just makes a mole hill into a mountain. Quite often, I had to look the other way.

A couple of things have happened since we've been out of office where I really got whizzed off and tried to answer them. One was that the *Washington Post* reported, as you know, that I had tapped Reagan's telephone when he was living at Blair House. It was a horrible thing to contemplate that an incumbent President would tap his successor's telephone. Then we had to spend a great deal of money, which we really didn't have, in finally forcing the *Washington Post* editors to the wall. In lieu of a libel suit, which they certainly would have lost, they finally apologized and withdrew. But Ben Bradlee did not. Ben Bradlee has never admitted that he was wrong. It was only Kay Graham and others who finally admitted it. This is the kind of thing that is there. I don't know how to correct it. The press is culpable, but I have to say to you again, I don't know if I would change it. I don't think that the press ought to be subservient to a President. I think the adversarial relationship is good, the investigative tendency is beneficial for our country, and in balance, I don't think I suffered any more or as much as say Johnson, or Nixon, or possibly even Jerry Ford. It's just a part of our system. I guess that's part of democracy and it's unpleasant at times, but in balance, good.

FENNO: I have a slightly different twist, I think, Mr. President. I wanted to ask you a couple of questions about the problem of support generally and the places where you might have gotten support. Not exactly the party, but perhaps in pushing forward your views. One question has to do with the Georgia delegation in Congress. Other presidents have sometimes found it useful to use the members of their delegation, particularly the House and maybe the Senate, to deal with congressional issues, eyes and ears, and lieutenants and so forth. I wonder if you could say something about your relations with your Georgia delegation as a set of supporters or potential supporters?

CARTER: I had several meetings with the Georgia delegation, either private breakfasts at the White House or even before I went to the inauguration. We had a tacit understanding that if I really needed them on an issue of importance that I would let them know directly and they would make every effort to support me even though it was damaging for them at home. But if I didn't really need them, that I would permit, I would say permit that it would be known, that they would vote in accordance with what they thought was best for them and their own constituents. I think we worked it that way all the way through my four years. I didn't have anybody on the Georgia delegation, maybe to answer your question more specifically, who was my spokesman in the House or Senate.

On defense matters, Sam Nunn is almost pre-eminent and was when I was there. Although he's a junior senator, in matters that really require knowledge and study, Sam Nunn even then was pre-eminent. Senator Stennis would tell you the same thing. If he didn't understand something, he would go to see Sam and say, explain to me how this works or what's going on. Sam was a staunch supporter there. On agriculture matters, of course, Herman Talmadge was. And Herman and I have known each other for a long time. I was never a Talmadge supporter, although my father was. But I never did support Talmadge when he ran for the Senate. When I got to be president, the first thing I did was to have a meeting at Herman's home in Lovejoy with the congressional leadership and whenever I asked Herman on a difficult issue for support, he gave it to me. He was not a forceful leader. I depended on Bob Byrd in the Senate and I depended on Tip O'Neill and Jim Wright primarily in the House. As you know, we had our leadership breakfasts. But the Georgia delegation was not senior enough to have committee chairmanships except for Senator Talmadge. The senior member of the Georgia delegation in the House was a congressman who was elected when I withdrew from the congressional race in 1966 to run for governor. Jack Brinkley has now resigned. So they didn't have the seniority positions to make them important. And I don't think that if I had asked one of them to be my spokesman it would have been particularly fruitful for me. The closest one to me there was probably Wyche Fowler from Atlanta and on occasion I would depend on him to help.

FENNO: But he didn't have much seniority?

CARTER: No. None of the House members had much seniority. None of them had a committee chairmanship or even a subcommittee chairmanship. Herman was the only one who had a committee chairmanship. But they came through. I don't have any complaints about them. The most crucial test was on the Panama Canal treaty. Herman and Sam were strongly opposed to the Panama Canal treaty at the beginning. In fact, Talmadge had signed a resolution in the fall of 1976 against any change in the Panama Canal treaty. I think there were forty-four senators who signed that resolution and Herman was one of them. But eventually, they both voted for the Panama Canal treaty.

YOUNG: Was that one of the occasions when you called upon them?

CARTER: Yes, that was one of the occasions. I put my whole life on the line on the Panama Canal treaty. And the House members supported me on that too. It was very difficult. The thing that people have forgotten is that after the treaty was ratified, we still had that legislation to get through the House. It was a horrible experience. But on those crucial issues where life or death was at stake, Frank Moore would go to them and say, this is something that the President really needs, can you do it? If they said no, then I would call them on the phone and try to add my voice to Frank's to let them know that I really needed them. And I'd say their support was adequate or even better.

YOUNG: I don't know whether it was Frank or somebody whom we talked to and we asked a question like that, what is good congressional relations, and he said, I suppose good congressional relations is when you've got very bad relations because that means you're getting something done. Which is another way of dealing with the question.

JONES: I'm very interested in this matter of what a crisis does to some of the rest of the government and your position in regard to the rest of the government. I suppose the hostage crisis was the principal case, but there might be some others too. Is it so totally preoccupying that all other problems slip away? Does it become possibly an advantage in the sense of leverage, not the crisis itself obviously, but in building support or can it not be used in that way?

CARTER: With the one exception of the Camp David thirteen days, I don't recall any time when I didn't have a multiplicity of conflicting responsibilities on my desk or in my mind. I never could deal unilaterally with any issue because of always these different things. I don't know if any of you have ever been in financial trouble, but there were a couple of years when I first came home when I thought I was going to have to go into bankruptcy and be embarrassed and go back in the Navy or the Electric Boat Company or somewhere and get me a job. And no matter what happened, if it was a beautiful day or if my older son made all A's on his report card or if Rosalynn was especially nice to me or something, underneath it was gnawing away because I owed twelve thousand dollars and didn't know how I was going to pay it. If I couldn't collect my bills that month, I couldn't pay for the fertilizer I'd already sold. It was a gnawing away at your guts no matter what good, other things were going on.

Well, that's the way the hostage thing was for me for fourteen months. No matter what else happened, it was always there. It was painful because I was failing to accomplish what seemed to be a simple task to get those hostages home, and the personal responsibility I felt for them was there. But I couldn't ignore them and didn't ignore all the other routine jobs of the presidency. So there was no way to separate the two. It was just an overlaying of feeling, distraught, or ill at ease, or uncomfortable. Even when we'd go to Camp David and I had a fairly relaxed weekend, I was always thinking about the hostages and getting them home. That kind of a chronic crisis was uncomfortable, but it never did interfere with energy legislation and that sort of thing. We were fortunate in not having any serious, acute crisis like a war, or a matter where I thought my nation's security was in danger, or an embarrassment, or the revelation that was true. I didn't have any acute crisis that really pressed on my mind.

TRUMAN: I want to get in one question that goes back to the congressional relations thing. I'm not sure you didn't answer this this morning, but I'm not certain that you did. You say in your book when you're talking about the fifty dollar tax rebate, as it was developing in the spring of '77, you had made the decision to drop it or to abort it. And you say that you notified the key members of the leadership in Congress of the decision that had been taken. Was there consultation with them on the pending cancellation? Were they in your counsels about the possibility that that was going to get withdrawn before Christmas?

CARTER: Some of them were. I almost lost a friend in that episode with Ed Muskie, who was the chairman of the Budget Committee. And although I had consulted with Bob Byrd and with some of the others about it, I didn't consult with Ed Muskie before he got the word. He was very aggravated about it because he was still fighting to line up votes to pass the fifty dollar tax rebate when I decided that it was better for us not to have it at all. I have a tendency like every other human being to rationalize what I did. If we could have gotten the fifty dollar tax rebate and implemented it early, which was our original commitment, I would have gone ahead with it. But by then I think it was May, was it that late?

NEUSTADT: April, way into April.

CARTER: We thought we were going to implement it by April, put it right into effect like that and stimulate the economy and get some jobs going. We didn't get it. There was some doubt at the time I cancelled it that we could get the votes in the Senate. It wasn't a sure thing at all. More and more members of the Senate were coming to me and saying, Mr. President, this is late, I'm not sure we can get the thing through, the best thing to do is not to put forward this fifty dollar tax rebate because the economy is already recovering and the job programs are going over well. Let's just drop the thing. But I think that uniquely in our administrative circles among the leadership was Lance and me and Blumenthal and when I finally said, well, we'll take the political consequences of reversing our position, at that time, a lot of the members of Congress were eager for me to do so. But a few of them didn't get notified on time.

Another problem that you have when you make a decision like that is that you can't have simultaneity of notification. Some people just get the word before others do. Some of the key members of Congress might be at home on the ranch in Wyoming or up in Maine fishing or something and then you try to put into operation calling two hundred people as rapidly as you possibly can. Invariably, you'll miss two or three of them. And they'll forget that they were out on a fishing boat. All they'll know is that their subcommittee chairman knew we were going to do it and they didn't. That's one of the most difficult problems you have. In this case, the answer was we notified them as soon as I made a decision. We missed Ed Muskie for some reason, but many of his fellow senators were eager for me to cancel that proposal.

TRUMAN: One thing that you don't mention in the book although you talked about the 1980 campaign and leading up to it is the problem, if it was a problem, that you faced for the first time in your career running as an incumbent. You'd always run from the outside looking in. But this time you were running as an incumbent. Did that present any special problems to you? Were you consciously aware that this was a different role and perhaps there was conflict with at least your past or practices that was implicit in this?

CARTER: Yes we discussed that several times, the exceptional difficulty of having to defend not only all of your policies that had been put forward among consumers with deregulation of oil and gas, for instance, and the responsibility for the hostages not being released. I think incumbency was inherently a restraining factor on me and on our campaign organization. I hadn't run that way before. I was in the Senate and was reelected, but I didn't have any opposition for reelection to the Senate, the Georgia Senate. I think as far as presidents go, it is a deleterious factor to be in office. As far as a congressman is concerned, it is an advantageous factor because you have so many goodies to hand out to your constituency in the form of letters returned, attendance at weddings and funerals and barmitzvahs, checking on social security, and sending out mailgrams and letters. You have a great opportunity as an incumbent congressman to campaign for two years at public expense. A president has just the opposite. He's responsible for everything that aggravates people. So it was a new experience for us and we did consider that several times.

TRUMAN: Did you make any special concessions to that or rather make any special allowances for that difference?

CARTER: I tried to. We thought we were going to have the economy in very good shape in October. I remember back in March and April, I was getting projection from Charlie Schultze and Bill Miller that the inflation rate would be down to 5 or 6 percent by October. Of course, the unemployment rate was down too. We underestimated the impact of the oil price increase that later just ran over the whole world and boosted inflation and interest rates. As I pointed out in the book, that was one of the major factors that resulted in our defeat. The other one was a schism in the Democratic party, and I will always believe that the hostages being held and a sense of impotence and incompetence that was generated from those hostages not being released, those were the three factors.

TRUMAN: It sure was no help, there's no doubt about that.

CARTER: No.

TRUMAN: Was this concern about the awkwardness of running as an incumbent one of the reasons you made the decision in January not to withdraw from the debate out in Iowa?

CARTER: No. That wasn't the reason. I had decided even with the hostages held to go to Iowa, as you probably know. When the Soviets went into Afghanistan, that further aggravated the situation and I had a plateful of congressional responsibilities too. My final decision was a close call. My final decision was, I may not have put it in the book, that I would go to Iowa as a president, and I would come back as a candidate.

TRUMAN: Yes, that was the sentence that I read and that's the reason I hooked it into this problem of running as an incumbent. I was struck by that sentence.

CARTER: I thought in dealing with the Soviets in Afghanistan, with the grain embargo, with a possible boycott of the Olympics, with secret aid that we were giving to the Afghan rebels, with the hostage situation, that I would be best served as a candidate and also our nation would be best served if I didn't become an active campaigner that early. Once I got into a political debate which would obviously be nationwide television and absorb the consciousness of all political scientists and others interested in government, with Jerry Brown and Kennedy, I could never go back then to the role of being the president instead of the candidate for reelection.

TRUMAN: I'm puzzled by that frankly, because it's always seemed to me to a degree, obviously not an extreme degree but to a degree, one of the curious inescapabilities of the American presidency is that the president, except in his final term, in a sense has always got to be a candidate. The American people tend to understand and, if it's the right word, forgive the candidate because he's the president.

CARTER: That may be true. I looked on it the other way, as more of an onus than an asset. But I can't sit here today and tell you that I made the right political judgement during 1980 by holding myself aloof from the primaries. I didn't do that at all after the convention. I was a full-fledged campaigner after I got the nomination and I won the nomination, as I say, with about a two-to-one margin over a formidable opponent during the primary session. So I'm not sure that the political judgment was ill-founded. But I think that if I had been more free in going around the country, not particularly campaigning but explaining my policies to the public in town meetings and local TV interviews and that sort of thing, I would have been better off than to be stigmatized by the so-called Rose Garden isolation allegations. I think in balance that I would probably have been better off politically to have been more free with my movements and my travel and my talks.

JONES: Mr. President, all that followed Camp David and I guess I don't quite understand the argument at Camp David. Was it, the people you mentioned, was that a Washington-based analysis of your performance or was it an analysis based on public opinion polls?

CARTER: It was a fairly unanimous recommendation. Jody could answer this question better, but you know I had a group of governors there, governors that were closest to me, Jim Hunt, Dick Riley. They, plus the so-called political wisemen that I just mentioned, two or three of them, there was an agreement among them that I was being overexposed to the press and to the public. And it's hard for you or me to go back to the feeling we had in the summer of '79, of being belabored by or in contravention to the press. We had been through a whole series of events, first Bert Lance and then Hamilton and then the warehouse, Peter Bourne, all that kind of stuff, we were kind of. . . .

JONES: There was a sensitivity there.

CARTER: It was a sensitivity, but I still relished and looked forward to the press conferences because I thought that was one avenue that I had to reach the American people directly without my comments being screened through the press. But our afternoon press conferences didn't help. I could understand that because by the time the evening news came on they didn't show the reporter asking the question and me answering it. They showed the reporter asking the question and they would have a picture of me up there on the screen with my mouth moving. A reporter, Sam Donaldson or Judy Woodruff or somebody, would be telling the American public what I claimed to be saying or what they thought I should have been saying or something. It was really a frustrating sort of thing. We had a few press conferences at night to reach the studio audience directly. But the networks were very reluctant to do that.

JONES: Was there any substitution recommended by these people?

CARTER: No. The general recommendation, I think, was all-pervasive. You're over-exposed, Mr. President. You're having too much access to the press. You're talking about things that sometimes are inconsequential. You need to just address the public directly or through the press when something of major importance is there. Part of this argument was derived from the fact that I had made, I think, five nationwide speeches on energy and the reason I cancelled that energy speech was because the public had turned themselves off. Pat Caddell's definitive poll, he ran one of the most definitive polls I guess anybody has ever done, showed that instead of convincing the American people that the energy crisis was real and that Congress should act on it, I had been to the public so many times it was like the guy crying wolf. They didn't believe it any more. Not only did they not believe it, they had gone past the point of ignoring it, and they were actually aggravated by it. So we were losing ground by my going back with this fairly unpopular harangue, we've got to do something about the energy situation. That was part of the reason for their argument, that I was over-exposed.

JONES: But that leaves the president doesn't it, I mean where is the president to go at that point if one cuts back on press conferences, and the speeches and the repetition are not getting through?

CARTER: Well, the outcome of that week was this speech that the press called erroneously the "malaise" speech. I never used that phrase. It was a press thing that came out. It was the most successful speech I ever made. It had the largest viewing audience and the highest approbation of any speech I've ever made in my life. Immediately following that, I made two other speeches, one on putting forward our energy policy and then I went to I think a CWA convention or UAW convention, I've forgotten which, in Detroit and had a town hall meeting and every question was about energy, something they never would have mentioned. Shortly after that, the Congress finally passed the bill. But it was a successful effort.

I still felt free to call a press conference any time I chose. But instead of doing it on a discipline basis, it was kind of a hit-or-miss basis. Jody's natural inclination was to procrastinate on everything. The incentive for having the press conferences was on a disciplined, every-two-week basis was gone. I don't think now that it was a good decision. But it was a decision that we reached almost with unanimity.

THOMPSON: We've been asking everyone about the so-called "malaise" speech and among ourselves there seems to be a divided jury as to whether it was the right speech or the best speech. Some of us think that it's a speech that we'll go back to again and again in the future because of the enduring truths that it stated. But did you make that decision despite some counter-advice and were you reinforced, if that is the case, by the advice of this outside group that you brought in in a major way?

CARTER: The decision not to make the original, scheduled energy speech was made by me and Rosalynn. I don't think we had any support for that decision at the beginning except Pat Caddell who was convinced that it was counter-productive. Jody was aggravated about it, Stu Eizenstat was aggravated, Fritz almost went into a tizzy. Fritz almost lost control of himself about it. But after I went through the days of relaxation and consultation at Camp David, I felt better and better and I felt at ease. I think it changed my outlook. I spent an enormous amount of time writing that speech and I enjoyed it. I would meet with governors and economists and mayors and representatives of minority groups and the members of Congress and distinguished energy chief executive officers in government.

THOMPSON: Even at least one clergyman.

CARTER: Yes, a group of clergymen. I had about fifteen clergymen, the top ones that I could identify in the nation, and everybody came, nobody refused to come. It was an interesting experience. Somebody could write a whole book just about that week. It was really remarkable.

YOUNG: Including the economists.

CARTER: The economists were kind of dry, I guess. Very little help. No help. But anyway at the end of that experience, we had put together what I thought was a good speech. When I go back and read that speech, I did it when I was writing the book, I still think it's one of the best speeches in its text that I've ever given. I delivered it well. My heart was in it. I had written a lot of the phrases and knew them almost by heart and the response was good. It was a speech that needed to be made. Shortly after that by the way, Giscard d'Estaing in France made a similar speech about the deleterious effect of loss of confidence of people in government and how there ought to be a major national commitment to a specific issue to prove the efficacy of government and the strength of one's nation. That was the basic thrust of my speech. I thought it was a good speech. And I believe that it paid dividends. This was quickly frittered away by me in the way I discharged Mike Blumenthal and Califano; I handled that very poorly. And it came immediately after that. But that was one of the results of the Camp David discussions, that those two cabinet officers ought to be replaced.

McCLESKEY: I'd like to come back to something you said this morning almost at the beginning when you were talking about first going to Washington. You used the term "a different way of governing." You followed that almost immediately with some description of your southern background, the fact that you were a newcomer and so on, and if that's all you meant, then I'm clear on it. But I wonder if you were thinking as well of something more than just the fact that you were different from other presidents in terms of background? Were you really trying to come at it, did you see that you were coming at it, the governing process, in a fundamentally different way?

CARTER: I'm not a good enough historian to answer that question adequately, but I never have known a Democratic president and I guess I've studied the Truman administration more than any other because he's the one I admire most. He had a lot of issues that came up during his term that were directly affecting my own administration. I ran as an outsider. I had studied the techniques of governing of the other presidents, and I knew that my arrangement of staff was different from some of those others. Also, the reason that I was elected was because I was the epitome of an adverse reaction to secrecy and misleading statements and sometimes betrayal by the president of the public, since Watergate and Vietnam and the CIA and so forth. I wanted to have an open administration. As an engineer and as a governor I was much more inclined to move rapidly and without equivocation and without the long, interminable consultations and so forth that are inherent, I think, in someone who has a more legislative attitude, or psyche, or training, or experience. So for all those reasons, I think there was a different tone to our administration.

I had adopted, I'll use the word pious again, I think an attitude of piety that aggravated some people, but also was the root of my political success in 1976. People wanted someone who wasn't going to tell another lie, who was not going to mislead the public and who was going to try to reestablish, in my judgment, ethics and morality in international affairs. That's what I offered, and that's what I tried to carry out. I was obsessed maybe to excess with the need to carry out all my campaign promises. We kept a record of every campaign promise that I made. We even published it, as you know. Stu Eizenstat was the one who evolved our campaign policy and he kept a record of everything I promised and when we'd been in office a few weeks, we published the darn thing, which was probably naive in a way, but it was restraining on me. I would go over with Stu Eizenstat or with Jack Watson, Ham every now and then, a list of the things that we had promised and when we thought we could fit them into our agenda to get them accomplished. We had a very heavy agenda of items that I thought would be beneficial for our country. I can tell you with complete candor that we didn't assess the adverse political consequences of pursuing those goals. I didn't think it was particularly foolhardy. I thought eventually our good efforts would be recognized and our achievements would be adequate to justify my reelection. But I was not under any misapprehension about the adverse consequences of things like China normalization or moving into Africa or getting involved with the Mid East when everybody else had had little success or moving toward the Panama Canal treaties and so forth. We had a complete agenda and we just tried to fit it all in together.

I tried to draw a distinction too between the use of the cabinet as a nationwide group of distinguished and experienced statesmen who, in effect, ran the departments without interference from me and a small loyal staff that would extract from them advice and counsel. A lot of that, as Dr. Neustadt would know, is not innovative. It's not a major change in what some other presidents have done, but the conglomerate totality of it was different compared to other presidencies. And we were in a different time. The press was inquisitive, there was this sense of distrust, and confidence in government was shaken. I felt a particular need to reassure people that we were honest and benevolent and moral. The human rights policy was one way to epitomize this new attitude. I'm not claiming that all those attributes were well-advised or right, but that's the way we looked at our responsibilities. And we tried never to deviate from it. A lot of my advisors, including Rosalynn, used to argue with me about my decision to move ahead with a project when it was obviously not going to be politically advantageous, or to encourage me to postpone it until a possible second term and so forth. It was just contrary to my nature. I felt like I was . . . , I just couldn't do it.

TRUMAN: Were there any major issues that came at you, I don't mean issues such as the ones that were in your campaign promises, but issues that came at you during the first couple of years that would have involved legislative action that you did deliberately postpone or put off to a second term or put them off indefinitely?

CARTER: No, not to a second term. There were a few cases where we couldn't interfere with the congressional consideration of the Panama Canal treaties, for instance. One notable example that I mention in the book is normalization with China. I did not want to have changing the Taiwan relationship and changing the Panama relationship in the Congress at the same time. I still believe that they would have both been defeated. So we did on occasion modify our lists of current agenda items so there wouldn't be that conflict. I can't recall a single issue on which we made a decision that we would wait until a second term or postpone it completely because it was politically damaging or potentially damaging.

YOUNG: At some point, there was an effort to make a Geneva conference on the Middle East thing with the Soviet Union involved, and then it moved into another arena and obviously became yours. Something that you would undertake against much advice. I noticed a sentence in your book that said you became hardened against that advice and as stubborn as I can ever remember in going ahead with it. I wonder how that shift occurred from the Geneva context into your personal responsibility with your own briefings and everything, your own learning in preparation for that experience?

CARTER: Well, even after Sadat went to Jerusalem, the presumption was that he was laying the groundwork for a Geneva conference to be chaired by me and Brezhnev. It was long after that that I decided that we would never have a Geneva conference. We had no hopes of putting one together. Only then did I come to realize in that early spring of '78 that the entire Mid East peace process was going to fail. I couldn't see any alternative to bringing Sadat and Begin together. And once I came to that conclusion, then I had two options. One was to abandon the Mid East peace process altogether and admit failure on a major project that I had undertaken, or to jump into it with both feet of my own. I didn't have too much of an argument with my advisors about bringing Sadat and Begin to Camp David.

The biggest argument I had with my advisors, it got kind of ugly, was almost a year later when I decided to go to Jerusalem and Cairo, because that made me so vulnerable. You know, here was a president traveling halfway across the world and failure was much more politically damaging and embarrassing to our country than going to Camp David and having those other two leaders come in and fail. I don't know how to express it exactly, but I was out on a limb literally, and figuratively, I was way out on a limb. That was a major argument. But again, I thought that we had reached a point of extremism where it was either do that or fail. I think that Jody and Ham, Jody was the most strongly adverse to my taking chances like that, although I think Jody's inherently bolder than Hamilton. But Hamilton was much more amenable to things of that sort than was Jody. Once I made a decision I was awfully stubborn about it. I think if I could have one political attribute as the cause of my success, to begin with, it would be tenacity. Once I get set on something, I'm awfully hard to change. And that may also be a cause of some of my political failures. I just can't say for sure. Stubbornness is not always an attractive attribute.

TRUMAN: When it succeeds it's called courage.

THOMPSON: Jim, will you read your other quote? It seems to me so much of a better way of saying your view on morality in politics than the moralistic thing that sometimes you're tagged with. The one about at Camp David and going out to think.

YOUNG: Oh yes. "I craved intense exercise and lonely places where I could think and sometimes pray." That is a fascinating experience to read about. It is unique in history.

CARTER: I can't imagine a similar event occurring in history.

TRUMAN: Not very many cases where a President of the United States has himself sat down with the old pen and drafted a peace treaty.

CARTER: I don't know what Theodore Roosevelt did off the coast of Maine. He negotiated some sort of settlement between Japan and the Soviet Union. I don't know if he met with the leaders or what.

TRUMAN: He did.

NEUSTADT: Well he didn't meet with the leaders.

TRUMAN: No he met with their ambassadors. But he negotiated. I don't think he wrote it out in longhand.

CARTER: No, I'm sure he didn't.

NEUSTADT: He didn't have nearly as much trouble.

CARTER: No. They weren't as intransigent then as they are now.

TRUMAN: In that case it was easy; they both wanted out.

CARTER: But it was an exciting event. It could have gone either way. And I'm not sure where it's going now. It's a basis for peace if they all ever want it badly enough. I'm afraid that Begin has decided that he's going to ignore the Camp David commitments and just confiscate the property in the West Bank. If that's his presumption, which I suspect, then it's going to be very difficult to make any progress. My judgment is that some of the Arabs are ready to negotiate, but they've got to have some indication that the Israelis will do so in good faith.

YOUNG: We political scientists, probably too much of the time, studying presidential personality and character, focus on the question, how does someone's personality and character affect their four years in office? It occurred to me that maybe we make the mistake by never asking that question the other way around, which is what I want to do now. How does the experience of the presidency really affect you personally? Does it isolate you or does it educate you in some special way, does it exhaust you or exhilarate you, or does it change you?

CARTER: While you are there?

YOUNG: While you are there and now that you're looking back on it.

CARTER: Well, obviously, it's the most intensive, educational process imaginable. You have such a large number of things to learn about simultaneously, you can either avoid the learning process, or you can jump into it with enthusiasm. I did the latter. I was eager to know about the matters that were my responsibility. I was exhilarated by it and gratified by it, even in retrospect since I didn't have two terms and was defeated. I still look on it as one of the most pleasant and gratifying experiences of my life. There was never a time that I was there that I was in despair or felt hopeless, frustrated or, I have to say with an element of humility, that I felt inadequate. I never felt that somebody else could be doing a better job at particular times than I was. And I always did my best. I had a few principles that guided me. One of them was not to duck an issue that I thought was important to my country for my own political benefit. I possibly carried that to excess. But I think I grew in the job and I obviously learned a lot about my country and about the world.

I learned a lot about human nature, my own and otherwise. It brought my family closer together than we'd ever been before. We shared the criticisms, the achievements, and the successes and failures. It was like a team. Even Amy was part of it. The whole family level of awareness and breadth of our experience and the multiplicity of new friendships and relationships with human beings was very large. In every way, I think it was a wonderful experience. Now I'm perfectly at ease with myself. I don't have any regrets. I wish I had been re-elected, but that aside, (it's a pretty good aside), but with that exception, I feel completely happy with the whole situation. I'm grateful that I had a chance to serve. As far as I was concerned, it didn't hurt me. I don't think it made me age, although at the end of my term, I was so exhausted from the negotiations I just hadn't had any sleep or rest at all for three or four days. I was just like any other human being would be—exhausted. But I don't think I suffered any adverse consequences. This week I ran thirty miles. Still in good shape.

YOUNG: If you had been re-elected, do you think, (this is very iffy but why not), do you think that if this conversation were being held four years hence instead of today, that we would be seeing a very different kind of administration, a different kind of presidency in terms of its way of working?

CARTER: From Reagan's?

YOUNG: No. From yours, from your early one. I'm sure on the latter.

CARTER: I think so.

YOUNG: You think it would have been different? The second term would have been substantially different?

CARTER: I believe so. It would have been much more devoted to consolidating the changes that we made, of implementing environmental decisions and educational decisions or deregulation decisions, accommodating some of the economic matters that had evolved, taking advantage of the new energy laws. I think we would have consummated the SALT process and moved on to the next phase. I think that we would had success in the Middle East because I was aware and was deeply committed to it and I wouldn't have had the political constraints on me of a first-term president in these areas.

I think I could have done a lot more with a statesman-like aura rather than an aura of a political opportunist or one who was running for an election. I think it would have been a much more sedate administration with not so much innovation and not so heavy an agenda. By the time we went out of office, we had already put forward our proposals on the major issues that were before us. I would have understood the Congress better. I think I would have had a better relationship with the press the last four years by not being a candidate for re-election. But I've often mentioned to Rosalynn when we're walking in the woods or something now that we would have had our share of economic and other problems, we would have had our share of confrontations and failures with the Congress, and many people would be saying, gee, if Ronald Reagan had just been elected, we would have had zero unemployment and the inflation rate would be down and so forth. So you know I'm not misleading myself about the easy days of a second term. I think the sense of crisis and the sense of urgency and the sense of pressing on multiple issues would have been removed from me and the possibility of being a political candidate would have also been removed. But I read, I think in Truman's biography that the last seven years that Roosevelt was in office, he never got any legislation through the Congress of any consequence. We might have been frustrated too in dealing with the Congress on a second term. I can't say. But I would have enjoyed another four years. There were some things that I would like very much to have completed, like SALT and the Mid East and energy.

YOUNG: It must be quite a frustration.

CARTER: It is. Part of life.

YOUNG: I think we've come to the end of our time.

CARTER: I figured you'd run out of questions eventually.

YOUNG: I'm sure we've learned much and still need to learn more, but our time is up, it's been a long day, and a most enlightening one for us. Mr. President, I deeply appreciate the generous time you've given to us, and the thoughtful, conscientious way you have responded to our questions and concerns as scholars in search of understanding about the presidency in your time and ours.

17

PLAIN TALK FROM PLAINS, MAR. 24, 1985

60 Minutes, Mike Wallace

This interview was conducted in Plains, Georgia, by Mike Wallace who, unlike most post-presidential interviewers, does take a combative stand. Wallace baits Carter to talk about President Reagan. Carter rises to the occasion and gives a negative evaluation of the Reagan administration. In another interview, Carter points out that CBS taped about one and one-half hours of conversation on a wide range of topics, but only broadcast this brief segment that was critical of Reagan. Carter notes that the vast majority of the interview did not mention Reagan at all.—*Editor*

MIKE WALLACE: We spent last Monday in Plains, Georgia, with Jimmy Carter, the 39th President of the United States, and he was surprisingly candid on the subject of Ronald Reagan. He devotes his days now to writing, fishing, farming and teaching and says that he's happy doing it, that he doesn't look wistfully at Washington and the power that resides there. His Democratic Party has turned its back on him and he acknowledges that the American people would just as soon forget the Carter years.

This isn't—these aren't easy questions to ask, sitting in a man's living room, but the Carter image, the political image, is that of a loser. Why?

PRESIDENT JIMMY CARTER: Well, it may be easier to ask the question than it is to answer it, but I'll be glad to answer it. Well, the last—my last political encounter was with Reagan in November of 1980, and I

---

lost and I think that's the image that still remains in people's minds, that I was not re-elected.

WALLACE: You must be very jealous, in a sense, of Ronald Reagan.

PRESIDENT CARTER: Not really.

WALLACE: Jealous of the fact that he is—I mean if—if his is the "teflon Presidency," nothing sticks—

PRESIDENT CARTER: Mine was the opposite.

WALLACE: Yours was the "flypaper Presidency."

PRESIDENT CARTER: I think that's true. When I was there, there was no doubt who was responsible.

WALLACE: The buck stops here.

PRESIDENT CARTER: I was—I was responsible. And now there is a great doubt about who's responsible, and Reagan has been extremely successful, more than any of his 39 predecessors, in not being responsible for anything that's unpleasant or completely—or not completely successful.

WALLACE: How does he manage that, Mister President?

PRESIDENT CARTER: Well, he's blamed me for his $200 billion deficits. He's blamed me and Ford and Nixon for his lack of understanding of the Lebanon crisis, saying that this intelligence network was not adequate for him. He's blamed the Congress for his withdrawal of the Marines from Lebanon under, you know, very damaging circumstances, and—and he is—has never accepted responsibility for lack of progress in Middle East peace or a lack of progress on alleviating the problems of the poor and so forth. And he's been remarkably successful in telling people, you know, everything is okay, at least as far as I'm concerned everything's okay. It's okay for—for the Marines to be embarrassed and damaged in Lebanon, it's okay to have $200 billion deficits, it's okay to have $120 billion trade imbalances and so forth.

WALLACE: He doesn't say it's okay, Mister President.

PRESIDENT CARTER: He said it's okay with him and—and—and that, you know, he's not responsible, don't associate him as President with any of these problems. We have now almost doubled our nation's debt since Reagan has been in office. When I left the White House, the United States of America was the greatest creditor nation on earth. By the end of this year we'll be the greatest debtor nation on earth. And we're now seeing a wave of economic suffering in the agricultural community of our country which is the most evident first indication of Reagan's policies. I think the second indication will be a continued deterioration in the banking and financial institutions of our country. So, you know, what will be the Reagan heritage is too early to say. I cannot think of a single international or diplomatic achievement that's been realized by Ronald Reagan.

WALLACE: President Carter has written a new book on the Middle East called *Blood of Abraham*. We asked him what bold new moves he might undertake there now if he were President.

PRESIDENT CARTER: There is no reason why George Shultz can't sit down with—with Yasir Arafat, if they want to make a bold new stroke.

WALLACE: If who wants to make a bold new stroke?

PRESIDENT CARTER: If the United States wants to make a bold new stroke and the people in the Middle East.

WALLACE: Would you recommend that now?

PRESIDENT CARTER: Yes, I think that would be a good move, yes.

WALLACE: What is going to—what's going to be the outcry in Israel if such a meeting were to take place?

PRESIDENT CARTER: We could make—well you know there—there has to be a willingness to face outcries, and I don't see any way for any substantive progress to be made in the Middle East peace process without the Palestinians being intimately involved in the process.

WALLACE: But it's not just the Middle East that worries him. It's war and peace. You think we're closer to war today than we should be?

PRESIDENT CARTER: I think we have let the world know that our country is no longer the foremost proponent or user of negotiations and diplomacy, and that our country's first reaction to a troubled area on earth is to try to inject American military forces or threats as our nation's policy.

WALLACE: Human rights under Ronald Reagan.

PRESIDENT CARTER: Well, Reagan has basically abandoned our nation's commitment to the human rights policy that we espoused.

WALLACE: Why? Because he's a callous man?

PRESIDENT CARTER: I think part of it was a natural adverse reaction to my administration's policies. One of his first moves, for instance, was to send Mrs. Kirkpatrick to snuggle up to Pinochet in Chile and to the military junta in Argentina, who had been responsible for more than 10,000 deaths through those who disappeared in the middle of the night. And this was a clear signal that went over the world that the previous human rights policy under my administration was being changed. I don't know what his motivations are, but the result has been that the world now sees our country as not being a champion of human rights, but as being dormant, at best, in the face of persecution.

ROSALYNN CARTER: I think this President makes us comfortable with our prejudices.

WALLACE: That's not very nice, what you're saying.

ROSALYNN CARTER: But it's the way I feel, and I think it's true.

WALLACE: Despite rumors that she might run for governor of Georgia, Rosalynn Carter says she has no political ambition. But she is no less candid about President Reagan than is her husband.

ROSALYNN CARTER: I think he's been devastating to the country and—

WALLACE: How? How has he devastated the country?

ROSALYNN CARTER: Well, I wouldn't trade places with him in history, with Jimmy and Ronald Reagan, for anything in the world, unless— I'll qualify that because he could correct some of those things. But the big budget deficit that I think is going to—that my grandchildren will have to pay for, that's going to hurt us forever. He did not even have a single gesture of good will toward the Soviet Union the whole first four years.

(The Carters singing a hymn in church)

WALLACE: Since they left Washington, the Carters have returned to a simpler life in Plains. On Sundays, they and their daughter Amy, now near college age, worship at Baptist services. The President teaches Sunday school here, frequently attended by large groups of visitors, tourists.

PRESIDENT CARTER (addressing Sunday school class): " . . . might have my joy fulfilled in themselves." How much joy were the—were the disciples going to have? Not much.

WALLACE: And after church, the President patiently poses for pictures and signs autographs for folks who have stopped by to meet Plains' sole tourist attraction. Twice a week, he travels to Atlanta where he teaches liberal arts courses as a Distinguished Professor at Emory University. But his roots, and his heart he says, are in Plains. Still, though, he will talk politics when prodded.

PRESIDENT CARTER: Good to see you! Just fine!

WALLACE: Is hands-on political experience a must for a President? Could a Lee Iacocca conceivably be as good a President as a Jimmy Carter or a Ronald Reagan?

PRESIDENT CARTER: Well, I know he could be as good as one of us. Whether he could be as good as both of us I really don't know, but I think that that sort of approach to—to American life that Lee Iacocca has exemplified would be very beneficial in the—in the White House.

WALLACE: But he's never been elected to office. Does that necessarily put him beyond the pale for the Presidency?

PRESIDENT CARTER: No, because he would have to go through a very torturous and difficult political campaign to get there, and so that— his absence of experience in the political field would obviously be— be filled while he was running for President.

WALLACE: Sounds like Jimmy Carter is going to run an "Iacocca for President" campaign.

PRESIDENT CARTER: I have an admiration for him.

WALLACE: You do?

PRESIDENT CARTER: Sure.

WALLACE: One of the personal low points of his presidential years, he acknowledges, was his collapse while jogging in a mountain marathon. Do you remember this, Mister President?

PRESIDENT CARTER: Sure.

WALLACE: Do you think that that, in the final analysis, that episode did you any harm politically?

PRESIDENT CARTER: It probably did. I think that that showed that I had tried something I couldn't—that I couldn't finish and that I had attempted something where I didn't succeed.

WALLACE: And it had nothing whatsoever to do with politics or governmental affairs or—

PRESIDENT CARTER: Well, you know, politics is a matter of image, and the image that I had attempted something that—that I didn't accomplish I think did have political connotations.

WALLACE: His mother, Miss Lillian, died two years ago. He took us to the Carter burial plot in Plains. You were very, very close to your mother.

PRESIDENT CARTER: Yes, I was. Momma helped shape my life. Mother, even in the difficult years of racial segregation down here, Mother was the—I guess was the token liberal, the token integrationist around Plains. And she was always the champion of the underdog. And at that time, of course, the blacks were the underdogs. So, Momma was—she was really inspirational. When—after my father died, Mother kind of blossomed forth.

WALLACE: Miss her?

PRESIDENT CARTER: Yes, very much so, particularly when I—you know, early in the mornings. I used to go out before daybreak and Momma and I would just talk about politics or—or sports or family affairs and kind of watch the sun come up together in the mornings, even when she was in her last months. She knew she had cancer and she knew that she wouldn't live very long, but she was always an exciting companion.

WALLACE: You know, I have one memory on television of watching you and Ted Kennedy on the platform back in 1980. Was that a bitter time for you? And does any of that bitterness remain toward Ted Kennedy?

PRESIDENT CARTER: Well, I don't think—well, in fact, maybe "bitter" is the right word. We didn't feel, and I still don't feel, that Ted Kennedy had any reason to challenge me as an incumbent Democratic President and therefore destroy the unity of the party, which is so crucial. And about the only time the Democratic Party has a chance to be unified is when there is an incumbent Democratic President.

WALLACE: Mm-hmm.

PRESIDENT CARTER: And I think that—that the primary season, with Kennedy never giving up, even until the convention assembled, gave us a tremendous obstacle to overcome in—in the fall election. But I think that it would be highly unlikely that Ted Kennedy would ever be approved as a potential President by the American people. He's always done best when he didn't have a chance to win.

WALLACE: So, you think that next time around, whatever is the image of Ted Kennedy in the mind of the American people, it will not have changed sufficiently for them, for the Democratic Party, to give him the nomination?

PRESIDENT CARTER: That's right. That's my expectation and also my hope.

18

LEGITIMATE PRIDE, APR. 1985

Leaders Magazine

The tone of this and almost all subsequent interviews changes dramatically from the combativeness that characterized the presidential interviews. Carter has now earned the respect of his interviewers and can talk about the good deeds of his post-presidency.—*Editor*

QUESTION: How will the Carter Center differ from other think tanks, and where will it be in two years, and in the future?

CARTER: A former President has two or three things to offer to make it special. In the first place, we are making it nonpartisan, a bipartisan effort on all major projects. We've already embarked on some: one on Mideast peace—President Ford and I co-chair this effort, which will be ongoing; the second is on U.S.-Soviet relations, with an emphasis on arms control—again, President Ford is co-chairman with me. The center's audience, we hope, will be a worldwide audience. In this country, of course, we'll deal through media of all kinds, with documentaries, interviews and things of that kind that would let a maximum audience discern what we're doing. We'll have eight endowed chairs at our center that will concentrate on matters that we consider to be of major importance to our country and to the rest of the world: Middle East peace, Soviet relations, health care, education, environmental quality—including updating the Global 2000 report—and human rights. We'll have international scholars who'll come to work for an extended period of time, but not on a permanent basis. These will be experts in the field of their particular study. The Carter Center is a part of Emory University, just as are the law school, medical school and theology school. In every case our senior scholars and those who assist them at the Carter Center will also be teaching either at Emory or in one of the 23 colleges and universities in the Atlanta area. We still have funds to raise, to endow the different chairs of study, and that will be a continuing effort until we reach our goal of about $15 million. We've raised enough money now to build the Presidential Library and the Center itself, but we've just begun our effort to raise funds for the endowed chairs.

QUESTION: What are the three most urgent problems in world health, and what are your solutions?

CARTER: We've now completed the first phase of our health-care project. We discerned the 13 most severe causes of mortality and morbidity in this country. We've also quantified the gap between what we know how to do to prevent those afflictions and what we are actually doing. Out of this, we have identified five or six of the major causes that can be prevented. The single most urgent problem in this country is cigarette smoking, causing more than 1,000 unnecessary deaths each day. Probably by the end of this century, cigarettes will be the major cause of unnecessary illness and death throughout the world. There's a rapid increase in the rest of the world in the smoking of cigarettes. Cigars and pipes, too, are pretty severe causes of cancer in the mouth and larynx. Of course, obesity, lack of exercise, excessive consumption of alcohol and other threats to health are also causes of concern.

QUESTION: Don't both the Bible and the Koran say there will never be peace in the Middle East?

CARTER: I think that by selecting certain partial quotes within the Bible and the Koran you can find that statement, but I think that the Bible, both the Old Testament and the New Testament, teaches that there should be peace among people. The goal should be peace. Whether it will be perfect peace, no one knows. I doubt it.

QUESTION: Should genetic engineers and others who manipulate the basis of life be restricted in any way?

CARTER: Yes, they should be restricted in some way. There needs to be, first of all, a realization of priorities of health capabilities. We have limited funds for research for prevention of illness and death and also for the treatment of illness once it occurs. I appointed a special commission when I was President to deal with the ethics of euthanasia and the prolongation of life beyond its normal span and, to some limited degree, with the use of genetics to create a so-called superior being or something of that kind. There will be a natural reluctance on the part of both government officials and medical leaders to tinker with the quality of human life by selective genetic breeding and things of that kind. But at the same time, the use of genetics as a means to reduce afflictions and birth defects will be permissible and acceptable.

QUESTION: Is there a role for religion in government?

CARTER: Yes. I never have found any incompatibility between my religious beliefs and my oath of office to the laws and Constitution of the United States. But politics ought not to be used to try to shape a definition of religion. We should not define our nation as one dedicated to a particular religion, and religious leaders should not emphasize their own personal political beliefs as a definition of what is a proper Christian or interfere in the freedom of people to make their own choice politically. In the past few years there's been an escalation in effort, particularly by the television evangelists and the so-called right wing or extreme fundamentalists, to emphasize religious beliefs as a definition of what is a proper Christian, and also to inject their own particular political beliefs into the religious field. Jerry Falwell and others, for instance, equate a proper Christian with one who is against SALT negotiations with the Soviet Union, or against the Panama Canal treaty, or against the establishment of a department for education or for mandatory prayer in schools. Some of them also feel that you can't be a proper Christian unless you're in favor of minimizing the effect of the public schools. They've now maintained that the public school system is the focal point, or the birthplace, of "secular humanism," which is a threat to Christianity itself, and therefore, things that would weaken the public school system are thought to be admirable. I deplore very strongly these kinds of theoretical pursuits in theology and religion. While they are more of a threat now than in the recent past, they are likely to be transient in nature.

QUESTION: What taught you the most about succeeding in life?

CARTER: I have never been afraid of taking a chance or facing the possibility of defeat, and I've always done the best I could. I've never been particularly grieved or disheartened when I tried something and it wasn't completely successful if I had done my best. I've had an underlying stability in my life derived from my community, family and religious beliefs. There hasn't been any one dramatic thing in my life that has transformed me. One of the things that shaped my life was realizing that I have one life to live on this earth, and I ask God frequently not to let me waste it and to let my life be beneficial for my fellow human beings in His kingdom.

QUESTION: What do you think is the single most important thing to teach children?

CARTER: I think the most important thing to teach is that we should not accept unnecessary limits in our own lives. The most severe limit is most often the one we place on ourselves by not striving for greatness, or by not attempting to utilize our talent, ability and opportunities to the utmost. A refusal to meet life's challenges with vigor and determination can severely restrict one's vitality.

QUESTION: What do you feel is your single greatest accomplishment to date?

CARTER: Two hundred years from now when people consider my name, I would like them to equate it with peace and human rights. I hope that for the remaining years of my life I can continue to pursue these two goals—human rights in its broadest sense and the use of our great strength for the benefit of peace in this world. I don't know to what extent history will show that I have been successful, but I would hasten to add that my life is not yet over.

QUESTION: How can society be developed to respect people who are not winners?

CARTER: Society has to be careful how it defines winners and losers. The leaders in our society who do the defining tend to assume that winners are those who are most similar to us, who have fame, material wealth and some publicized success. But there are others in life who are perhaps even greater winners in the eyes of God: those who are humble, self-sacrificial, unselfish, who care about others and who are filled with charity or love. Quite often these people are not known, are not famous, don't have a notable accomplishment in their lives and have little material wealth. I'm always cautious about deciding that people are losers, even though they haven't reached the same level of achievement that I've defined for my own life. The so-called winners must be sure that their actions don't denigrate the accomplishments of others. It's not always proper for so-called successful people to look down on unsuccessful people and ask, "What's wrong with you people?"

QUESTION: What can a leader do to avoid corruption?

CARTER: The adherence to simple ethical standards—my preference would be founded on religious belief—is a good prohibition to corruption.

QUESTION: Is it even possible to avoid corruption in politics?

CARTER: Yes. I don't believe that Harry Truman was ever corrupt. He was meticulously honest and I think many other leaders have been the same. Politicians are no more exposed nor susceptible to corruption than those in other areas of life such as journalism, business and commerce, medicine or education. You can violate the ethics or standards of your own profession because of avarice, greed or selfishness just as well in one profession as another. But politicians are probably the most severely scrutinized and publicly criticized when they err.

QUESTION: Is the greed that propels the businessman to sell more products so he can make more money so that he can do better things for his family a good part of avarice and greed or are they only bad words?

CARTER: I think that avarice and greed are both bad words. It's a matter of priority. Jesus said that it's easier for a camel to go through the eye of a needle than for a rich man to get into Heaven. Someone who's obsessed with making money to the exclusion of other goals in life has likely forgone the possibility of acceptance in God's kingdom. We each establish our own goals in life, and if you put the acquisition of money as your top priority in life, then I think that's where the danger comes. This could lead to the downfall of politicians and business leaders as well. If the accumulation of riches is the only purpose in life, then that's avarice or greed, and inherently that is bad. I hasten to add that one can be quite successful as a business leader under our free enterprise system without being consumed with a desire for riches.

QUESTION: What do you believe are the key issues that will determine the future of society?

CARTER: The major challenge now is to try to discern as best we can what the changes might be in the future, and to react accordingly. At the Carter Center one of our major purposes will be the analysis of societal changes concerning such matters as population growth, the erosion of land, destruction of forests, waste of natural raw materials—and the opportunities to protect the quality of life and to adjust to changing times with a minimum of suffering or deprivation. This may let us understand better the causes of Third World debt, revolution and massive starvation. Our economic competitors in countries like Japan and Germany are doing this very effectively. We need to do the same—for many obvious reasons.

QUESTION: Does the public in the United States really appreciate freedom?

CARTER: Freedom, liberty, justice and equality of opportunity are things that we appreciate, but just to clasp them to our breast and say we're so proud to have these things in the United States is not enough. We have an obligation to see where they are not available to others, and then to decide what we can do about it. How can we share these great blessings of freedom and democracy with others? How can our nation be a shining light of inspiration? How can we use our influence in a proper way to correct deficiencies that exist in the lives of others? In the future, our nation is probably going to move in that direction more than it has in the past and certainly more than right now, because we can husband those advantages in isolation only in a counterproductive way. The more we try to retain these benefits to ourselves alone the more they are in danger. We can't shape other people's lives; there has to be a limit on what we can do. But to recognize the interrelationship that exists among nations, the extremely poor and the extremely rich, is a mandatory thing for us, and in the recognition, the sharing and the enhancement of quality of life for us and others, that's where the *legitimate* pride in America comes.

19

"ONE MORE HELICOPTER . . . ,"
MAY 12, 1986

USA Today, Barbara Reynolds

Reynolds treats Carter as the "elder statesman" and elicits opinions on a diversity of topics such as the Libyan air raid, Middle East peace, and the "Teflon" quality of President Reagan. In this interview, Carter admits that Reagan is a better politician than he.—*Editor*

USA TODAY: Since you left office, terrorism has increased. Would you have ordered the air raid on Libya?

CARTER: No. I don't believe so. It's hard to say, not having been in the White House, what I would have done, but I think there's a better way to approach the threat of terrorism

USA TODAY: What's the better way?

CARTER: First, it's necessary to understand the motivations of terrorists. What are their goals? What causes them to be willing to sacrifice their own lives and the lives of innocent people? It's fairly obvious that terrorist leaders like Khadafy want publicity. They want stature, they want to be placed on an equal basis with the leaders of major nations. They want to be famous. And they want to intimidate their enemies by making it uncomfortable or impossible for American tourists to travel and difficult for U.S. business to compete abroad. And I think that mounting a bombing attack in response to terrorist acts gives the terrorist leaders most of those goals: fame, publicity, stature, importance, popularity. And it has intimidated American citizens.

USA TODAY: So you think the Libyan bombing raid will be counterproductive?

CARTER: I think it might prove to be. It also tended to separate us from our European allies, although that schism was at least partially healed at the Tokyo summit. But there are other ways to deal with terrorism.

USA TODAY: How did you deal with Khadafy?

CARTER: We had a few outbreaks of terrorism when I was president. Almost every week there was an airplane hijacked. And Khadafy was responsible for a lot of it. He was receiving hijackers in Libya and making heroes out of them. So at the Bonn economic summit in 1978, the president of France and I decided to try to get the other leaders to join us in doing something about it. We drafted a letter: We told Khadafy if you accept any more hijacked planes, or if you don't return the hijacked plane to its owners and the hijackers to justice, we will never again permit a Libyan plane to land in any of our nations and will never permit any of our planes to go to Libya. It was a private, unpublicized letter, signed by me, and the leaders of France, West Germany, Italy, Great Britain, Canada, Japan. Khadafy knew we meant business. He knew that if all airline travel between his country and ours was terminated, this would be a devastating economic and political blow, and he never again accepted another hijacked plane. And we carefully did not reward him with publicity, we treated him as a criminal. We acted together, and it was effective.

USA TODAY: Did you try that kind of strategy again?

CARTER: Yes—Iran. After our hostages were taken, after about a week or so, the Ayatollah Khomeini announced that he was going to put all the American hostages on trial. He was going to determine which ones were guilty of spying, and then he was going to execute the "guilty" ones. I tried to assess how to protect our hostages without rewarding Khomeini with additional publicity. I prepared a message to the ayatollah, and I got the leaders of Germany, France, Italy, and Great Britain to join me. I told him, if you put the American hostages on trial, we would interrupt all trade and commerce between Iran and the outside world. If you injure or kill a hostage, we will respond militarily. Khomeini knew we meant business. We didn't send a public letter, we sent a private message to him. And he never put an American hostage on trial; he never injured or killed one.

USA TODAY: Your mistakes in office brought you a lot of criticism, but President Reagan seems to be able to shake off criticism. Why?

CARTER: I never have quite understood this phenomenon myself. In the first place, we have a different political philosophy. I am more in tune with Harry Truman; I had that sign on my desk, "The buck stops here." It was my government; I took responsibility for it. President Reagan has a different philosophy. He avoids responsibility, successfully, for anything that's unpleasant or unpopular or disappointing or embarrassing or a failure. It's never his fault. It's always the fault of his cabinet members, of Congress, his predecessor in the White House, or some foreigner. Never his fault. And third, I would say that he's just a better politician—than I am, or was.

USA TODAY: You admit that?

CARTER: Sure.

USA TODAY: A better communicator, or—

CARTER: He's just better at politics. You know, he's kept his popularity very high, yet he's had no detectable achievements in foreign policy. We've had unprecedented deficits, unprecedented trade imbalances, many members of the administration have been embarrassed by improprieties and so forth, and he's come through it all unscathed. He just knows how to handle the political arena better than I did.

USA TODAY: How will history judge your presidency?

CARTER: I feel at ease with history. I think historical analysts will actually assess what I did in office, what sort of standards we followed, and in other nations our administration is looked upon very favorably. I don't have any concern about how President Reagan is treated—I'm sure we'll find that he's treated very well by history. But I feel that our record will stand the test of time.

USA TODAY: Looking back on your term as president, do you have any regrets?

CARTER: Well, I wish I'd sent one more helicopter to Iran—there's one. I think that would have changed the course of election history in 1980. You have to remember that in November, 1980, President Reagan got less than 51 percent of the vote. That's a fact that a lot of Americans have forgotten—there was no overwhelming mandate then for Reagan. And I think had our hostages in Iran been released early in the year, that I would have won the election without much of a problem. Who knows, it's just a matter of conjecture.

USA TODAY: When you were in the Navy, you worked on nuclear submarines. Could there be a nuclear accident like Chernobyl in the USA?

CARTER: Yes, it's possible. Somewhat similar events have occurred in England, and in Canada. When I was working in the nuclear submarine program, there was a disaster of this kind in Canada, a place called Chalk River. Subsequently, I went up there with my crew of men who were assigned to the second atomic submarine. Part of our duty was to assess the damage to the core of the nuclear reactor. We went into the center of the core, and we were permitted to take the maximum dose of radiation, which then was probably a thousand times higher than it is now. We have nuclear reactors in this country, not designed exactly like those in the Soviet Union, but without massive containment buildings that could keep the results of an explosion on the premises. We've been remarkably fortunate in this country that there has been minimal injury or death to human beings. It's always a possibility, although unlikely.

USA TODAY: Should we abandon nuclear power?

CARTER: No, I don't think so. I think that we ought to reassess the safety factors. After the Three Mile Island accident, I appointed the most competent group that I could find to investigate the causes and to tighten up safety. We have an extremely high level of safety consciousness in this country now.

USA TODAY: In your new book, *The Blood of Abraham*, you argue that to achieve peace in the Mideast, it will be necessary to find a homeland for the Palestinians. Are you satisfied with the way the Reagan administration has dealt with this?

CARTER: No, there's been practically no initiative taken by the Reagan administration in the last five and a half years to deal with that basic problem in Palestinian life, and until the policy in question is resolved, as Israeli Prime Minister Begin agreed at Camp David, I don't think we can expect to see an alleviation of the tension in the Middle East.

USA TODAY: You said not long ago that the Camp David peace process had come to a screeching halt. Do you still feel that way?

CARTER: The Camp David accords, concluded in September, 1978, were the first step. Then it took us about six months to negotiate a peace treaty between those two countries. After I left office, there was practically no effort made to pursue the opportunities that Camp David provided. President Reagan did make a very fine speech on the subject in September of 1982. But there's been no follow-up. And as far as the Palestinians are concerned, there's been no tangible effort made at all. The only thing that President Reagan did do of an appreciable nature was to send the Marines into Lebanon, which was a very serious tragedy. I think the Lebanese experience was so unpleasant that it may have discouraged the Reagan administration from any further real involvement.

USA TODAY: Do you think there is too much mixing of religion and politics today? Should a person's religious preference be stamped on public policy?

CARTER: No. I'm a Southern Baptist, and I have always believed in a total separation of church and state. And I think the injection of religion into politics is not good for this country: The Moral Majority trying to say if you voted for the Panama Canal treaty, you are not a Christian; if you negotiate with the Soviet Union, you're not a Christian. Those kind of things to me are ridiculous. I think you've seen a tremendous loss of popularity for people like Jerry Falwell, who's now had to change the name of his organization from the Moral Majority to something different. My belief in Christ is so important in my life, that it's unshakable. I don't accept human definitions of what I have to believe, you know, to be a Christian.

20

KOVACH ON CARTER, APR. 1990

Southpoint, Bill Kovach

Bill Kovach, an ex–newspaper editor, now with the Neiman
Foundation at Harvard University is an apparent Carter fan.
In the article preceding this conversation, Kovach notes
Carter's accomplishments as president and suggests that his
"post-presidency offers us a vantage point from which to re-
vise our judgment of his work as president."—*Editor*

KOVACH: Let's talk about the South, which you symbolize as much as
anybody. The South has finally achieved a nationally recognized political and economic strength. And I'm curious what it feels like to
see the Republicans capitalize on that regional development, after
decades of dominance by the Democratic Party in the region.

CARTER: I think the Republican achievements are exaggerated by the
press primarily because there is so much emphasis on the presidency
itself. Who wins the White House is looked upon as evidence of the
orientation of a state. Georgia, for instance, with the exception of
voting for me twice, has voted Republican, I think, since 1960. But
both of our U.S. senators are Democrats. All of our ten congressional
members except one are Democrats. And probably 85 percent of
both houses of the legislature are Democrats. All the state officers
are Democrats. So, the Democratic Party is still a commanding presence in Georgia. But the image is that Georgia had shifted Republican. I think it's not because of party affiliation; it's because of the relative effectiveness of the candidates who are running for president.

KOVACH: That seems to be based on the ability of the candidates to
develop and discuss policies that were true to the Democratic Party

---

heritage but still in tune with a more conservative outlook for the American people—as you did when you ran in '76 and in '80.

CARTER: Exactly. I don't see any incompatibility between the conservative heritage of Southern politicians—let's leave out the race issue for a moment—and what the Democratic Party can and ought to do to win the White House. Southerners and many others believe in a strong defense; they believe in minimal intrusion of the federal government into local and state affairs; they believe in a strong free-enterprise system. But at the same time the people of this region are in favor of environmental quality; they are in favor of government support for education, for health care. I think they favor human rights, government support of foreign countries.

There is still a disturbing element of racism in our country, in my opinion, which is relatively concealed except for the final result, the tabulation of votes. And ever since 1964 when Barry Goldwater subtly introduced states' rights into the campaign, there has been a feeling among many white voters that the Republicans would best protect them against affirmative-action programs and other social programs designed to compensate for the ravages of racism. Obviously there are exceptions to the case, but it's still there. And I think, for instance, when President Reagan made his opening campaign speech on states' rights in Philadelphia, Mississippi, this was not an accident. It was a clear and a very subtle message concerning civil rights. And this is still a factor in the South. There are a lot of Southerners who think the government has gone too far in compensatory education, in integration of schools and social programs.

KOVACH: As a candidate and a president who ran a campaign and a government based on an open discussion of issues, facing, on the other side, the manipulation of symbols, the very powerful symbols like the speech in Philadelphia, Mississippi—how do you run a campaign on an even basis in that atmosphere?

CARTER: I think the American people detect an effort to address difficult issues during the campaign. I don't think I ever avoided issues of that kind in my '75–'76 campaign. And I won over what was generally accepted to be almost insurmountable obstacles. Nobody thought I was going to win. I think it's a matter of human nature not to want to confront unpleasant facts.

There are some inherent political advantages to the Republican side because if you have high inflation it affects everyone and if you have high unemployment it only affects those who are directly unemployed. I think the Republicans have been much more competent in assessing those distinctions in the political campaign environment than have the Democrats. And also with President Reagan and President Bush, not only are they very avid to ascertain what the public-opinion polls show to be attractive or not, but they have been much more able, especially President Reagan, to avoid any responsibility for the unpleasant attributes of the presidency, for unnecessary sacrifice on the part of the American people or an unpleasant foreign development or a failure or mistake. He successfully secluded himself from relationships with those kinds of unpleasant or unpopular issues while he was in the White House. It was always someone else, sometimes a cabinet officer, most often the Congress. Sometimes his predecessors in office. And this was a very effective means to keep President Reagan in office. And I think it's something that the Democrats have not addressed adequately.

I don't feel discouraged about future elections. Obviously a lot of it is the performance of President Bush in office, a lot of it is fortune, what's going to happen of an uncontrollable nature, a worldwide shortage of oil that would drive inflation rates and interest rates up or some unpleasant overseas adventure shortly before election time. But I think if we can come forward with a candidate who can be conservative on defense and local responsibility in federal government activities on the one hand and progressive on civil rights, human rights, environmental quality, education, health care, I think that kind of campaign would be successful. One other point is that the identity of the candidate we choose as our nominee is crucial. The platform has to be evolved by the candidate himself. He either accepts or rejects particular facets of a platform that was written at the Democratic convention. So, in effect, it's identity, the character, the philosophy of the candidate we choose that is the key.

KOVACH: When you were talking about the success with which the Republicans were able to keep the president somehow separated from policy problems, you said the Democrats haven't studied that or learned enough from that. What do you think the Democrats can learn from those techniques?

CARTER: I haven't successfully addressed that issue. I'm the only Democrat who has served in the White House in a long time. And I obviously got the reputation as a Velcro president. If something went wrong in our country, I was the one who went before the public and said, "We've got to make this sacrifice on energy consumption" and that sort of thing. And I think if I were president again, I would have done the same thing. My political advisers and my wife were always saying, "Don't get involved in that, wait until a second term. Don't address this issue because it's obviously and predictably unpopular." But it wasn't my nature. And I don't say I'm right. I didn't get re-elected.

But I think more careful attention to public opinion without violating the principles of good government, that's what the Democrats should do. And I think a wise incumbent Democratic president who has learned from the Bush and Reagan administration and also learned from mine will find a kind of balance of frankness and honesty and I think political courage in not avoiding difficult issues on the one hand, but still be more aware of and sensitive about public reaction. I don't think that's an impossible task. It's one that I didn't resolve successfully. But I don't see any reason why a future Democratic president can't do it.

KOVACH: Where do you see the new Democratic Party leaders developing? Who do you see out there?

CARTER: One that comes to mind is Senator Bill Bradley. [Another is] Chuck Robb. It's hard to know about Mario Cuomo. There are others who have been totally concealed from the public eye, as I was three years before I was elected, a governor who has a tenacious commitment to campaign who might come forward with an attractive image. Members of the House and Senate—Sam Nunn would obviously be the most popular in Georgia, maybe in the South.

But I don't think any candidate is going to win without the strong support of the South. The last two Democratic campaigns the South basically ignored—it didn't feel compatible with Walter Mondale and Mike Dukakis.

KOVACH: Has any party chairman had any discussions with you about the shape of the party? Are you consulted by Ron Brown?

CARTER: Yes, he's called me several times. He writes me on occasion. A leading group of Democrats representing the party has made arrangements to rent the Carter Center for one day. But I play a minimal role in the party. We are very careful that everything that we undertake as a project at the Carter Center is totally nonpartisan or bipartisan in nature. So, when I deal with the Middle East, [or] when I supervised the Nicaraguan election, I always bring in a prominent Republican to serve as cochairman. We're very cautious not to be identified as a Democratic center. Also, I've refrained from any involvement in the Democratic Party primary process. I don't go out and endorse or raise funds for candidates just because they served in my administration or supported me when I was running for president. I think within the bounds of loyalty and propriety as a Democrat, I devote my efforts to other things.

KOVACH: You've been described as probably the most successful former president in the history of the country in writing a new chapter in the use of the position. The conflict-resolution center may be the most exciting international prospect at work here. What's current on your agenda?

CARTER: We are just getting started with conflict and dispute resolution. And we've decided almost exclusively to deal with internal civil disputes, the reason for this being that there's a vacuum there. It's very difficult, if not impossible, for the U.S. government or the Soviet Union, Great Britain, France, and so forth, or international organizations to work harmoniously between a government that's recognized officially on the one hand and a revolutionary group that's fighting against that government. There's no way for that civil war to be addressed in most cases. This is a role that we hope to fill increasingly as time goes on. We are now involved in the dispute between the Ethiopians and Eritreans.

We've had two substantial negotiating sessions, both of them successful. We've been involved in the Sudan revolutionary war. I was called down to monitor the Panamanian election last May, trying to resolve conflicts there with the election. And the election unfortunately was made fraudulent by Noriega. We have been involved in some other issues in a very private way, between Tibet and the government of China, and in some lesser degree . . . in Afghanistan and Kampuchea. In every case, I'm very sensitive not to duplicate what is being attempted by the United Nations or any major government.

KOVACH: Are you optimistic about the chances for some major positive development in the Third World?

CARTER: One of the most severe problems in the Third World is that for the last 20 years the annual production per capita of food grain in Africa has gone down. Also there has been about three or four calories per day decrease annually in the nutrition of Africans, which means that compared to 20 years ago, they have 70 less calories daily. And it was already marginal. We would like to reverse that trend.

So that's the kind of effort that we try to initiate well beyond the borders of the Carter Center itself. One key to the success we have is that we have people like Dr. Norman Borlaug and Dr. William Foege, who are preeminent in their field. And secondly, I have a direct relation, as you know, with the heads of governments. And we sign an official contract between them and us. We are able to cut through red tape.

In human rights we do the same thing. We work very closely and very privately with the major human rights organizations in Europe and in this country. They come to us with particularly disturbing cases or with seminal cases that would have impact in the future. And we get too many requests for a two-person staff. The ones that we think are worthy of our attention, I habitually go directly to the head of the nation involved and say, "It's been reported to me that this is going on in your country. . . . I would like for you to investigate and if they are accurate to correct the abuses and if they are not accurate, let me know." In a surprising number of cases they agree.

KOVACH: You've got so many irons in the fire. Do you have any time for yourself?

CARTER: We spend two or three days a week in Plains, usually the weekend. I take care of the timberland areas that we have in our family. We have to deal with our own family personal problems and the interrelationship among our children and grandchildren. We habitually find time when we go on trips to do things that we enjoy. We go fly-fishing for a half a day in the countries that we visit or we go out bird-watching. Every Christmas we take the entire family—there are 15 of us—off for a week to someplace where we have a good time and where the family pretty well stays together for those days. This year we went to Belize.

We have climbed a couple of mountains. In 1988 we had business in Tanzania, so Rosalynn and I and two of our sons and three of our grandchildren climbed Mount Kilimanjaro. We've climbed in Tibet. One week a year, as you know, we go off and build houses, Rosalynn and I, along with a group of volunteers. It's now gotten to be kind of a fraternity or sorority or club.

KOVACH: Are you working on another book?

CARTER: Not yet. I have two books in the bookstores now. We keep very detailed notes about things relating to human rights, to Third World problems, to conflict resolution, some of them quite exciting and quite interesting. Rosalynn sits in on my sessions when I meet with PLO leaders or Arafat or Shamir or others in the Mideast or when we were in Ethiopia this year or Khartoum or with the revolutionary leaders. She takes detailed notes and transcribes them later. We have all that as potential material.

21

A CONVERSATION ON PEACEMAKING WITH JIMMY CARTER, JUNE 7, 1991

James Laue

This conversation between Jimmy Carter and the late Dr. James Laue, Lynch Professor of Conflict Resolution at George Mason University, took place in Charlotte, North Carolina, on June 7, 1991. It was part of the fifth National Conference on Peacemaking and Conflict Resolution. In this conversation, Carter discusses lessons learned from a variety of conflict situations both during and since his presidency. Of particular interest are Carter's insights regarding the Camp David peace initiative.—*Editor*

DR. LAUE: Our conversation will cover a number of themes relating to peacemaking as a profession and a practice. We have received questions from participants here at the conference and we will include as many of those as possible near the end of our discussion.

Let me remind you, Mr. President, that you see gathered in front of you, probably the biggest concentration ever under one roof, people who are dedicated to peace and peacemaking—not only as a set of techniques in mediation or problem-solving, but as a deep and central part of their existence. We have here mediators, peace activists, policy-makers, agency officials and scholars, among them representatives of many foreign countries in the Eastern Bloc, South Africa and elsewhere. I would like to focus on the principles and lessons you have learned from your work on the international as well as the local level. You all know, I'm sure, of President Carter's activities

Reprinted with permission of the National Institute for Dispute Resolution, 1726 M Street, NW, Suite 500, Washington, DC 20036. Call (202) 466-4764 for futher information.

in Habitat for Humanity. In fact, he has built a number of houses here in Charlotte.

PRESIDENT CARTER: A couple of years ago we came to Charlotte and built 14 homes in one week, and Charlotte has kept up that progress. Last month Rosalynn came here and joined a group of women. They built an all-women's house. No man touched a hammer or drove a nail. As a matter of fact the only thing the men did was serve lunch and sweep up in between. One building inspector was the only man on the work site. Rosalynn is very proud of that. We enjoy the Habitat work.

DR. LAUE: I would like to start by asking you to tell us how your own personal commitment to peacemaking developed. What life experiences, skills and activities did you have that led you to the deep commitment to peace that so few people have? How did you get interested in this as something one could actually do, instead of just hope for?

PRESIDENT CARTER: I think anyone who is a North Carolinian, or comes from South Carolina, Georgia, Alabama or Mississippi would realize that people of my age who reached positions of some political responsibility during the civil rights years were confronted with one of the most tortuous, self-inflicted wounds that a society could suffer. To watch the slow evolution into racial harmony—to see the elimination at least of legal discrimination—was something that was both emotional as well as memorable. Out of civil rights came a commitment to human rights.

There's no doubt in my mind that the greatest violator of human rights that we know is armed conflict. This permeated my thoughts as I was preparing for the Presidency. We had prepared a long list of things that we thought might be notable or needed in the conflict resolution field. At the time we didn't use that phrase very much. But we brought to the White House, in a receptive era—not as a credit to me, but as an adverse reaction to Viet Nam primarily—an eagerness to deal with the 35 years of estrangement with China, the 10-year deadlock on the Panama Canal Treaties, the 25-year post-war period of hostility between Israel and Egypt, the lack of progress on intercontinental missiles agreements with the Soviet Union, things of that kind. We had a heavy agenda. I think that most of it grew out of the inseparable relationship between war and the basic human rights of survival, the absence of suffering, a stable home and food to eat. And I think that we still have, on a global basis, a tragedy I'd like to cover a little bit later, Jim. Even these professionals, who devote their lives to conflict resolution, may not be aware of how serious it is.

DR. LAUE: Thank you, President Carter. We will indeed return to that theme.

Since many people identify your peacemaking efforts particularly with the Camp David Accords, may we spend a little time talking about the major elements that led to a success at Camp David—the preparation, the parties who were there, the kind of personal relationships that developed? You have written extensively on this and many people here have read your work, but I wonder if you might comment further.

PRESIDENT CARTER: The book to which Jim refers is *Keeping Faith,* which still is on sale.

One of my great disillusionments when I reached the White House was to see how inadequate was—and still is—the international mechanism by which peace can be brought to a troubled area. The science of waging war is very highly developed, but waging peace is still in the embryonic stage even at this point.

Anwar Sadat was my best friend. He and I were intimate friends. His wife was a friend of Rosalynn's, his children have been friends with my children, his grandchildren even with my grandchildren. Sadat, on his first visit to the White House, made it plain to me that he would do anything I asked him to do concerning the peace process. It was almost like a blank check. Out of that grew the capability of exchanging ideas that was permanent until his death. When Sadat finally went to Jerusalem there was a euphoria that, I think, was almost global in scope, but the next meeting in Ismailiya only lasted 20 minutes. It was obvious that Begin and Sadat were totally incompatible personally. Rosalynn and I were resting at Camp David one day, on Friday night or Saturday, I don't remember. She said, "If we could just bring those two guys to Camp David—in this 125 acres on top of the mountain—and lock them up for a couple of days, together, maybe we could make some progress." Out of that, I talked to our advisors and we extended the invitation.

They did come to Camp David with their chief advisers. I think it was a harmonious environment because Egyptians and Israelis who had been devoting their adult life to killing each other were required to swim in the same swimming pool, watch the same movies, play on the same tennis courts, throw horseshoes together, sit on the same rock and talk. That was all part of it.

There was a very detailed mechanism by which we prepared. Hal Saunders, Assistant Secretary of State in my Administration, who's here sitting at the head table with us, is familiar with this. I went out to Idaho, down the middle fork of the Salmon River, the week before we went to Camp David. I took with me two large books, each several inches thick, with individual psychological analyses of Begin and Sadat. I mastered those books that were prepared by a staff of about 30 people in the national security apparatus, analyzing how Begin and Sadat responded to pressure, where their origin was, to whom they were obligated, what political commitments they had made, their basic commitment to truth or to exaggeration, how they responded to outside pressures—that sort of thing.

When we got to Camp David it was a well understood relationship. However, I found very quickly that the two men were still incompatible. The first three days we sat in a tiny room in my cabin, but the last 10 days Begin and Sadat never saw each other. I went back and forth. I was with Begin while Sadat slept. I was with Sadat while Begin slept. We didn't get much sleep on the American side. Hal Saunders was a big part of this.

To be very frank about it, Sadat was almost completely accommodating, much more so than other members of the Egyptian delegation, who thought he was going too far. Prime Minister Begin was the most reluctant member of the Israeli delegation. But we prepared a single text document, well known in theory, that was moved back and forth between the two men, and eventually, they reached agreement. I think that the Israeli public was heavily committed to peace at that time. When Prime Minister Begin, during the last few hours, saw that if he rejected the final proposal it would not be acceptable in Israel, that war would continue if he didn't do two or three very tiny things. Then, he did indeed, agree. As you probably remember, that was just the Camp David Accords, a framework for peace that laid a groundwork that still is applicable. It was six months later that we negotiated a peace treaty.

That treaty has been meticulously observed. The marshalling of adequate preparation, a harmonious environment, a dedicated mediator, with many people like Hal Saunders closely associated, public support back home—these are some of the factors that went into a very complicated agreement.

DR. LAUE: Can you tell us about any particular turning points in the process when you clearly saw it moving from difficulty and polarization toward an agreement?

PRESIDENT CARTER: Yes, there were a couple. One was quite emotional. Prime Minister Begin, as I said, had not seen Sadat nor, vice versa, for 10 days. Prime Minister Begin had given up on success. He sent over eight photographs of himself, Sadat, and me that had been taken at Camp David for me to sign for his grandchildren. He just wanted my signature. My secretary, Susan Cloud, had gotten the names of those eight grandchildren for me and I put each name on one of the photographs and signed them. I took them over to his cabin to tell him good-bye, because he had been absolutely adamant. He had taken a blood oath that he would never dismantle an Israeli settlement. That was it. He looked at those eight photographs and tears began to run down his cheeks—and mine—as he read the names. I went back to my cabin. In just a few minutes, he sent his Attorney General to tell me that he was going to look at it again. So we evolved a proposal that Begin would not authorize the dismantling of a settlement. They had to get the Israeli settlements off of the Sinai. The way we did it was to let the Knesset, the Israeli parliament, make that decision. Prime Minister Begin promised me that he would not try to persuade the Knesset against it, and he stayed mute. The Knesset voted 85 percent to dismantle the settlements.

I might point out parenthetically, as a footnote to history, that most of the members of the Likud leadership in Israel now did not vote for the Camp David Accords and also did not support the treaty with Egypt later on. Unfortunately, that is one of the problems that we face now. You can see that there is a personal, emotional factor that goes into a final success story, which is all too rare, and also that you have to search for different avenues when you run up against a blank wall. You have to be innovative and get a lot of outside help to find some alternative route that might bring you to the same goals.

DR. LAUE: Let's talk about the situation today. I wonder what reflection you have done on Secretary Baker's efforts, whether you would predict success in at least getting to the table for that effort soon, or are the blockages too great?

PRESIDENT CARTER: As you know, the primary effort in Secretary Baker's last four visits has been just to get some kind of meeting to take place, which I think is notable. I'm not going to try to be completely objective today; I'll be subjective, if you'll permit me. You probably remember that in the last 10 years there has been very little concentrated, persistent, clear effort from Washington to bring about progress on peace. Secretary Schulz got involved for a few weeks in the Lebanon situation and then got burned. He basically withdrew. It's been a hit and miss proposition there.

I don't think we will ever have peace in the Middle East until the United States does provide, not only enlightened and clear, but also consistent and persistent influence to a maximum degree on everyone that we can influence. Pressure is not a good word to use, but influence is, I think, an adequate word.

I admire what Secretary Baker has done. I have talked with him on the phone. In fact, shortly before he made his last visit, I wrote a fairly definitive private letter to him and to President Bush giving my own ideas on what might be done. Secretary Baker asked me to intercede with some of the key parties and I wrote them a personal message, so I stay involved to some degree.

Now, of course, I think we have a great opportunity. But a major problem, to repeat what I just said, is that most of the members of the leadership in Israel now, in the Likud coalition, have taken almost an oath that they will never relinquish one square inch of the West Bank and Gaza. That is an almost insurmountable obstacle unless they change their minds. The other issue is the promise in the Camp David Accords of full autonomy for the Palestinians. I put down "autonomy" on my yellow scratch pad at Camp David. Prime Minister Begin said, "Not autonomy, but full autonomy." The Palestinians have zero autonomy.

I think that good faith measures on both sides to build up confidence between them would be great. All the universities have been closed in the West Bank and Gaza for more than three years. The Palestinians can't meet and talk about politics. They can't vote. They can't levy taxes. They can't make out a budget. They can't dig a well. They can't plant an orange tree. They can't collect their own garbage. They can't run their own elementary schools. Those are the kind of things that the Israeli leaders could unilaterally grant without hurting Israel.

On the other hand, the PLO ought to remove the elements of its charter that calls for Israel's destruction. The Palestinians could very well pledge that in the Intifada their commitment would be peaceful in nature, that they would abhor and terminate all violence. Some of the key Arab leaders in the region could lower, or remove completely, the trade embargo they've imposed against Israel. You can see that there could be a step-by-step demonstration of good faith that hasn't yet come. The bottom line is that potentially it is better now than it was—primarily because Israel has not only good relationships with the United States, but also with the Soviet Union now, because of the release of the Soviet Jews and other things. Diplomatic exchanges have taken place between Moscow and Jerusalem. When I was in the Middle East last year, President Assad in Damascus told me that he was ready to negotiate directly with Israel on the Golan Heights. He would be willing to accept a demilitarized zone there under the aegis of an international conference and he was willing then to let the United States and the Soviet Union be the convening parties. Now he has backed off somewhat on that commitment with Secretary Baker. I think Israel could accept that as well.

The basic question now is two-fold. One, can the United States play only an observer role at an international conference? This is what the Arabs insist upon. Israel has refused. The other thing—how long do you have the bilateral, two-nation discussions deadlocked before you come back to the plenum group for more instructions and more help? The Israelis say never, unless you have unanimity. The Syrians and others say that if there is a deadlock in the bilateral negotiations, you need to come back within 30 days. I would like to see both sides back up on those attitudes. You see they are relatively insignificant.

But it is not a hopeless case. I know a little about it from experience and I'm not naive, but I'm not without hope. The reason I have a glimmer of hope is that the people of the region want peace. The Israelis want peace. The Syrians want peace. The Palestinians, God knows, want peace. The Lebanese want peace. The Jordanians want peace. The obstacles are the political leaders. Finally, the Camp David framework—I suggest you all read it. It's only eight pages long. The Camp David framework is still a viable document. It's not a Biblical text. It can be modified. But even the Likud leadership paid lipservice to the Camp David Accords. It is a viable document that has been officially endorsed by the parliaments of Egypt and Israel.

Dr. Laue: I think one very important thing you've done since your Presidency is to take the experiences and lessons of Camp David and turn them into an institutional form which can promote peace. Would you tell us a bit about the work of The Carter Center, which I know many people here are interested in—the programs in health and disease eradication, as well as in peacemaking, particularly the formation of the International Negotiation Network and plans you may have for it?

President Carter: The Carter Center has three basic guidelines. One, we do not duplicate what others are doing. If the United Nations, or the Brookings Institution, or the U.S. government, or Harvard University, or George Mason University can do something—we don't do it!

Secondly, we are totally non-political in nature, especially when we are addressing a difficult issue. When we have had Middle East peace conferences at The Carter Center with Palestinians, Syrians, Israelis there, I have invited President Gerald Ford, or Henry Kissinger or Howard Baker, or some other very prominent Republican to come in.

Third, we don't undertake a project purely as an academic analysis, although I see that as a very beneficial activity. Unless we think that there is a possibility for a direct action from a conference or from a consultation, we don't do it. So, in the process, we bring together experts on a subject in the same forum, people in positions of authority who can actually implement the recommendations or ideas that are forthcoming. We try to maintain an objective, non-political environment.

We have two or three basic types of activities. One is humanitarian projects. I'll give you a few examples. In Africa for the last 20 years, every year the production of food grain per person has gone down. For the average African person there are 70 fewer calories per day than 20 years ago, and they were already bordering on starvation. So The Carter Center has helped to orchestrate a program in Africa to increase food production in a wider range of countries to learn and to expand in the future. We have very successful programs, for instance in Tanzania (I was there just a couple of weeks ago), Sudan, in Benin, Togo, Ghana, Zambia, and other countries. We just work with small farmers. We've been able to increase production of corn or maize per plot (which is about an acre or acre and a half) from five or six bags to 25 or 26 bags average.

Another thing we do is work on health programs. Obviously starvation through malnutrition goes to the question of agricultural production, but we have 26 major health programs at The Carter Center, most of them international in scope. Let me give you several examples. We have the Task Force on Child Survival, now in its sixth year. It is designed exclusively to immunize children of the Third World against polio, measles, diphtheria, typhoid and whooping cough, and to use oral rehydration therapy to counteract diarrheal diseases. We formed a task force, bringing people together who, in the past, have not been compatible. The World Health Organization and UNICEF, for example, were not only not compatible—they were sometimes antagonistic. But in our task force they and others now work together as a team.

Their success has been extraordinary. When we began five and a half years ago, only 20 percent of the children in the Third World had been immunized against these diseases. Last December, we passed the 80 percent mark—an absolutely astounding result! We have also organized a task force on disease eradication. The only disease that has ever been eradicated is smallpox. The director of our Center, Dr. William Foege, is the one who put together the smallpox eradication program. He was head of the Centers for Disease Control for 10 years. We now have a task force on disease eradication. We identify those diseases that inflict human beings, and we decide, theoretically, which ones can be eradicated totally. Not very many can. Then we ask what the impediments to eradication are, and try to overcome them.

Beginning last year, we targeted two diseases for eradication. One is guinea worm. Today about 10 million people have guinea worm. The Carter Center is leading the fight to eradicate guinea worm. The other is polio. We expect to have polio eradicated by the year 2000. We had our last case of contagious polio in this hemisphere, we believe, this past January. So, eradication of disease is a major Carter Center goal.

We also have special programs on Soviet media and on the Middle East peace process, and human rights programs, as well. I won't go into those.

A third program that Jim asked me to mention addresses the question of conflict. When I was president, I was bogged down in many ways, trying to bring Zimbabwe out of Rhodesia and dealing with the Soviets on various matters, negotiating the Panama Canal Treaties, and Camp David, and the Peace Treaty between Israel and Egypt, and normalizing relations with China and so forth, but I became increasingly aware that most of the conflicts on earth are not even acknowledged. This is a horrendous truth.

Under Dr. Dayle Spencer at The Carter Center, we now work with Uppsala University and others to analyze the conflicts that exist in the world. I think the last report I got from Dr. Spencer counted 112 conflicts. Thirty-two of those are major conflicts. We define a major conflict as one within which at least a thousand people have died on the battlefield. In some of these, like Ethiopia and Sudan, hundreds of thousands of people have died. That is a tragic fact. Most significantly, not a single one of these major wars is between two nations. They are all domestic, civil wars. This is intriguing, but it is a tragedy in that, with a very few exceptions, the United Nations or the Organization of American States, the Organization for African Unity, the Commonwealth countries, the U.S. government or the British government—all are precluded from dealing with them because it is totally improper for an official of government or an official of the United Nations to communicate with revolutionaries who are trying to change or overthrow a government that is a member of the United Nations, or to which our ambassadors are accredited. This means that almost all the horrendous wars in the world are not even known about. There is no concentration of effort on how to end the wars. The revolutionaries and even the troubled governments quite often don't know where to turn.

We are trying to fill this vacuum with the International Negotiation Network. We include in this effort George Mason and Harvard and Uppsala and the World Conference on Religion and Peace and many of you. We are trying to put together an adequate effort to let the world know, firstly, that these wars are taking place; secondly, the horrendous personal ravages of these wars; thirdly, that there is hope for peaceful resolution of these wars. Then we try to involve a mediator that might take an interest—sometimes me, sometimes others.

Sometimes we go to the OAS, sometimes we go to the United Nations—but we would rather have individuals do it. If they don't, we would like to fill the vacuum. That is our ambition for the future.

One very fine thing we have learned is that there is an alternative to negotiation or mediation or arbitration. In most of these conflicts, it is almost as difficult to get people to negotiate or to accept a mediator as it is to reach a final agreement. The easiest one to understand is the Israelis and the PLO. You can't get them to go into the same room, or to sit down and acknowledge the legitimacy of the other. So the tremendous, new emerging possibility on the global scale is the holding of elections.

The Carter Center has been involved in this hemisphere. We held the elections in Panama, Nicaragua, the Dominican Republic and Haiti. We have just finished helping out in Suriname. This fall we will run the election in Guyana. Some of these elections, as you know, either prevented war—or in the case of the Contra war in Nicaragua, I think we helped to end the war. We brought in, when the people would accept them, the United Nations and the Organization of American States. In Guyana, they won't permit those organizations to come in, so we have invited the Commonwealth countries to join us. They have never participated in elections, but they will.

You have seen this same thing happen in Namibia. It is likely to happen in Angola. Dayle Spencer spent a week in Liberia. I think, in the future, we may see this technique for resolving the conflicts in other countries, even including Ethiopia, Afghanistan and Kampuchea. But in the meantime, the wars are going on in Burma, and Mozambique and Somalia and the Western Sahara and so forth. I could go down a long list of wars that are not even recognized and nobody is doing anything about them. We want our work at The Carter Center to bring these to public visibility.

We need all of you to help us. We hope that next fall, or maybe in January, we will have the first conference at our Center that will be highly publicized, just to let the world know this is a major problem that has not been previously recognized. There is hope for peace in these troubled regions. We want to take the most deadly intra-national conflicts and try to orchestrate a clear plan for addressing each particular conflict, because they are all different in scope. That has not been done. We hope that our work will bring attention to many trouble spots in the world where problems have not been seriously addressed.

One final point. When I was inaugurated there were seven million refugees in the world, according to the United Nations High Commission on Refugees. Last year there were 30 million. That doesn't count the Kurds or displaced persons who don't cross a border. That is a symbol of a problem in the world that we are not yet adequately acknowledging or addressing.

DR. LAUE: Thank you. We have about 15 or 20 minutes left and I do want you to have the opportunity to comment on some of the specific intervention initiatives that you and The Carter Center have undertaken, and on some principles and lessons that you may have learned from this work. I wonder if you could give us a brief word on your work in the Ethiopian/Eritrean conflict: how you selected that as an area that might be useful for intervention from yourself as a former President, the way in which you approached it and where you think it stands now? There have been some dramatic developments there in the last few weeks.

PRESIDENT CARTER: One of the freedoms that we have at The Center is being able to deal with revolutionaries and also unsavory incumbents. . . .

DR. LAUE: We all have some candidates for you to deal with, I'm sure.

PRESIDENT CARTER: I'm speaking exclusively of foreign nations.

DR. LAUE: Of course.

PRESIDENT CARTER: In the case of Ethiopia, we did not have an ambassador there, and still don't, as a matter of fact. We have a representative, but not an ambassador. But I felt free to go meet with then-President Mengistu. I was asked to go in by the United Nations High Commission on Refugees, by the Red Cross and others to try to do something about refugees in the northeast from Somalia, and in the southwest from Sudan. I got acquainted with Mengistu. In the meantime, I also met in Khartoum nearby, with the leaders of the Tigrean revolutionaries and also the Eritrean revolutionaries. And, to make a long story short, we got all of them to agree to have peace talks for the first time. We couldn't take on all of them at once, so we worked on the conflict between Eritrea and Ethiopia. The Italians finally took on the Tigrean/Ethiopian negotiation. In the meantime, the Tigreans formed a larger coalition, since they are a very tiny portion of the Ethiopian population, and they have been able to triumph militarily. Now Mengistu, as you know, has flown out and gone to Zimbabwe.

Our hope now is that there will be a consummation of the proposal that I consistently made to Mengistu when he was in office, to have an internationally supervised election, to let there be a united Ethiopia, and when that has occurred, later to let the Eritreans decide through self-determination their own role.

Sudan is perhaps an even worse case. In 1988, there were 260,000 people who died because of the Sudan war. This is an almost unequaled tragedy in history. We happen to have a very effective program in Sudan in wheat production. We are making Sudan, I believe, self-sufficient in wheat production. That will happen in three more years, working just with small farmers in a closely defined irrigated area. So I have an entree into the Sudanese ultra-conservative Muslim government. On the other hand, the revolutionaries live in the South—the Sudan People's Liberation Movement.

I was teaching Sunday School one morning at Maranatha Baptist Church in Plains when John Garang, the head of the Sudan People's Liberation Movement, came in to my Sunday School class with four or five other people. We spent all that Sunday talking about what we can do to have peace talks. I hope that eventually Sudan will see the advisability of resolving the conflicts. The revolutionaries do not want independence. All they want to do is to have a united country. That's a way we get involved.

In the case of Panama, as you know, once Noriega stopped supporting the Contras and had a falling-out with Washington, our ambassador to Panama and all his staff were prevented by the White House from having any communication with Panamanian officials. But I didn't have that restraint, and after we had been involved in some other work in Panama and Central America, Noriega sent me a letter asking me to come in and conduct an election.

Now, I don't want you to tell anybody outside this room, but when people don't want to negotiate with adversaries, there is a tremendous element of self-delusion among naive politicians who think they can win a public office. It is human nature to believe that if I want to run for mayor or for governor, or for Congress, or for President, that if the voters just have an honest procedure and if they know me, and know all those other people running, they are going to vote for me. Back in 1988 we had been invited to run elections by Noriega, who thought he was going to have an overwhelming victory. His candidates only got 22 percent of the votes and he killed the election result. Of course, the people who were elected are now in office.

The Sandinistas did the same thing. I was in Ghana for the corn and health project there. I got word from the foreign minister of Ghana that Daniel Ortega wanted me to come in and run the election in Nicaragua. He thought he was going to win. He wanted us to come in and certify the legitimacy of his victory. Again, he lost.

We had the same thing happen in the Dominican Republic when the opponent to Balaguer, Juan Bosch, thought he was going to win and we went in. We were reluctantly permitted by Balaguer to come in. Again, the guy that invited us lost.

The point is, that this is a way, a new possibility of dealing with a conflict if negotiation or mediation is not possible. I think there is a growing awareness now within the United Nations and the OAS and others of fair elections as a way of dealing with conflict.

DR. LAUE: Thank you. Now I want to ask you to reflect on some of the principles you believe have emerged from this work—lessons that you might share with these peacemakers. I've caught one already, which is that if you get called in to observe an election, the person that calls you in loses. I don't know if we will enshrine that in the theory of this field, but there may be other lessons you would like to share with us from your work.

PRESIDENT CARTER: I think the major problem that has not been overcome, and will not be overcome in official channels, is a willingness or ability to communicate freely with both sides, as I have mentioned. To reemphasize a point I made, it is totally improper for any UN official even to talk to a revolutionary who is trying to change or overthrow a member government. This means that you cannot even let the revolutionaries know that there's a hope for a peaceful settlement of an issue. The first need is to devise some mechanism by which you can communicate with both sides freely. In most cases, it is better to do it without publicity, in order to avoid embarrassment.

When a public announcement is made, it ought to be joint and no one person should get credit for it. This was the case with the Eritreans, who first suggested peace talks with Mengistu. I went and talked with Mengistu and told him about this. He agreed. The next day, he had his parliament announce that they were taking the initiative on peace talks. So you have to let both sides take credit for any move toward peace.

Then, once you do get a process started, either mediation or an election process, there has to be a clear definition of the role of outside observers. In the case of the Eritreans and with the Sudanese, they wanted us to keep transcripts of every word spoken in the negotiating sessions. That's important because the later revelation of the process is an incentive to both sides to be a little more flexible and more reasonable.

Another very important principle is to exclude the press totally during the process of negotiation, or to get a firm commitment from both sides that they will not comment on the negotiations taking place. That was what we followed at Camp David and both sides thought we had the phones tapped. I never did ask my subordinates whether the phones were tapped. I don't think they were. But there was a secrecy there because if you had let, for instance, Prime Minister Begin or his Foreign Minister, or anyone else, go out every day and give the press an update on what was going on, we never would have made any progress. I think there has to be an element of confidentiality existing between the two adversaries and the mediator.

It is very important to set time limits on the end of the talks. There were 500 sessions between North and South Korea, as you may remember. I don't know how many we have had in the conventional arms talks in Europe. But there has to be some time limit. In the case of Camp David, we just had to leave Camp David and everybody knew the time limit.

There is another important consideration. I would say the best way to evolve a procedure is for the mediator, if one is accepted, to prepare a document that encompasses, at the beginning, what is mutually agreed upon. It's surprising, even if a war has been going on 30 years, to see how many points the two sides do agree on. The differences quite often are minuscule in comparison, but then you've got to start dealing with the minuscule things. They become paramount. The semantics are very important. In the case of Sudan, the semantical problems are enormous. John Garang, the leader of the Sudanese revolutionaries, admitted that to me last month when I met with him in Nairobi. The semantics are important.

Another thing that has to be understood is the importance of public opinion back home. We were running public opinion polls in Israel every four days during Camp David. Begin would tell me the people back home "will never accept my doing this." I would say, "Mr. Prime Minister, here's a poll that was run day before yesterday in Israel. Sixty-three percent of the people approve of this." It made an impact. I think that public opinion back home is a very important element. You have to remember that in a war the people are suffering. The leaders quite often are not suffering. Saddam Hussein hasn't suffered. As many as 200,000 Iraqis have died and the country is destroyed. He has not suffered. The people want peace. That's the point I made about the Middle East. If you can marshall the people's desires for peace as a pressure on the recalcitrant negotiator, that is very helpful.

The last point: once an agreement is made, it needs to be convincing as far as implementation is concerned. The use of the United Nations observers in the Sinai was a very important element of the Peace Treaty there and will be important in the future. Sometimes there is cost involved. The only thing I promised at the end of the Peace Treaty was that I would pay two billion dollars of the cost of moving Israeli airfields out of Egyptian territory. That was all I promised. Sometimes you have to make some kind of financial arrangement.

Those are some very quick, off-the-cuff considerations—some of the lessons we learned.

DR. LAUE: We have, unfortunately, just a few minutes left because President Carter does need to get back to Plains to finish mowing the church yard.

PRESIDENT CARTER: I finished that this morning.

DR. LAUE: Of course! I would like to ask you for quick responses to some of the questions that people at the conference submitted. First, any comment on the role of grass-roots and non-governmental groups in peacemaking? What is the best way in which they might complement and parallel official initiatives?

PRESIDENT CARTER: I realize that many of you in this room are involved in community conflict resolution. That's very important. It is a truism in our country, in our system of government, that changes in attitude and policy come from the local level first, then the state level and ultimately the national level. This was the case, as you remember very well, in the environment. Years ago, when a city had a bad garbage dump, or a local stream was polluted, the state government had nothing to do with it. But when a local government corrected a problem, it eventually became a state challenge and an achievement. The states had disparate approaches to environmental control and the federal government finally did something uniform.

That's what is so important about the work that you do—raising issues at the local level. If you never are involved in Sudan, or Burma, or Sri Lanka, or the Western Sahara, the fact that you are doing a good job in Charlotte, North Carolina, Atlanta, Georgia, or Idaho means that people get the awareness—the conviction that, in spite of serious disagreements, there is a successful way to resolve a dispute where both sides win. That awareness can help to change national and even international policy.

DR. LAUE: A participant from Great Britain suggests that U.S./Cuba relations are moving forward. Would you like to mediate U.S./Cuba relations to normalize them?

PRESIDENT CARTER: [silence]

DR. LAUE: Thank you very much.

PRESIDENT CARTER: We have proposed to Castro that to cap his career—positive or negative, I'll let you make a judgment on that—he could bring to Cuba democracy, with honest public elections. My belief is that Castro might very well be elected if there were an honest election. I don't know. But anyway, if he thinks he would be elected—that's all it takes.

DR. LAUE: That's right. And you know what would happen.

PRESIDENT CARTER: Yes!

DR. LAUE: That is, if your track record holds . . . you know what would happen. Here's a question in another vein. One of the biggest obstacles to resolving conflict is "exploitation of Third World peoples by corporations and their shareholders." How would you deal with that? Are structural changes needed?

PRESIDENT CARTER: One thing that I didn't cover earlier that this brings out is: what is the cause of the conflict at the beginning? Sometimes it is ethnic hatred. Sometimes it is direct abuse of human rights by a powerful oppressor who doesn't want any dissenting voice. Quite often though, in a surprising number of cases, it is the deterioration of the quality of life of people. This can result just from deforestation or soil erosion or the siltation of streams. It can result from air pollution or the movement of people from agricultural regions into cities. It can come from a lack of land reform. Disillusionment can be another cause of serious conflict. Many people around the world—while they may not agree with our government's policies—they have a great admiration, almost a reverence for American life. But they may be the ones who receive shiploads of toxic waste in 50-gallon drums because American companies cannot find a place in our country legally to bury them. You see those drums sitting alongside the road in a poverty-stricken country where some guy has been bribed to take them. Or they get infant pajamas that are inflammable because a company that has been prevented by American laws from selling inflammable pajamas to American kids ships them overseas to dispose of them instead of burning them. They get chemicals or medicines that are prohibited from sale in our country by the FDA because they are harmful to human beings. The drug companies, instead of disposing of them, sell them in Zaire.

These are major breakdowns that not only affect international relations, but also generate despair and distrust of even good faith and honest efforts that we might make to provide those people with more peaceful, fruitful and enjoyable lives.

DR. LAUE: I know it will be tough to deal with this question in a short time, and we do have only a minute or so. Any particular advice to give to this group of kindred peacemaking spirits about what they ought to be doing, about their potential assistance in the International Negotiation Network or other activities?

PRESIDENT CARTER: I know that Dayle Spencer will be contacting some of you as we prepare our conference. Quite often, the outcome of a consultation or a conference is just to issue a document or to make recommendations for other people to carry out. It can be a beautiful document, leather bound with photographs of prominent people who appear on the program, but if you look at it five years later, nothing has happened.

What I hope to do at our Center in a few months (Dayle and Bill Spencer and I will work out a date very shortly) is to bring together a number of people and analyze the international conflicts that I have described for you in hasty terms today. What can be done about each individual conflict and who would be the best person or group or organization to be responsible? How can we form task forces to deal with them?

I would say that the main point of the Charlotte conference for you, in your own realm of responsibility, is to actually resolve to take action, to reach out to others who do not know about your role. Avidly seek publicity on your local television or radio station. Invite in the editor of the newspaper. I know that Madeleine Crohn yesterday had a conversation with the editor of the *Charlotte Observer*, which is a wonderful newspaper. She taught him, in just a few minutes, some theoretical and practical applications of dispute resolution, with which he was not familiar, and those are reflected in an editorial today. If the world public, the U.S. public, your own local public can be acquainted with what you are doing and the achievements that you are reaching, that is the key to future success. Even though you solve a problem between blacks and whites, labor and management, city government and employees, students and faculty, on occasion to your great satisfaction and gratification—you cannot imagine how broad a realm of unaddressed similar questions there are because people don't know that this kind of service is available. I would say, publicize what you do. Be prepared for people to come to you. If you hear about something, be aggressive. Go see both sides. If you get too much to do in your local communities, you can always call Jim Laue and others and say, "Send in some help!"

I hope that you will consider The Carter Center a part of your life. We would like to have you visit us, to talk to us, and we hope to join with you in an increasingly effective way in the future to resolve the disputes that I've outlined for you. We have failures. We have successes. Even out of failures you can learn a lot and prepare for future successes. That's what I pray we can all do—bring peace among people.

DR. LAUE: Thank you so much, President Carter, for being with us.

22

LIVING FAITH, DEC. 19, 1996

C-SPAN, Robert Fulghum

This interview originally appeared on the C-SPAN 2 cable
television program *About Books* on December 19, 1996 following the publication of Carter's book, *Living Faith. About
Books* airs every weekend on C-SPAN 2. (More information
regarding *About Books* is available on the World Wide Web at
http://www.c-span.org). Robert Fulghum, a clergyman and
author, eschews the normal kinds of questions that a journalist might ask President Carter—the kinds of questions
that we already know the answers to—and probes for information that is not in the public eye: "Things about the life
we don't see as much, things that are a little more private."
The interview is one of the kindest on the part of the interviewer and one of the most revealing on the part of Carter
that appears in this book.—*Editor*

MR. FULGHUM: I was in an author's conference a couple of years ago
and a man named Sammy Cahn stood up—the songwriter—and he
said, "I'll show you what fame is. I'm going to start singing, and when
you recognize what I'm singing, join me." So it was quiet, and in a
very small squeaky voice he began singing, "Kiss me once, kiss me
twice, and kiss me once. . ." and everybody joined in and sang
the whole song. And he said, "I wrote that. That's fame." (*Audience
laughter.*)

When you walk into a room, nobody asks who you are and no
one asks what you do. We know who you are (*audience laughter*) and
we know what you do and you have the same kind of fame. Who you

are and what you do is carried around in the hearts and minds of these people. So I'm not going to ask you questions along the lines that we all know most of the answers to. We watch your public life a lot. But I'd like to ask you some things about the life we don't see as much, things that are a little more private.

We were backstage talking about—in fact, I had a very short ten-minute lecture on the poetry of Dylan Thomas. So we both, we both share—but I ask you the question: Are you still writing poetry?

MR. CARTER: Well, the answer's yes. I started writing poetry when I was a child [*unclear*], and when I was in submarines, I would write poems to Rosalynn, and most of which were thrown away, either by her or by me. And then, about six years before I published my volume of poetry, I decided I would learn some of the techniques of it. So, I got a couple of professors from the University of Arkansas to give me advice and eventually published a volume of poems. And I still keep poems on my computer, word processor. All of 'em are in the phase of evolution, and sometimes you reach a point where that's as far as I can go and it stops; but I keep on writing poetry, yes.

MR. FULGHUM: Has any other president of the United States written poetry?

MR. CARTER: Yes. Ah, Abraham Lincoln wrote some poems and one other. I think John Adams was the other poet. Two, uh, two presidents have written poems that were published. I thing maybe Abraham Lincoln's after he died, but yes. So I'm the third, or maybe there are others that I don't know about.

MR. FULGHUM: Another side of your life that none of us ever see is— [*After some adjustment to the microphones, the discussion continues.*]—So, I was going to ask you, what do you do in your woodshop, and is this something you do alone, and what do you make?

MR. CARTER: Well, I write a number of hours every day when I'm home, but I've been a woodworker all my life. I make furniture. I, ah, in fact, we have a mountain cabin in north Georgia; I made every piece of furniture in the house, beds, chifforobes, chairs, tables and so forth. We have a fundraising effort at Crested Butte Skiing every year and each year I make something in my woodshop to auction off. This year—first time I've said it publicly; you're in on a real secret— I went back to the colonial days and I cut down a hickory tree in my back yard, took photographs all the way through, and used nothing except tools that were available three or four hundred years ago. And I'm making two beautiful rakes and two pitchforks, bending the wood in steam and so forth. So this is what we're gonna auction off this year.

MR. FULGHUM: Can you cook? (*Audience laughter.*)

MR. CARTER: I can cook hickory enough to make it bend. (*Audience laughter.*) A couple, a few years ago I made a chess set. I carved an entire chess set and made a beautiful box for it to go in and Rosalynn lined it with velvet, and we auctioned it off.

MR. FULGHUM: Amazing. Well, another aspect of your life that we haven't seen, except in one sense you've always been a teacher by the life you've led, but every Sunday you teach a Bible course. And I was reading a description of your techniques as a teacher and I was struck by your Socratic style. Tell us a little bit about your teaching and what you think of the role of a teacher.

MR. CARTER: Well, I started teaching Bible classes when I was eighteen years old when I was a midshipman at the Naval Academy. Every Sunday in the Navy Chapel I taught (*pause*) young girls of officers and men stationed at the Naval Academy. And I teach now in our own church in Plains that we attend, Maranatha Baptist Church. I have about ten members in my church, regular, but I have between two hundred and five hundred visitors every Sunday. (*Audience laughter.*) Most of them only come once. But I have about one out of six visitors that are Baptists. I have people that come from all over this country. One Sunday I had visitors from twenty-eight foreign nations. I generally have anywhere from five to fifteen pastors of churches that come to listen to me but also to argue with me about the Old Testament and the New Testament. I have a good many people that leave my Sunday School class and tell me, "I've never been in a church before in my life." Some of them are tourists on their way to Florida, uh, or from Florida. So it's a very exciting teaching process and I learn as much as I teach.

MR. FULGHUM: That's, that's what good teachers are about.

Let me shift a little bit and go in another direction. We know a lot about your family, in a sense. I remember when you were first elected, and it, it seemed like it was a cast of unbelievable characters. There was Miss Lillian who was rather outspoken, and then your sister Ruth who was an evangelist, and your sister Gloria who was a leather biker—or maybe that's exaggerating a little bit—and then there was Billy, of course. I thought people were making this up. I couldn't believe you had . . .

MR. CARTER: Let me tell you, one day the reporters came to Plains and asked Billy, "Billy, don't you think you're kind of a peculiar character?" And he says, "Well, I've got a mother who's seventy years old in the Peace Corps. I've got a sister in her late fifties who's a leather biker; she rides a Harley-Davidson all the time. I've got a sister, an-other sister that's a holy-roller preacher. I've got a brother that thinks he's gonna be president." (*Audience laughter and applause.*) He said, "Why do you think I'm peculiar?" (*Audience laughter.*)

MR. FULGHUM: Well, we know about these people and we know about Amy because she was there. But when I ask people, "How many chil-dren do you think Jimmy Carter has?" they all stop at Amy. We don't know much about your sons, and you mention them in this book. Tell us a little bit about your sons—where [sic] they're doing, where they are.

MR. CARTER: Well, Jack is my oldest son. He's twenty years older than Amy, and he, he was in Vietnam for three years and then he came back and got a degree in nuclear physics and he graduated from law school. Now he works for an investment company in Bermuda.

MR. FULGHUM: Married?

MR. CARTER: Married; has four children, four of my nine grand-children.

My second son Chip is also in international trade and invest-ment. His wife is an accountant. He's got two children. He was born in Hawaii in 1950.

My youngest son Jeff has three of my grandsons. He and his wife have never had a date with anybody else, even during high school years. Jeff is a very successful computer programmer. He writes very advanced computer programs.

So they're all nice—we take all our family off on a Christmas va-cation which Rosalynn and I pay for. We'll be leaving the day after Christmas. Amy got married this year so we gave her the right to choose where we go, ah, and she chose the Florida Keys. So, we'll have twenty-two Carters and Carter in-laws going off, and my wife and I are footing the bill. That's why I need to sell more copies of this book. (*Audience laughter.*)

MR. FULGHUM: Buy a book. Send Jimmy Carter to Florida this time. (*Audience laughter.*)

The other person that we don't know a lot about, because he was dead after you were in office, is your father. But you speak about him a lot in here. Tell us a little more about your father.

MR. CARTER: Well, my daddy was, uh, had faulty eyesight. He was a first lieutenant in the First World War in the army. He was a stern disciplinarian, a tremendous athlete, a good baseball pitcher, one of the best divers in Plains, a good tennis player, whom I never de-feated. He was, uh . . . he gave me orders when I was a child which I carried out or suffered the consequences.

When I became a father I emulated my daddy. I was a naval officer. I gave my three boys orders. If they didn't carry my orders out, they were punished. And it was only later in an incident I describe in this book when my oldest son finally made me realize that I was not a good father. This was after he came back from Vietnam and got married and went through law school and so forth; I still looked on him as a child. And we were hunting out in the woods one day, walking behind the bird dog; and Jack turned around with tears running down his cheek—it was obviously a very difficult thing for him.

He said, "Daddy, I've been wanting to tell you for years. I think the way you treated me as a child almost ruined my life."

And I, my reaction was anger at this ingrate; all I did for him, he didn't appreciate. So I went home and told my wife about it, and it took us a long time to realize that we were not good parents. And it took us about two years before we could get reconciled with my oldest son. I would talk to Rosalynn, Rosalynn would talk to his wife, his wife would talk to him, he would talk to his wife (*audience laughter*), but now we get along fine and he will be one of the twenty-two who will be going with us after Christmas.

MR. FULGHUM: I think that's one of the most remarkable things about you, that I know of, is that a lot of us can do things in public with the rest of the world, but to carry that out in your own home is often a most difficult thing. You tell a story about the conflict that you and Rosalynn had about sleeping in the same bed and having a heat problem. And I thought it was one of the more charming stories because it has a great truth about conflict resolutions in it. Will you share that story with us?

MR. CARTER: Well, a few years ago, Rosalynn and I wrote a book together called *Everything to Gain: Making the Most of the Rest of Your Life,* which Rosalynn asked me to mention is still on sale (*audience laughter*); and it told about our setback when I lost the election, reelection for president. I found out I was in bankruptcy, Amy had left home; uh, it was a very difficult time in our lives. So we decided to write a book together and it almost ruined our marriage. We could agree on ninety-seven percent, but the three percent became paramount. We couldn't even communicate with each other about the book except by writing ugly notes back and forth on the word processor.

And Rosalynn writes very slowly, very carefully, doesn't go to the next sentence until this one is perfect. I write very rapidly. And Rosalynn looks on my writing as a rough draft (*audience laughter*). Rosalynn, Rosalynn's writing is as though she had gone to Mt. Sinai, God had given her this tablet. (*Audience laughter.*) Any word that's changed is painful, so we couldn't agree on the book, literally. And our publisher finally took those three percent of the paragraphs and he said, "O.K. I'm going to divide 'em up. This paragraph is yours, Jimmy. This paragraph is yours, Rosalynn." (*Audience chuckles.*)

So if you buy the book, you'll notice that some paragraphs have a "J" and some paragraphs have an "R." (*Audience laughter.*) We never could agree. So we finally sent the book off to the publisher and we felt, well our marriage is saved. And after that we could not agree on anything. We'd go to bed at night—it was in the wintertime. Rosalynn would say, "Jimmy, it's too hot." I would say, "Rosalynn, it's too cold." And I finally went off on a trip thinking our marriage was on the verge of destruction. I came back and Rosalynn met me at the front door with a smile on her face. She said, "Jimmy, I think we've solved our problem. We've had the electric blanket hooked up backwards." (*Audience laughter and applause.*) This is a true story.

MR. FULGHUM: We've all been there. That's why we're laughing. (*Audience laughter.*) We have to go back there tonight, some of us, too.

Let me shift a little bit away from that, and to your book which is again—this is my book (*audience laughter*), but the reason you want to buy this book is to send the Carter family to the Everglades or Key West.

MR. CARTER: And that's part of the privileges of being the host. You can hold up your own book. (*Audience laughter.*)

MR. FULGHUM: There are two of many, but two things I want to pull out of your book that really struck me as quite surprising—to go off in another direction. You say on page 169, "Of all the industrialized nations, we are"—speaking of the United States—"by far the stingiest in sharing our wealth with others."

Now that's an astonishing statement. And I was listening to NPR tonight coming down, and some comment was made about the Japanese being the leader in the world in giving away funds and support. Now, this is quite a surprising change of image. I mean, a lot of us would say, "Wait a minute. Did you really mean that? Are we that stingy?"

MR. CARTER: We are. In total amount of money given, regardless of the size of the country, Japan is number one, France is second, Germany is third, United States is fourth. Every time an American citizen gives a dollar, a Norwegian citizen gives twenty dollars. We're by far the stingiest nation on earth. We, we had a poll not long ago—I didn't do it, but it was done nationwide—asking American people how much of our gross national product, or budget, rather, do you think we give in foreign aid. The average answer was fifteen percent. "How much do you think we ought to give?" "Five percent." "How much do we actually give?" (*Audience murmurs.*) "Three-tenths of one percent." And I don't think the American people know this. But it's true, and if we have a Christian faith, or a Jewish faith, or a Muslim faith, in sharing with a poverty stricken people, our nation above all the developed nations on earth, violates this principle. We are the stingiest nation in the world. I don't think that is a [sic] attitude or preference of the American people, but it is a fact.

MR. FULGHUM: Wow. You tell a lovely joke that I'd like to make sure you tell it rather than I—on page 209, about the man who had thought he had given away a lot of money and was going to heaven and was getting credit for this; would you share that with us?

MR. CARTER: O.K. Well, in my Sunday School classes which, as you said, is a kind of give and take, I try to use a joke sometimes to illustrate a point. And as you know, the writer of James said, "Faith without works is dead." You can claim you're a church member, you can claim you're a Sunday School member, you can claim you're a minister or whatever; but what do you actually do?

And this man went to heaven. When he got there, St. Peter met him along with an angel, and they asked this fellow, "Tell us, why do you deserve to come in?"

And he said, "Well, I've been a member of church all my life, and I've been a Sunday School teacher. I've been a deacon, or a steward."

And St. Peter said, "Yes, but what have you done for other people?"

And the guy said, "Well, back in the Depression years, a bunch, a family of hobos came by my house and I had my wife fix up a whole sack full of sandwiches and I gave it to them. It probably was worth fifty cents."

And St. Peter said, "That's interesting. Anything else, more recent?"

And the guy said, "Well, as a matter of fact, just a couple of years ago, one of my neighbors had his house burn down. And I had a table on my back porch that I wasn't using, and I gave it to him. It was worth at least a half a dollar."

St. Peter told the angel, "Go down and check and see if this guy's telling the truth."

And the angel went down and came back and said, "Yes, St. Peter, he's telling the truth. What should we do?"

And St. Peter said, "Give him his dollar back and tell him to go to hell." (*Audience laughter.*)

MR. FULGHUM: I sense that that's something of the attitude that some of the other countries of the world are saying of us now.

MR. CARTER: (*Laughs.*) I hadn't thought about that, but it's true.

Mr. Fulghum: I think it surprises a lot of us to realize how negative we have been toward the United Nations. We are a billion dollars behind. Why is this?

MR. CARTER: One and a half billion.

MR. FULGHUM: One and a half billion.

MR. CARTER: And we don't pay our dues to the World Health Organization even.

MR. FULGHUM: Why?

MR. CARTER: (*Pause.*) I think it's politically unpopular because of the atmosphere in Washington now to give any support to an international organization, including the United Nations. And so the American people pride ourselves—I'm not speaking of you, but other American people (*audience laughter*)—in punishing the U.N. because we don't think they represent the U.S. accurately, or we think they're trying to dominate our military forces overseas, or because we think they waste money in their organizational structure or—all these are impressions implanted in our minds by candidates for public office, including Republicans who run for president or Democrats who run for president. So, we have been instrumental in forcing out Boutros-Ghali—we were the only nation that wanted him to leave—and now we have a new Secretary General, whom I know quite well, Annan from Ghana, who's gonna be a good man.

But I think this is the essence of it: we just don't want to support the U.N. or any international organization, and it's a political environment that we see now in Washington.

MR. FULGHUM: If the French were to take this same stand, or the Germans, or the Japanese, or the Russians, we would not find it acceptable.

MR. CARTER: We would condemn them.

MR. FULGHUM: Yes.

MR. CARTER: We certainly would. And one of the rules that has been proposed is that if you don't pay your dues, you don't have, have a vote; a rule that would suit me fine. (*Mr. Fulghum laughs.*) We ought to pay our dues.

MR. FULGHUM: You get to go places in the world that many of us have never been and cannot go; for example, behind the walls of Korea. What's it like inside Korea?

MR. CARTER: Well, in 1994, as some of you will remember, the Koreans were purifying uranium. And there was the fear they were going to build a nuclear arsenal. And so, the United States and North Korea were incompatible. In fact, the U.S. had a law passed under President Reagan that no American official could communicate directly with any official of North Korea or P'yongyang. Kim Il-sung was a dictator then. And he wanted me to come over and talk to him and try to resolve the issue. So I got permission from President Clinton to go as a private citizen.

My wife and I went to Seoul first and met with the South Koreans to try to put their minds at ease. And we went across the DMZ to P'yongyang, and met with Kim Il-sung and came back, we were the only, we were the first human beings that had made that trip in forty-three years. And we found Kim Il-sung quite eager to resolve the differences with the rest of the world and with the United States; and he agreed with everything that I proposed.

Ah, the next morning, he and I and Rosalynn and his wife went on a boat trip for about five hours, and I suggested that he let me extend an invitation to the President of South Korea for a summit meeting. And after a few minutes of exchange, he said, "O.K."

So, when I got back to Seoul, I did this: Kim Yung-sam agreed; they arranged to have a summit meeting for three days there. All the details were worked out for the 25th of July, 1994. But on the, I think, the 7th of July, Kim Il-sung died, unfortunately, and it hasn't been done. And since then, the two sides are irreconcilable.

But P'yongyang was a, is a beautiful city. It's a tightly closed society, maybe the most closed society on earth now that Albania has opened up. Kim Il-sung was very complimentary about Christians. In fact, Billy Graham had been there a few weeks before I was. When Kim Il-sung was in a Japanese prison preceding the Korean War, Christian missionaries had helped to keep him alive. In fact, Billy Graham's wife Ruth was educated in North Korea, in P'yongyang.

MR. FULGHUM: I didn't know that.

MR. CARTER: And Kim Il-sung was very proud of this fact.

So, even in the most, among the most despised and condemned people in the world, there is a possibility, I think, or a need at least to communicate with them and to give them a chance to correct their mistakes or to help bring peace, or to stop human rights abuses or to open up those closed societies, I think.

MR. FULGHUM: So, you have hope for Korea?

MR. CARTER: Yes, I do. Unfortunately, when Kim Il-sung died, a few students in Seoul, in South Korea, put on black arm bands to express condolences at his death. They were arrested and put in jail because, according to the South Korean laws, they had violated security law. And this lack of respect for Kim Il-sung, was and still is deeply resented in North Korea.

And, of course, Kim Yung, Kim Chon Il, who is the son of Kim Il-sung, knows that I'm very eager to come back if and when they are ready to have any sort of peace talks with South Korea. I hope it can be done.

Mr. Fulghum: Speaking of peace and reconciliation, you are going to be very close during your Christmas holidays to Cuba.

Mr. Carter: Yes.

Mr. Fulghum: And, by my lights, I see an incredible tragedy building there, that we, with initiative, could change or head off. Any thoughts or feelings about Cuba and its future?

Mr. Carter: I think one of the most—if I could use the word "stupid"—things that our government has ever done, is to pass the Helms-Brighton Law, which not only closes down any communication with Cuba, but also imposes severe punishment on any of our allies and friends around the world who do communicate or deal with the Cuban people or with Cuba. And I think that the best way to address a closed society like this is to open it up and to let Cuban-Americans go back to their native land and visit with their relatives, and to let American tourists go there and so forth. I think it'd give the Cuban people a glimpse of what freedom can mean.

Also, when we punish Cuba so severely—they have about thirteen million people—we don't permit food or medicine to go in there from the United States. We try to restrict any trade with them. We make Castro a hero for many people, not just in Cuba, but around the world, as a David standing up against a Goliath, and Washington.

This is, by the way, is not a new attitude of mine. When I had only been in office two months in 1977, I opened up all travel for American citizens to go to Cuba and vice versa. And we opened up an entry section, which is just one step short of a full embassy in both Havana and Washington. And those offices, by the way, are still open. But I think it's a very good possibility that in the future Cuba will become more and more inclined to a democracy.

I'm very pleased, by the way, that the Pope has decided to visit there, I think, this coming year. I think it will be another step in opening up the situation.

Mr. Fulghum: One of the things that people associate you with is Habitat for Humanity; but I don't think people understand how much of yours—that's just a volunteer—they call you their "number one volunteer." But the place where you really do most of your work is the Carter Center.

Mr. Carter: Yes. We only put in, we only build one house a year, my wife and I; and that's one week a year, with other volunteers.

MR. FULGHUM: Tell us more about the work of the Carter Center. Give us an idea of the size of it, what's the budget, and how many people, and . . .

MR. CARTER: O.K. Well, unfortunately, the budget is more than twenty-five million dollars, which I have to raise every year. I'm always raising money for the Carter Center.

MR. FULGHUM: Buy this book. (*Audience laughter.*)

MR. CARTER: Right. The Carter Center has three principles. And I'll be very brief. One is that we don't duplicate what anyone else is doing. If the United Nations or the World Bank or the U.S. government is doing something, we don't do it. Secondly, we are non-partisan. And third, we just take on action programs. We go where other people don't want to go. For instance, we have Carter Center programs in thirty-three nations in Africa.

For the last ten years the Carter Center has coordinated the immunization of all the world's children, and we've jumped from twenty percent to eighty percent of the world's kids who are immunized against polio, measles and so forth.

We have another task force that analyzes all the human illnesses to see which ones might possibly be totally eradicated from the face of the earth. And we've targeted two now. One is polio, which is known by all of us, and the other one is Dracunculiasis or Guinea worm. And the Carter Center is in charge of eradicating Guinea worm.

We're looking at a few others now, one is Onchocerciasis or River Blindness, another one is measles, another one is rubella, maybe in the future I would say malaria. So we're trying to eradicate these diseases.

Another thing that we do is to try to improve the Africans' ability to raise food grains. We now have three hundred thousand small farmers in a Carter Center program to increase their production of corn and wheat and millet and sorghum. We were able the first year to triple their production. We started this program when Ethiopia was starving, when they had the big rock concert to raise money for Ethiopia in 1986. We've been in Ethiopia now almost four years and Ethiopia has now become self-sufficient for the first time in corn production—they call it maize. Next year they'll be exporting maize, and next year they'll be self-sufficient in wheat production. That's the kind of thing the Carter Center does.

Another thing is that we analyze all the world's conflicts. In an average year about seventy wars break out. All the wars in the world are civil wars. There are not any wars anymore between two nations. And the United Nations was founded about fifty years ago to deal with wars between countries. So, since we are involved in immunizing children, eradicating Guinea worm, dealing with River Blindness, planting corn, when two warring groups decide they want to have peace talks, quite often they come to us and ask us to do the mediation to end the war or to prevent a war.

So, those are some of the things we do overseas.

MR. FULGHUM: How many people are involved in working for the Center? Do you even know?

MR. CARTER: About, a little more than two hundred.

MR. FULGHUM: Two hundred?

MR. CARTER: Yes.

MR. FULGHUM: And there's a special connection with Emory University?

MR. CARTER: Yes. The Carter Center and Emory University have a marriage, an equal marriage. In fact, ten members of the, of the Emory Board of Trustees serves [sic] on our Board of Trustees and I choose ten members; and those twenty people make the basic policies for the Carter Center.

MR. FULGHUM: Frequently when the spotlight is on a troubled situation and a lot of attention is given and a lot of people go, and we think that's solved and the press turns its attention elsewhere—I was wondering what the Carter Center does about looking back; for example, how are things going in Haiti now that we don't have the spotlight on Haiti anymore? Do you feel useful for what you've done there?

MR. CARTER: We had a very successful election in Haiti when Aristide was elected, we helped monitor, carry out their election. Seven months later he was overthrown, stayed out of, of the country for three years. In 1994 we had thirty thousand troops poised to invade Haiti. I got Senator Sam Nunn and Colin Powell to go with me and got permission from President Clinton, and we went down and negotiated a peace agreement where General Cedras stepped down and went to Panama, and Aristide went in. Unfortunately, when Aristide went back in, he didn't try to reimplement democracy. He tried to dominate the next election and discourage any opposition. And he wouldn't let us come in or anyone else come in and monitor the conduct of the election. Haiti is still a basket case economically. And Haiti is one of two nations in this hemisphere that has not had successful elections. Cuba is the other one—Cuba and Haiti.

Mexico's elections have not measured up to our standards of success because one of our standards that is very difficult is for all the major parties to agree to accept the results of the election. (*Audience laughter.*) That hasn't happened yet in Mexico. But lately two states in Mexico have had successful elections where the opposition party won, and in the summer of 1997 there will be nationwide elections in Mexico. And we hope that for the first time Mexico will have honest, fair elections that are accepted by all the major parties. So, that's the kind of thing, we monitor elections all over the world, too.

MR. FULGHUM: All of this activity that is in the world of the political realm rests on your faith. You make this very clear, always have made it very clear. I'd like to shift now to that element in your life and ask you a very short question, but that in fact, has a bit of a long lead-in.

We know you are a man who's trained in science, a nuclear engineer. You deal with quarks and facts and all these things. We also know that in your special faith you give a fairly mainstream Christian description of Jesus as your Lord and Savior, being born again, God, the Lord of the Universe. I wonder, given what you see about facts and what you see about faith, if the most recent information the last couple of years, of these incredible photographs from the Hubbell deep space eight to twelve million years ago, we now realize that there must be fifty billion galaxies. Does that size of the universe affect your notion of God and Jesus and your faith? Big question, but . . .

MR. CARTER: Well, I'll give you a quick answer. It strengthens my confidence in God Almighty as the Creator. The fact that human beings have not previously understood the, the scientific fact doesn't mean that the facts have not always been there. And I don't fall with the presently accepted theory that the universe began with a big bang theory from what they call a "singularity." Where did the singularity come from? I think it came from God the Creator. And if God created the universe from the big bang theory or from a cycle of expansion or contraction or whatever, to me it just makes God more awesome and more, and more mystical and more profound and more believable. And when you look at the, at the minutia of, ah, under microscopes of subatomic particles, again these are things we're just now discovering. So, it doesn't shake my faith; it strengthens my faith.

As I said in the book, I don't think there can possibly [be] any incompatibility between God the Creator on one hand and scientific discoveries on another. There are places in the Bible, even in the New Testament, that says [sic] "the four corners of the earth." The fact that we now know that the earth is round, it doesn't mean that the New Testament about salvation and justice and peace and love and compassion are [sic] incorrect. And just because we now know that evolution took place over a long period of millions of years doesn't mean that we don't, that we doubt that God created the universe. It just means that the people that wrote the Bible didn't know about, about the scientific discoveries. When Galileo discovered that the earth was not the center of the universe, that was the thing that shook the religious world. But I notice that even in the last two months that the Pope has come out and expressed a belief in Darwin's theory of evolution.

MR. FULGHUM: Yes, yes.

MR. CARTER: A wonderful thing. I figured that the Pope read my book. (*Audience laughter.*)

MR. FULGHUM: Speaking of your book and moving into this subject a little deeper, you may—I'll read a part of a paragraph that I really found quite stunning, and I'd love for you to elaborate on it: "Jesus liked to have a good time. Some of His parables include memorable and funny events, and Jesus enjoyed outwitting those who were hostile to His teachings. He gave answers to questions that destroyed their arguments, embarrassed His tormentors, amused and enlightened His spectators." And this is the sentence that grabbed me: "As far as give and take is concerned, He could have taken over easily from David Letterman or Jay Leno." (*Audience laughter.*) Now, there's a concept I hadn't run into from a Southern Baptist before, certainly. And we were laughing about this backstage and wondered how He would feel about ratings and I said, "He could have any ratings He wanted." Tell me, tell me, that's a rather amazing statement. Tell me a little more about it.

MR. CARTER: Well, so many people think that Christianity is a depressing belief that removes humor and joy and peace and exhilaration; and I think that when you go through the parables of Christ when He was oppressed apparently by lawyers and by Pharisees and Sadduccees, and so forth, He always came out on top by telling a story or parable that turned the tables on them.

Of course, the most despised people in the world at that time were the Samaritans, who were looked upon as traitors to the Jewish faith, they weren't permitted to go in the temple, they were black, as a matter of fact, and a shadow of a Samaritan falling on a devout Jew's feet were [sic] cause for purification, and Jesus when He was asked, "Who are my neighbors?"—when He said, "Love your neighbors; who are your neighbors?"—gave the report of a guy that was beaten up on the road, left abandoned by his robbers. A Pharisee came by and walked on the other side of the street. A priest came by and walked on the other side of the street. Along came a despised Samaritan. What did the Samaritan do? He picked the guy up in his arms; carried him to the nearest inn; gave the innkeeper money; said, "Nurse this man. I'll be back to take care of him." Then He asked the lawyer who was criticizing Him, "Who was the neighbor to this man that was beaten up by thieves?"

That's the kind of parable all the way through the New Testament that shows that Jesus really had a sense of humor and enjoyed turning the tables on His adversaries.

MR. FULGHUM: I have a photograph of a drawing on my wall in three places, three different studios where I do some work, and it's a photograph of Jesus as a man, laughing, great roaring laugh, very Semitic, long—have you seen this?

MR. CARTER: No, but I'd like to see it. Take a picture and send it to me.

MR. FULGHUM: Well, I'm surprised you didn't see it because it was in *Playboy* magazine is where I got it. (*Audience laughter.*)

MR. CARTER: Well, I don't subscribe to *Playboy*, but I'm glad to meet someone who does. Unitarians can take *Playboy* (*indistinct; audience laughter obscures words*).

MR. FULGHUM: I bring this up because you did. You're in your seventy-second year now. How are you doing on the "lust" front? (*Carter and audience laugh.*)

MR. CARTER: I was—my poetry book—I was signing a book in a bookstore nearest to Harvard University and a very solemn crowd was there, obviously in love with great poetry (*audience laughter*), and one beautiful young woman came by, about 25 or 30 years old, and the crowd got quiet because she was speaking with a pretty loud voice. She said, "Mr. President, if you still have lust in your heart, I'm available." (*Audience laughter.*) And I turned blood red. I was so embarrassed.

This was an interview I did with *Playboy*—older people would remember—in the campaign of 1976. I was asked by the *Playboy* reporter, when I thought the interview was all over and his tape recorder was turned off, "You think you're perfect, being a born-again Christian, how can you hope to govern average people who have a lot of faults in this country?"

And I said, "That's not my belief at all. Jesus preached against judging others and against exalting themselves." And I made the mistake of quoting two verses in the Sermon on the Mount; one where Christ says, "If you have hatred in your heart against a brother, then you should not criticize someone who commits murder," and He said, "If you look on a woman with lust in your heart, you shouldn't criticize someone who's actually committed adultery." So, the next question was, I guess, predictable. The *Playboy* reporter asked, "Have you committed adultery?" And I answered that. And he said, "Do you have lust in your heart?"

And I said, "Yeah, like all men, when I was young, before I met Rosalynn, I looked on beautiful women and I'd wish that they'd go all the way and have sex with me and so forth." And I forgot about it. Then about two months later—well, a month later—I was on a train trip from New York into Pennsylvania and every reporter on the train had a *Playboy* magazine (*audience laughter*), which is still the best selling issue of *Playboy* in history. (*Audience laughter and applause.*) And, ah, really.

MR. FULGHUM: And you didn't even have to take your clothes off. (*Audience laughter.*)

MR. CARTER: No. And I was eighteen points ahead of Gerald Ford at that time. In ten days I dropped fifteen percentage points because of that *Playboy* interview.

MR. FULGHUM: I wonder if anybody has ever asked Gerald Ford if he has lust in his heart? (*Audience laughter.*)

MR. CARTER: I don't know. I think I exhausted the subject. (*Carter and Fulghum laugh.*) That shows how innocent the American people were, you know, twenty years ago.

MR. FULGHUM: I have been living in the last year outside of the country, in Greece. And recently I was speaking with a Greek Orthodox Archbishop. And he had seen this photograph that I have—which, if you've not seen it, I'll make sure you get one. I think you'd like it very much—and we got—the Greek Orthodox Church has been carrying on the—well, apologies to anyone who's here, but this is my opinion—one of the longest running funeral services in the history of religion. I mean, it's really a grim and sometimes, uh, deal—and I said, "The Jesus that you're dealing with here is not the Jesus that I read in the Bible. It's very clear that Jesus was a man, a whole man, not a part man, a man with special privileges, a man with discounts, a whole man, who had . . . And that meant that He ate food, He went to the bathroom, He sweated, uh, everything. And even at the end—"; and this Greek Orthodox is looking at me as if I'm absolutely crazy, it's without any possibilities. But my understanding of your image of Jesus is this whole man. Whatever else He was, He was above all this man.

MR. CARTER: Exactly, laughed a lot, suffered a lot, prayed a lot, felt discouraged, was very humble, abandoned by His best friends, was not adequately articulate on occasion, He couldn't convince even His own disciples to be loyal to Him, was condemned and scorned, punished, died and then, of course, resurrected. But I think during His lifetime on earth—about thirty-three years, I think—He was, in every way, a human being.

MR. FULGHUM: I know this is a little irreverent, but I think there's probably some truth in it, but He was Jewish. We know He was a good storyteller, and Jews under pressure tell wonderful jokes, and often on themselves. And I've often thought that somewhere in the collecting of the life of Jesus that there's a missing chapter of the humor, of the wit of Jesus, because I can't imagine as whole a man as He was to be, that He didn't laugh and tell hilarious stories. The man who could produce wine at a wedding like He did was bound to got some good jokes to go around with it. (*Audience laughter.*) And that doesn't make Jesus less attractive. It makes it more, to know He was that whole . . .

But speaking in that particular subject, I spent some time in Istanbul in this year away, and was talking to some people who are very moderate members of the Islamic community and they said that they resented the fact that, Americans especially, were always looking upon all of Islam as if it were just the radical, fundamental, crazy aspect of Islam. But when they looked at Christianity, they saw a lot of radical, crazy, angry, mean—and we all see this. What's going on in the Christian community that generates this anger and hate that I see?

MR. CARTER: I cover that a good bit in the book because it bothers me, a Southern Baptist who's seen what I consider to be our basic, fundamental beliefs change: total separation of church and state, which has not been broken down with the Christian right, in effect, going to bed with the Republican party; of the priesthood of the believer which means that each individual can relate to God directly, the autonomy of the local church, the pastors of the churches being servants and not masters, things of this kind. And I think there's a trend around the world, not only in Christianity, but perhaps in Judaism and also in Islam, toward fundamentalism. And I think that's an extreme step-by-step case when one of us or a group of us thinks that we understand the teachings of God perfectly, we are blessed because we are superior, we naturally believe that anyone who disagrees with us is wrong. The next step is that if they are wrong, they are inferior; and when carried to an extreme case, they are even subhuman. And the taking of another person's life who disagrees with us and our interpretation of God is made, even ordained by God. And we see these internecine battles take place, like in between Protestants and Catholics in Ireland, and the holy wars that are now almost dividing the Jews in Israel. And of course, the not quite so bloody yet, wars that are going on in the Southern Baptist Convention and among other Protestant groups. So I think this is a trend that I hope is cyclical in nature. I hope it's kind of bottoming out now and we'll see a tendency for reconciliation and for healing of these differences because we all could share the kind of the things that St. Paul said of the unchanging things when the early Christians, as you know, asked Paul, "What are the things that are important? What are the things that never change?"

He gave an answer that was somewhat mystical. He said, "The things that you cannot see." Well, you can see a bank account, and you can see a beautiful home, you can see your name in the paper. What are the things that you can't see are the things, or what I think that Christ taught and that is justice and peace and humility and service and sharing and compassion and love. You can't see those things. And those are the things that, with which we all agree basically, and which shape the definition of a successful life, at least in the eyes of God.

MR. FULGHUM: I noticed recently the Southern Baptist Convention voted to formally begin proselytizing the Jews, which got the ADL, the Anti-Defamation League, all up in arms right away. What do you make of that kind of gesture that this is something new, Southern Baptists have now at least formally said they were going to do?

MR. CARTER: Well, you know, the Southern Baptists have forty-one hundred missionaries and one of them has been ordained to proselyte among Jews. You know I never have been comfortable trying to single out a Jewish believer to be converted to Christianity. I think, you know, that's something that shouldn't be emphasized. And a lot of Christians forget that Christ was a Jew, that Paul was a Jew and John and James and Matthew, all of them were Jews. And the early Church obviously was made up of Jews and Christians.

So, I think for the Southern Baptist Convention to announce that they are having a special program to proselyte Jews is divisive and it might even impede the normal decision by some Jews to become Christians. I think it makes it much more difficult if a Jew should happen to want to become a Christian. It separates Christians from Jews. I think it's counterproductive.

MR. FULGHUM: I think it was Dr. Adrian Rogers that you and I were trying to think of, and he was the one who said a couple of years ago that God didn't even hear the prayers of the Jews. And this is the same man who came to you and tried to get you to be born again by his terms, I think.

MR. CARTER: I think that was a man named Smith instead of Adrian Rogers.

MR. FULGHUM: Oh, Smith. O.K.

MR. CARTER: But I was very embarrassed as a Southern Baptist when, when the President of the Southern Baptist Convention made a speech and said that God didn't hear the prayer of a Jew. That was ridiculous, and embarrassing to most of us.

MR. FULGHUM: And it was Rogers who tried, come get you to give up your secular humanism.

MR. CARTER: Yeah. When he was elected President of the Southern Baptist Convention, I was President. In 1979 he came to the Oval Office, and I was very honored that the President of the Southern Baptist Convention had come to see me. But on the way out—

MR. FULGHUM: (*Laughs.*) That proves you really are a Southern Baptist.

MR. CARTER: Yes, I am. (*Audience laughs.*) And still am. But on the way out, he said, "Mr. President, I hope you'll give up your secular humanism and become a Christian again," or words to that effect. (*Audience laughter.*) I didn't know what secular humanism was. (*Fulghum and audience laugh.*) And I'm still not sure.

MR. FULGHUM: The secular humanists are confused, too.

MR. CARTER: I hope so. But I'm still a Christian and a Southern Baptist.

MR. FULGHUM: I realize I'm not all that old, this is my sixtieth year. But I realize—I began to think, well, what do I do with the next ten years of my life?—because I expect to be pretty healthy, but then I'm going to be seventy and worn out and beat up, and I realize you're seventy-two and looking pretty good. Do you think of your life in those terms of "how many productive years do I have?" And what are you planning for the rest of your time on this earth?

MR. CARTER: Well, I do; I think about it more now than I used to. One of the things I try to cover in this book is how we look on a life span and how many of us so greatly exalt the length of life as the most important thing.

But I hope that I'll continue to learn. I remember that one of my favorite theologians Paul Tillich said that religion is a search for the truth about ourselves, our relationship with God, our relationship with our fellow human beings, and Tillich went on to say the fact that, that when we stop searching, we lose our religion. And I hope

that, although I've come a long way in my Christian faith—I've re-
nounced God on occasion and been reconverted by my sister—that
I hope that I'll continue to search and to seek answers and to grow as
a Christian and as a human being. And I really honestly don't worry
about the end of my life. I feel that I have it well taken care of
through my faith.

MR. FULGHUM: How about your kids? Are they church-going Southern Baptists?

MR. CARTER: No. (*Audience laughter.*)

MR. FULGHUM: No?

MR. CARTER: No. My children were really turned off a lot by the division in the Church. And I'm lucky, I guess, in effect in living in a
little town where the thing to do is to go to church. We have two Baptist churches and a Methodist church and a Lutheran church among
the mostly white people of Plains, and then five churches among the
black people of Plains. We have common services sometimes. Nine
churches, we have a total population of seven hundred. (*Audience
laughter.*) So, if you don't go to church, you don't go anywhere; so,
and it's the thing to do and it brings us together; it's the center of
our social life.

But my children all live in different places in the world and they
don't have that inclination to go to church. My oldest son Jack,
though, has been a Sunday School teacher, very active in Evanston,
north of Chicago. I've gone up and helped him teach his Sunday
School class. And the others are all Christians, they just don't go to
church regularly, which I wish they would, but that's a decision for
them to make.

MR. FULGHUM: While you and I have been talking, people have been
writing some questions and ideas of their own and passing them over
and they've been sort of sorted out. Let's see what the community
has on its mind.

You have to understand, by the way, while we've got this little bit
of a pause in the flow of things that President Carter has to be on a
plane headed for Georgia at 10:40.

MR. CARTER: 10:20.

MR. FULGHUM: 10:20, excuse me. And they used to hold planes for
him, but they don't now. (*Audience laughter.*) So, we're going to finish
up some of our conversation here and then he'll be signing books as
you were told earlier. And we'll try to make sure that no one goes
home without their book signed.

Um, let's see—Oh, this is a lovely question. "Can you speak to us about the art of staying in love?"

You've talked extremely candidly and very usefully about a long love relationship, and its ups and its downs. What's the key? Give us your long secret. You're an expert in conflict resolution. (*Audience laughter.*)

MR. CARTER: When I showed Rosalynn a couple of early chapters of this book, she said, "No way are you going to put this in a book for other people to read." Because I did go into some of the problems that she and I had. And we have now, have finished fifty and a half years together, and we're more in love than we used to be. (*Audience applause.*) But I would say that the main secret of it is twofold.

One, I go into depth in the book about how to forgive another person, which is very difficult, one of the most difficult lessons I have to teach about twice a year: how do you forgive someone against whom you have a grudge? It could be a spouse, it could be a child, it could be a parent, it could be a former friend.

So, forgiveness is one thing and the other one is communication. How do you communicate with each other? And I think Rosalynn and I have been able to communicate and forgive because of our shared faith. A few times in our life we've had a crisis so great that we felt that we had to kneel together and pray out loud so we could hear each other. We could talk to God when we couldn't talk to each other.

And not too long ago, as a matter of fact, Rosalynn and I were still having some serious problems and I had taught a Sunday School lesson that made an impact on me; and I went out in my wood shop and I planed down a beautiful little piece of walnut about the size of a check; and I wrote on it, "This is good for an apology or forgiveness, whichever you prefer." And I signed and gave it to Rosalynn.

I said, "For the rest of our life you can present this to me and I will honor it." She presents it all too often. (*Audience laughter.*)

So, I've been thinking about getting a copyright and selling it. (*Audience laughter.*) The wives maybe could get their husbands to sign it, or vice versa.

So, I think a sense of humor, maybe, communication and forgiveness.

MR. FULGHUM: I know about your capacity for intelligent thought and your capacity for love and affection and things like that; but, also, what I know about you, I wouldn't want you really mad at me. And I wonder—your son, you mentioned this with your son. How do you deal with this very human thing of anger? What do you do?

MR. CARTER: That's not easy for me to do. And that's why I say that teaching a lesson on forgiveness, which I do every now and then, is very difficult for me. And usually when I teach the lesson, I try to think of someone against whom I have a grudge—it doesn't take too long (*audience laughter*)—and then in my Sunday School class I actually use that as an example and tell the Sunday School class what I'm gonna do, which is usually write a postcard or give somebody a telephone call, and say, "Look, we've been estranged, we don't get along well and let's try to resolve it."

One of the most famous ones involved a reporter in Washington. His name was George Will. And when I was preparing to have a debate with Ronald Reagan, my only debate, someone in the White House stole my book of briefings which described every question that I was going to ask or be asked and my answers to all the questions and my response to things that I thought Reagan might say. They gave it to George Will who used it to brief Reagan against me. And that was very difficult for me to forgive. And one Sunday morning I decided I would forgive George Will.

So, he had written a book about baseball, a very fine book about baseball, which I had bought on remainder. It only cost a dollar. (*Audience laughter.*) And I read the book and I wrote George Will and I said, "I've had this grudge against you ever since the debate with Reagan and I've read your book about baseball. I got a lot out of it and now I feel like we're even and I hope we can be reconciled."

And he wrote back and said he appreciated all of the letter except the fact that I didn't pay full price for his book. (*Audience laughter.*)

So, we were reconciled, but I think quite often it's not a difficult thing if we—I would guess that almost everybody in here has someone against whom they hold a grudge, and to make a telephone call and say, "You know, I'd like to work this out." Or write a postcard and say, "I'm thinking about you and hoping we can be friends." Just a simple thing like that can really change people's lives.

MR. FULGHUM: One of the things that's always struck me about you is that you come from what I think of as deep roots, peanut farmer. The word "farmer" comes up. I never heard you talk about the earth and the farming aspect of your life very much. Do you still get your hands in the dirt from time to time?

MR. CARTER: Yes.

MR. FULGHUM: What do you like to grow?

MR. CARTER: Well, we still grow about five hundred thousand pounds of peanuts on my farm. We also grow corn, wheat, sorghum, millet, soybeans, a little cotton, not all that much. Our main income comes from forest, from trees, and Rosalynn and I take care of our forest land.

We have the same farm that's been in our family since 1833. And we are deeply attached to this land, and that's one of the main things that's always pulled us back to Plains. No matter—after when I was in the Navy, after I became governor and served my term, after I left the White House, we always naturally have gone back to Plains. And of course, our church is there and our families are there. So, the soil, the earth is very important to me.

Every member of the Carter family for the last nine generations in this country have [sic] been farmers, and I'm the first one on my daddy's side that ever had the chance to finish college. But, so, I feel very deeply about my heritage as a farmer.

MR. FULGHUM: And when you're no longer around to farm, what will become of the Carter family farm?

MR. CARTER: Well, it now is in a partnership and all four of my children will own the farm. And I think, I know that three out of the four plan to move back to Plains; and maybe the fourth one, I hope, will come back to Plains. So I would, my preference, my children and even my grandchildren would still be attached to the land, but I can't put any restraints on them.

MR. FULGHUM: I suppose we would, especially during the Christmas holidays, find you walking through the Carter family land with grandchildren tagging along.

MR. CARTER: Yes. Always before Christmas, I take my grandchildren now, and some of my children, their parents; and we go wandering around the farm to find a nice Christmas tree on the farm somewhere. We cut down the tree and drag it back to the house and all of us decorate it together. We always look forward to Christmas.

MR. FULGHUM: What's it like in Plains, Georgia, at Christmas time? You obviously don't have snow, jingle bells and all that but,—

MR. CARTER: We jingle some bells (*audience laughter*), but we don't have snow. I talked to Rosalynn earlier this evening and there was— the guy that runs one of the local stores there has organized a choir and they were going around singing for people, and he had just informed Rosalynn that they were on their way to sing at our house.

I would say that Christmas in Plains is almost totally encapsulated in the Church, in the worship of Christ, the commemoration of the birth of Jesus; and, then, of course, we have Santa Claus.

We're kind of the foundation, the center of our own family. The day after Christmas, we're going on vacation together. Twenty-two of us going off to spend a week together. So, we . . . Christmas is a time to pull our family together.

Amy came along fifteen years after my youngest son. Rosalynn and I had a fourteen-year argument that I finally won. (*Audience laughter.*) So, we really had two generations in our family and then, now at our advanced age, you might say, we want our grandkids to know each other, and the whole family to be brought—so now, for the last ten or twelve years, every Christmas we bring our family together and go somewhere together. One year we went to Belize, one year to Panama; some years we've been on a Caribbean cruise. We go skiing in Colorado sometimes. And just do something together for a week. I think that's the essence of Christmas for us.

MR. FULGHUM: Do you go to church on Christmas Eve?

MR. CARTER: Yes.

MR. FULGHUM: A late night service?

MR. CARTER: Yes.

MR. FULGHUM: What are your favorite Christmas hymns? What do you sing?

MR. CARTER: Well, it's hard for me to know them all, but *Silent Night, Holy Night,* and some that are not church, Christmas—like *Coming Home for Christmas* and *First Noel.*

MR. FULGHUM: Do you like to sing?

MR. CARTER: No. I'm musically afflicted. (*Fulghum laughs.*) I'm not a good singer. On a few occasions I've been on the platform with Willie Nelson and he invites me up to sing *Amazing Grace* with him as a finale, but he always turns the microphone away from me (*audience laughter*) so people can't hear. So I'm not a good singer. I like to sing, though.

MR. FULGHUM: I'm not going to ask you to sing, and be glad for that. (*Audience laughter.*)

I actually picked up my book because I'm going to exercise a privilege. I'm going to read you something out of my book; but I'm going to read it—well, let me back up and say, I'm sure that we would all love to give you a Christmas gift. And you probably have an incredible clutter of knickknacks that grateful people have given you over the years; and there's not a thing, a thing that we could give you. But if you look across this audience of people who've come wanting to be here more than anyplace else tonight, to be in your presence—I mean, we would probably be glad to come and sit and watch you take a nap (*audience laughter*). Just reminding ourselves that you are real, and more real than real; and just to have the honor of your company for an evening is a remarkable thing.

We would like you not to forget us, and to understand that you never forget that all these faceless people who carry you around in their minds and hearts have only one gift to give you and that's their respect. And I would like to exercise the privilege of speaking for all of them by reading you something out of the book of mine called *Uh-Oh*. It's two or three years old.

"Just above the light switch by the door to the studio where I work, I often place a photograph, pinning it to the wall with a red push pin. When in a magazine or newspaper I find a particularly arresting picture, a visual image that provokes my mind, I tear it out and I put it by the light switch so I can see it and consider it as I come and go. Something to inspire me or to confront me.

"For most of the month of March, 1990, three photographs were pinned by the light switch together. The small one in color showed a middle-aged man doing some carpentry wearing aged, leather, high-top work shoes, blue jeans, flannel shirt, sweat-stained red baseball cap. And around his waist a well-used nail apron. In the picture he's working about eight feet off the ground, straddling a wall header while he nails it to the corner post. This man is framing a house. And by the look on his face, and the way he holds the hammer, it is clear that he not only knows exactly what he's doing, but intent on doing it right and doing it well.

"You and I see carpenters every day doing this common task— nailing wood to wood with hammer and nail and muscle and blood and sinew and brain. Men who say, when asked, 'What are you doing?' will reply, 'I'm in the construction business.'

"I like looking at this picture, bright sky, new wood, an ancient trade, something very honest, positive and fundamental going on.

"The second picture by the light switch is a grainy black and white news photo from the morning paper earlier in the month showing a middle-aged man in a short-sleeved, sweat-stained khaki shirt. The man is smiling the greatest of smiles. The other people in the picture are also smiling. The conclusion of an election is the occasion for the smiling, an honest election held in the powder-keg conditions in a Central American country. Nobody was killed during these elections for the first time; and the losers, for the first time, accepted the results, leading to a major change in government and hope for the people. The man in the shirt-sleeves was there risking his credibility and his brains and his skills and even his life to help bring about the impossible. He was there on his own, representing only himself and the concerns of people like him from all over the world, without any compensation other than the wages paid by conscience.

"The third picture by the light switch shows a man in a white shirt and tie. He is not smiling. The look on his face is a combination of vexation and determination. He has come once again as he has come again and again and again to meetings in the Middle East to get enemies to talk to each other face to face; not on behalf of his government or any government, not on behalf of any organization, but on behalf of peace and justice.

"It's the same man in each one of these pictures by the light switch by my door. And he is truly in the construction business, giving of his time and life to build houses for poor people, to build an atmosphere where free elections can take place, to build structures of peace in one of the oldest, harshest, and meanest arenas of conflict in human history.

"The man's name—well, you know—is Carter. He used to raise peanuts in Georgia, had a government job once; but he's gone back to being in the construction business and teaching. When historians settle up accounts in the twentieth century someday, his name will shine. He may not be in the list of great presidents. It's too soon to say, and history readjusts that all the time; but it is not too soon to say that he's the finest ex-president the country ever had and may ever have.

"Each night I finish my work and pause at the switch. I look at the three pictures, and the word that comes to mind is gallant. A high-spirited, courageous notion, this man knows how to lose and he has lost big. Forces beyond his control may have made him the wrong man for the wrong job at the wrong time; still he has lost as few men have in public. He might have tucked his tail between his legs and spent the rest of his life sorting papers, stacking books, fishing, playing golf. Others who have had his government job have done as little. But to lose and to be a loser are not the same thing. He knows, and we know, and besides, he still had work to do, tasks he accepts because of who he is and not because of any office he may or may not hold. He is proof that there is no limit to the amount of good a man may do if he doesn't worry about who gets the credit. He is not one of those the Bible talks about who gained the whole world and lost his own soul.

"And as I flick out the light switch, his example is not lost upon me. He has not yet won the Nobel Prize, but to him every day that he's alive, the prize of nobility is awarded by us all."

MR. CARTER: That was beautiful. Thank you. I'd like to have a copy of that.

(*Applause obscures brief comments as the program is concluded.*)

23

INTERVIEW WITH JIMMY CARTER, OCT. 17, 1997

Don Richardson

This teleconversation took place on Oct. 17, 1997. Carter was at home in Plains, Georgia, and I was in Huntsville, Texas. In the interview, Carter discusses his relationship with the media, his successes in the peacemaking process, his despair over the Middle East situation, and his view on the context in which his presidency should be judged.—*Editor*

CARTER: Good morning.

RICHARDSON: Good morning, President Carter. I gather from what Faye Dill said, you're at home in Plains.

CARTER: Yes, for one day.

RICHARDSON: Well, I'm going to start off with your relationship with media and journalists. Of course, during your presidency you were more accessible to the media than probably any other president. You had fifty-nine news conferences, scores of interviews with specific journalists that Jody Powell set up. Was it your impression that this unusual accessibility was ever really appreciated by the media?

CARTER: No, I don't think so. There was an assessment made by, I think, a professor from the University of Indiana about a year or two after I left office that showed that I had the most negative treatment by the media of any president who lived in this century—even worse than Nixon's during Watergate. I don't know if you've seen that study or not; but they analyzed all the headlines in both magazines and newspapers during the four-year period, whether the headlines were positive or negative or something—I don't remember the details—and I had the most negative. In fact, of the forty-eight months that I was in office, all of the news coverage, in balance, for forty-seven months was negative. The only positive was the first month when I was in office, when I walked down Pennsylvania Avenue.

But, even then I was—as Jody would tell you—I was always pushing to have press conferences more frequently because I enjoyed them. I liked the give and take and I could tell, obviously, that the news reporters—you can judge by their questions—were trying to catch me on things or test my knowledge or see if I had told them a lie or made a misleading statement, things of that kind.

I looked forward to that; but Jody was always, after the first few months, was on the side of "Let's not have so many press conferences," because I think, in balance, they were not helping very much—as far as making the people understand what I was trying to do and approve what I was doing. Then during the last year when the hostages were being held, that's all anybody wanted to talk about. And as you know, every night Walter Cronkite would say, "Two hundred and one days, still counting and the hostages are still being held," and they would show those pictures with bandages on their eyes. Then Ted Koppel's *Nightline* was a hundred percent on the hostages, and so that's when we decided to cut down on the number of press conferences.

There was also a very disturbing policy—and I think in retrospect, an amazing policy—that the press unanimously adopted during the summer and early fall of 1980. They would not cover any signing of legislation that I had proposed. Whereas, I remembered from my campaign against Ford in '76 that every time he would sign a bill, even those that he opposed—they were passed by the Democratic Congress—the press had a big coverage of it with ceremonies in the Rose Garden. But they embargoed those kinds of news stories as the election approached for me in 1980; and I kind of—I didn't think that was fair.

But, in general, you know, almost invariably, I enjoyed the exchange with the press and although Jody, my Mama and Rosalynn, for instance, would be kind of down on Sam Donaldson because he asked critical questions, I liked Sam and liked to have his questions.

RICHARDSON: It's been twenty-five years since Watergate. Since that time, our news media, it seems, have been a lot more adversarial, our politics more scandal-driven. For instance, if anybody knew about President Kennedy's apparently voracious sex life, nobody talked about it.

CARTER: That's true.

RICHARDSON: And Clinton today, fights on three fronts: he has the Paula Jones sexual harassment charge; he's continually contesting the special prosecutor's demand for White House documents; and of course, the investigation of the campaign funding gets hotter every day. Do you think the presidency can ever recover the esteem in which it was once held, and if so, what would it take to make it happen?

CARTER: Well, I think there was obviously an enormous achievement of investigative reporters in bringing out the Watergate facts. So after that, when I came into office, almost everybody was an investigative reporter. They were looking for things to be revealed in my closet. And then, I think that nowadays the press is still much more fascinated with the revelations than the general public seems to be. I think that Clinton is much more of a so-called "Teflon President" than Reagan was. I think it is because the public has just kind of gotten inured to sexual scandals and revelations and allegations and so forth, even [those] involving the campaign contribution things which you mentioned. I think there's much more fascination inside the Beltway with these things than there seems to be in the rest of the country. And this week, of course, everywhere Clinton goes—to Venezuela, to Brazil, to Argentina—every question he gets from an American reporter is about campaign contributions. And of course, this is disconcerting to him; but that just shows that the press is fascinated and the public is not.

RICHARDSON: There's a related question. You may have answered it. Do you think it really matters in the minds of the American people if the president has personal integrity, or what role should personal integrity play in American politics?

CARTER: I think it matters about integrity. But I think, first of all, loyalty to one's wife or to marriage vows doesn't seem to be as significant to the press—I mean to the public—because it doesn't necessarily interfere with performance of duty in the presidency. I think though, that if there is proof that any leaders in Washington actually violated the law when all of the allegations are investigated, I think that would still have a fairly substantial adverse impact on the election chances of Al Gore or on the permanent reputation of Clinton in the minds of the public and in the minds of historians.

RICHARDSON: I think so. As you know, I'm a university professor and I deal with young journalists every day. From your perspective, what advice would you give them to help them treat public figures fairly but still allow them to get their story, maintain the watchdog function that the press ought to have?

CARTER: I teach or lecture in the journalism classes at Emory University and I always tell them that I think that candidates for office or office holders ought to be fair game and they ought to be severely scrutinized, the facts ought to be published regardless, in a no-holds-barred fashion, that accuracy obviously is important. But I also point out that as a self-correcting factor in American journalism, in that, for instance, if a *Washington Post* reporter publishes an allegation against a public official, then for instance, the *L.A. Times* and the *New York Times* would be much more interested in proving the *Washington Post* made a mistake than they would in accepting the story and necessarily pursuing it further. So I think there is, on the responsible journalist—and I need not name them all—there is a very serious corrective factor or restraint on what they publish, because if they make a mistake, there's a serious adverse consequence to the newspaper or magazine and the journalist himself or herself.

So, and I think the candidates ought to be brutally assessed. This is the only chance that the American people have to size up the basic character of their future leader; and I think that it also requires the candidate to learn more about the nation, more about the issues, so that when they do make a campaign statement or promise that it's more likely to be accurate. So that long, tough, scrutinized campaign lets the people know more about the potential office holder; it requires the office holder to learn a hell of a lot more about the people and the circumstances with which they'll have to deal when they get in office. I wouldn't put any restraints on investigative reporters.

RICHARDSON: Good. Our students will be pleased.

A moment ago you mentioned the hostages. And of course, your last major effort in office involved countless hours negotiating the release of the hostages.

CARTER: Yes.

RICHARDSON: Of course, that was ultimately successful.

CARTER: Yes.

RICHARDSON: Peter Bourne, in his biography, states categorically that the Reagan campaign was conducting simultaneous negotiations to delay the release of the hostages until after the election. Were you aware of any evidence to support that claim? Is that something you can discuss?

CARTER: Well, you know, I've read, not only Peter Bourne's book, but also other books that make those allegations particularly involving the CIA, but I've never had any substantial evidence that would corroborate that presented to me. The thing that I can certify is that when we tried to inform Alexander Haig and George Shultz—Alexander Haig, particularly, who was going to be secretary of state—about what was going on with our negotiations to get the hostages released, they absolutely refused to accept any briefings. They did not want to be involved in anything that related to the hostages, even our efforts to get them freed. And made it clear to me and to our people: Ed Muskie and Brzezinski, Harold Brown, and others, Warren Christopher, "Don't involve us, we don't want to be informed, we don't want to be involved in any fashion." Obviously, when I was successful in getting the hostages released, Reagan was the one who welcomed them back, you know with—and making the statement that still kind of rubs me the wrong way, "Never, under my administration, will any hostages be taken," as though he was responsible for getting them freed. And the press there has made a tremendous issue out of the fact that fifteen minutes after Reagan became president that the airplane took off from the airport in Tehran with all the hostages on board as though Reagan was responsible for it.

RICHARDSON: In those first fifteen minutes.

CARTER: Yeah, in fifteen minutes, and he never had anything to do with it. His people refused to be informed about it. I had spent the last three days and two nights without even going to bed negotiating the details of their release. But the press, who ought to be more knowledgeable than that, have always said, "Well, the hostages were released under Reagan; they weren't released under Carter," and that sort of thing.

But I think that—I don't have any evidence presented to me, I say, any provable evidence—that Reagan was involved in trying to keep the hostages there. Whether his CIA director was involved, I have some very serious concerns. Talking about Casey.

RICHARDSON: Yes, I understand.

On an economics question, in 1976 you said that if you were elected president, you could have a balanced budget by 1980; which, of course, you didn't. And each president since then has taken on the budget deficit, some with more enthusiasm than others, but—

CARTER: Okay. Let me interrupt you just a minute. In the spring of 1980, we had a balanced budget that was approved by me and by the congressional leadership in the House and Senate. The bullet budget was absolutely balanced. We had a buffer zone there, in that if anything happened to unbalance the budget, automatically a five-dollar-a-barrel fee would be imposed on imported oil. It would be triggered if we went below a balanced budget. However—that was all agreed that was, I would say March or April, I believe. You can look it up in the records. However, we didn't anticipate that the oil prices would more than double in that twelve-month period.

RICHARDSON: Right.

CARTER: And the uncontrollable inflation, which was higher in other developed nations than it was ours, by the way, made it impossible for the budget to be balanced. And with the price of oil escalating so greatly, Bob Byrd and others in the Senate refused to give final approval to the extra five dollars a barrel that we had agreed to impose.

So, I just wanted to throw that in; but you haven't finished your question, I know. I'll answer it based on the fact that we didn't actually end up that year with a balanced budget.

RICHARDSON: Right. Well, the question basically is: Do you think this country can really live within its income or do we simply accept deficits as a way of life?

CARTER: I don't know if you read Fritz Hollings' op-ed piece this week. I think it was in the *New York Times*. You might want to get it and look at it. We don't have a balanced budget now. That's a bunch of baloney. There's about two hundred, almost three hundred billion dollars in Social Security Funds that are being allocated to the operating budget so that the Congress and Clinton can claim that the budget is balanced. But I think you might just take a few minutes to look up Fritz Hollings' editorial, his op-ed piece this week that points that out, rather than using my analysis for it. But the budget is not balanced and it's going to be horribly unbalanced if present trends continue when you get out to 2005 and 2010 and so forth. That was just a propaganda effort by the White House and the Congress to claim that the budget was balanced; primarily, so they could reduce taxes to some degree and increase some defense spending.

RICHARDSON: Changing the subject a bit, you're now engaged in many different peace initiatives. Of all the initiatives that you've participated in as president and as diplomat-without-portfolio, which ones do you think are most important and most satisfying?

CARTER: Well, I think the one that may have had the most far-reaching effect, which has not been really recognized too much, I think that our expedition to North Korea actually prevented a war. Don Oberdorf has just written a book about that, which you may or may not have read. Do you know Don Oberdorf? Do you know who he is?

RICHARDSON: No, I don't.

CARTER: Well, he was a *New York Times* top reporter in the Far East during the time I was president and following that. Oberdorf spent two or three years researching what happened when North Korea was prepared to develop a nuclear capability. And when Clinton and the

State Department were ready to impose, through the UN Security Council, sanctions against North Korea, the North Koreans had decided to go to war. And I went over, as you may or may not remember—

RICHARDSON: I do.

CARTER: —to Seoul and then to P'yongyang and negotiated an agreement for Kim Il Sung to stop his nuclear program and even to have a summit meeting with the South Korean president. That, I think, avoided a catastrophe; and the general who was in charge of our American forces in South Korea has confirmed what Don Oberdorf has written. In fact, Oberdorf had gotten a lot of his information from the general. Cho Luc is his name. So I think that mission had the most profound impact in that in the last minutes—the last days to be more accurate—it prevented a war on the Korean peninsula. That was in June, I think, of '94.

A few months later, of course, I went down to Haiti with Sam Nunn and Colin Powell, and I interrupted, I think, an armed invasion by 30,000 men. It would have cost a lot of casualties, certainly among the Haitians.

RICHARDSON: Yes.

CARTER: And so, I would say those two, plus the one at Camp David and then six months later the peace treaty between Israel and Egypt. Lord only knows what would have happened in the Mideast had Egypt still been at war with Israel.

So, I think those would be among the most significant.

RICHARDSON: More people know about the Camp David Accords, I suppose, than either Korea or Haiti.

CARTER: Well, there was some negative stuff about—the State Department has always resented it when I, you know, went to Korea and went to Haiti. But I never go without getting personal approval from the White House. So, even before I left South Korea, the State Department had issued a bunch of very negative stories to a reporter, a female reporter from the *New York Times*, whose name I've forgotten; but that clouded the public perception of what we were doing. But, I think that, in general, we've had fairly good support from Washington in the Carter Center's efforts to promote these things, particularly in countries where they don't give a damn.

RICHARDSON: Now, what is your assessment of the current Middle East situation?

CARTER: I view it with despair. . . . I really think that—I've known Netanyahu's position for many years. He was never supportive of the

Camp David Accords. He was never in favor of the peace treaty with Egypt. He claimed that I gave away the Sinai Desert, and gave away the oil wells that Israel had taken. Even when I was talking to him in Jerusalem at Rabin's funeral, it was obvious to me that Netanyahu was not in favor of the Oslo peace process. So, I'm in nothing but despair, and I think my feeling of despair is shared by probably a majority or substantial portion of the Israeli people themselves. Netanyahu's very nimble on his feet. He's a superb television performer, but I don't think he really is committed to the Camp David Accords, the peace treaty with Egypt, or the Oslo agreement. And unless you have that commitment on the part of Israeli leaders, no matter what the Palestinians do—and they have a lot of fault on their side—I don't think that any progress is going to be made. So, I think we just have to be patient and see what evolves inside Israel and their political situation before any more further progress can be made. I hope that Arafat will survive that long.

RICHARDSON: Certainly Camp David started a process that I would guess that no one in the world could have moved along as well as you did. That's my personal assessment.

CARTER: Well, the basic principles of the Camp David Accord are exactly compatible with the Oslo Agreement. And after I left office and when I began to see Arafat on a fairly regular basis, he always said the worst mistake he ever made was not accepting the premises of the Camp David Accord. And if you read the accords—they're not very voluminous—you can see that everything that was promised, or even dreamed about, in Oslo were agreed by Begin and ratified by the Israeli Knesset at Camp David.

RICHARDSON: Moving on to another one, it's kind of a multi-part one. When you went into office, Stu Eizenstat had a list of campaign promises actually published.

CARTER: I know.

RICHARDSON: They became the agenda for your presidency. Which of those items would you count as your most notable successes?

CARTER: I would say the deregulation of airlines, railroads, trucking, banking, and communications, which includes television and radio. During that four-year period, we deregulated all of those crucial facets of the American economy. That's one of them. Now the other one would be the Alaskan Lands Bill, which had been a hot potato ever since Eisenhower's term when Alaska was made a state. That bill, which was passed after I was defeated, by the way, when I was a lame-duck president, on which I worked for four years, as you probably know, doubled the size of our national parks and tripled the size of our wilderness areas. And although, since then, Alaskan members of the House and Senate have tried to undo the Alaskan Lands Bill, it has pretty well stayed intact. I would say that those are two of the things, on the domestic scene, that we did that have had the most profound impact, and I think, beneficial impact on America.

RICHARDSON: Would you include Panama in that list?

CARTER: Well, I would. You know, we are now approaching the time when the first Panama Canal Treaty will be implemented. It turns over control of the canal to the Panamanians. That process has been proceeding quite well. I've been down to Panama twice in the last few years. And of course, the second treaty covers a period from the year 2000 on and that gives us unlimited access, priority access to the canal during any time of crisis, and gives us a right to defend the canal against any external threat. So the first treaty and the second treaty of what I've described, I think that in general, it has been quite successful. And there's no doubt in my mind, or any responsible historian's mind that, had we not ratified those treaties, the canal would not be in operation today; it would have been destroyed. We would have had a war in Panama. And this was, as you know, a commitment first made by Lyndon Johnson. It was then a recommitment by Nixon and Ford, but when the time came to put it to a vote in the Senate, they all were much more politically wise than I and they backed away; but I pursued it to a conclusion. And it was by far the most severe political challenge I've ever faced in my life, much more difficult to get the Panama Canal Treaties ratified by two-thirds vote in the Senate than it was to get elected president.

RICHARDSON: And I think you expended a lot of political capital on that as well.

CARTER: Well, if you've read—I've summarized in my book, *Keeping the Faith*, of the U.S. senators who voted for the treaties that were up for reelection that year, there were twenty of them, only seven of them came back to the Senate. The attrition rate was almost as great two years later in 1980, and a hell of a lot of people voted against me and fervently opposed me because of the Panama Canal Treaties. And never does a month go by now that I don't get mail condemning me for the Panama Canal Treaties. So it was a very controversial and politically damaging thing to do. I think it was the right thing to do.

RICHARDSON: I think you took office under the most difficult circumstances in the twentieth century with the possible exception of FDR's first term. I think it's probably time to reevaluate the Carter presidency and my question is: In what context do you think that the Carter presidency should be judged?

CARTER: Well, let me give you a very self-serving answer. I didn't know what your question was going to be and I'll just answer it this way. We're now the only superpower on earth, right?

RICHARDSON: Yes.

CARTER: What is the measure of a superpower? I would say it is to be a champion of peace for ourselves and for everybody else in the world, where if there's a trouble spot in the world, like at Camp David or what used to be Rhodesia or Korea, that the United States is known to be and expected to be active in trying to negotiate or bring peace.

Secondly, I think human rights and democracy and freedom are a package. We ought to be raising the banner of human rights, freedom, and democracy in an undeviating fashion and supporting and protecting these rights of people whether they live in oil-producing rich states that are white folks or among black people where they're not any direct benefit to us. Another thing is, I think we ought to be generous in sharing our wealth with people who are suffering, and we ought to be protectors of the global environment. I think those are the four general measurements of a great nation, and I feel quite comfortable with what I tried to do as president and also with what I did as president. If we thought about it, we know we never lost a soldier in battle, we struggled for peace for ourselves and for other regions of the world, we've raised high the banner of human rights, we're generous in sharing our wealth with those in need, and we are protectors of the environment. So, I would say to answer your question—to repeat myself, in a very self-serving way—that's how I would characterize my presidency.

INDEX

ABOUT THE BOOK

Jimmy Carter participated in more than two hundred interviews between 1976 and 1996. In the twenty-three conversations presented here, highly regarded interviewers lead President Carter to clarify his public stands and private beliefs.

The dialogue created through these encounters demonstrates the growth of a principled man, encapsulating the major debates and concerns of the last quarter of the "American Century." Taken separately, the conversations provide a window on the recent past; taken together, they provide the basis for a new understanding of Carter the individualist and for a reassessment of an important segment of the political thought of our times.

The interviewers are Bonnie Angelo, David Broder, Tom Brokaw, Walter Cronkite, John Chancellor, Stanley Cloud, John Dancy, Sam Donaldson, Richard F. Fenno, Robert Fulghum, Murray Gart, Erwin Hargrove, Steven Hochman, Charles O. Jones, Bill Kovach, James Laue, H. Clifton McCleskey, Robert McNeil, Bill Moyers, Richard E. Neustadt, Dan Rather, Harry Reasoner, Barbara Reynolds, Don Richardson, Carl Rowan, Robert Scheer, Bob Schieffer, Hugh Sidey, Kenneth W. Thompson, David B. Truman, Mike Wallace, Barbara Walters, Curtis Wilkie, Judy Woodruff, and James S. Young.

Don Richardson is professor and chair of the Department of Public Communication at Sam Houston State University.